BRICK *by* BRICK

Building a strong *family* that won't lose their faith in a secular culture

BY THE REGNIER FAMILY

Brick by Brick:
Building a strong family that won't lose their faith in a secular culture.

Catholic Christian Outreach Canada Inc.
1247 Kilborn Place
Ottawa, ON K1H 6K9
Canada
www.cco.ca

Printed in Canada

ISBN: 978-1-989230-18-3

" [A] new generation of builders is needed. Moved not by fear ... but by the urgency of genuine love, they must learn to build, brick by brick, the city of God within the city of man."

-St. John Paul II

Acknowledgments

Our family gratefully recognizes the assistance of wonderful friends who have helped us in the preparations of this book.

Cristy Ombac-Orr – editing

Gillian Kantor – editing

Sara Francis – editing

Dean Schneider – final editing

Shayla Kirana – photography

Caleb Regnier – cover concept

Deana Fenwick – layout and design

Bishop Scott McCaig – foreword

The Regniers – André's family

The Hoffmans – Angèle's family

The Moreaus – Marc's family

The Doucettes – Elizabeth's family

The Heits – Alana's family

Dedication

We dedicate this book and entrust it,

and all families who read it,

to the intercession of the Holy Family.

Table of Contents

Foreword

Bishop Scott McCaig, CC

"The family is placed at the centre of the great struggle between good and evil, between life and death, between love and all that is opposed to love."[1]

St. John Paul II

Fittingly, it was immediately after being hit broadside by a well-aimed water balloon from one of the Regnier children that I was asked to write the foreword for this book. I didn't hesitate to say "yes", even as I sputtered in the deluge and ducked to avoid another onslaught of water-laden missiles. A book about raising healthy, faithful Catholic families in the tsunami of secularism that surrounds us? A book that presents solid principles to equip young couples in the midst of the 'battle for the family' that is raging in our culture? Fantastic idea! Count me in.

This family is uniquely qualified to do so. Their home truly is what St. John Paul II called families to become—a domestic Church. Indeed, what immediately comes to mind when I think of the Regniers, and families like them, is this quote: "Thus the little domestic Church, like the greater Church, needs to be constantly and intensely evangelized: hence its duty regarding permanent education in the faith … the family, like the Church, ought to be a place where the Gospel is transmitted and from which the Gospel radiates … the future of evangelization depends in great part on the Church of the home."[2] It is certainly true, as Pope Francis recently stated, that "the family which experiences the joy of faith communicates it naturally."[3] The Regniers are a wonderful example of this.

---

1. Pope John Paul II, *Gratissimam Sane (Letter to Families)*, 1994, n. 23.
2. Pope John Paul II, *Familiaris Consortio (The Role of the Christian Family in the Modern World)*, 51–52.
3. Pope Francis, October 27, 2013.

Whenever I visit the Regniers, we often engage in a massive backyard water fight around the pool. This is usually preceded by a few practical jokes, someone getting pushed into the pool with dry clothes, and my parking on their front lawn despite there being plenty of parking space on the pavement. (They always devise some retaliation when I do this and it has become a running joke.) The evenings generally include a hearty barbecue, good red wine, much laughter, impromptu catechesis, and perhaps even a few cigars. In winter, it is snowball fights and oven roasts but certain ingredients are always present: free-flowing conversation, joy, and Jesus. What gives them credibility to write such a book is this healthy combination of wholeness and the striving for holiness. Nature and grace both have their proper place.

Indeed, to my mind, André and Angèle have avoided the tempting extremes of legalism and permissiveness, and built their family on a healthy humanity and well-rounded faith. And the fruit is evident. Their children are missionary disciples who embrace the love of God and his saving mission as eagerly as they do. I consider the Regniers among my dearest friends and my own life as a priest and bishop has been richly blessed by them. Our friendship has now spanned many years. I have vacationed with them, ministered with them, watched their children grow up, and celebrated one of their weddings (and preparing for another). And I know that so many others have also been deeply blessed by them.

It is important to clarify, however, that they are not some "super family" beyond imitation like the Brady Bunch. They face all the difficulties that beset any committed Catholic family in these troubled times. They will be the first to admit that there have been many stumbles along the way. Like any family, they have had to forgive, reconcile, mature in grace, and heal. But they have been faithful to certain key principles that have enabled them to weather the inevitable storms and have drawn together in faith, hope, and familial love. I am delighted that they have chosen to share this wisdom with young families facing this same embattled and confused culture.

Pope Francis challenged modern Catholic families with this poignant question and subsequent challenge: "How do we keep our faith? Do we keep it for ourselves, in our families, as a personal treasure, or are we able to share it by our witness, by our acceptance of others, by our openness? We all know that families, especially young families, are often 'racing' from one place to another, with lots to do. But did you ever think that this 'racing' could also be the race of faith? Christian families are missionary families, in their everyday life, in their doing everyday things, as they bring to everything the salt and the leaven of faith!"[4] In my experience, this magnificently describes

---

4.　Ibid.

the mission of the faithful Catholic family in our time and culture. Not the closed isolation of withdrawal or the facile capitulation to the 'spirit of the age', but true missionary engagement! It is an engagement born of a living, robust, orthodox faith that cannot help but overflow in authentic love for others. As Catholic Christian Outreach itself models and proclaims so well, authentic spirituality and mission are inseparable. This is the beautiful and attainable ideal presented in this book.

I pray that all who read it will be drawn deeper into the radiant mystery of the Holy Family, and "may Nazareth teach us what family life is, its communion of love, its austere and simple beauty, and its sacred and inviolable character."[5] Like Jesus, may all children grow "in wisdom and stature, in favour with God and all the people."[6] And finally, "may Christ the Lord, the Universal King, the King of Families, be present in every Christian home as he was at Cana, bestowing light, joy, serenity, and strength."[7]

In Jesus, with Mary and Joseph,

+ Bishop Scott McCaig, CC

Military Ordinary of Canada.

---

5. Pope Paul VI, Homily in Nazareth, 1964. Quoted in the Catechism of the Catholic Church, 533.
6. Luke 2:52.
7. Pope John Paul II, *The Role of the Christian Family in the Modern World*, 86.

Meet the Authors

Introduction by André and Angèle Regnier

As the founders of Catholic Christian Outreach (CCO), we have been on an adventure for over 30 years of evangelizing and forming university students to be leaders in the Catholic Church. Our children have had the opportunity to meet many wonderful young people and join us on CCO retreats and missions over the years. To our amazement, God clearly called Marc, Joel, Elizabeth, Caleb, and Alana also to become CCO missionaries (which is incredible because we have a challenging call to live solely by providence on solicited donations!)

We suspect people might look in on our lives and assume that our CCO environment made things much easier for us to influence our children positively towards faith, but we understand it all could have easily backfired on us too. Because we have a background in evangelical Christianity, we have heard many stories of the bitterness and rebellion that can happen to children of pastors and missionaries. The 'turn-off factor' for kids is high when parents are that engaged as spiritual leaders. We were very intentional in our parenting decisions and we had our eyes wide open especially in regards to CCO, trying to avoid the pitfalls that all families encounter *as well as* those particular ones that hit missionary families.

In our ministry, and in our family life, we strove to follow the prompting of St. John Paul the Great to "build, brick by brick, the city of God within the city of man"[8]. We sought to lay firm foundations with God at the centre, then worked brick by brick to build the 'city of God' in our family life so it

---

8.   Pope John Paul II, *Address by the Holy Father John Paul II at the Evening Vigil with Young People, 27 July 2002, Toronto*, 4.

could thrive in faith and love. In this book, we have endeavoured to unpack *philosophically* and *practically* what we think worked in our parenting to foster a lifelong faith in our children. No doubt, you share this desire for your children as well.

You and Your Missionary Call

We hear many parents express their frustration with trying to get their kids to go to Sunday Mass. However, as parents, we must desire more than just this minimal action of getting them to Mass on Sunday (although it may seem that this is all that we can handle on a Sunday morning). Our prayer, hope and ideal should be higher and more magnificent. "A radical conversion in thinking is required."[9]

We should want our children to be nothing less than missionary disciples. As Pope Francis so often communicates, we are all missionary disciples by virtue of our baptism. If this is true, then we as parents need to start forming our children toward this necessary call from the moment of their baptism. The grace of baptism raises us up to be missionary disciples; to live otherwise will have damaging effects on our experience of faith and on the Church community, for we would be living our faith in a way other than who we are called to be.

When we speak of being missionary, we are not speaking of what would traditionally be understood as a professional position (priest, religious, overseas missionaries or even CCO campus missionaries). Being a missionary disciple is a *way of thinking*—a recognition that we are called to expand the kingdom of God by our actions and our words. It's a conviction that God desires for us to be a light to the world, salt to the earth. We see that our lives must bear fruit that will last. We are called to change the world. Living with such a worldview makes our faith exciting and allows us to see that our lives matter. Being missionary will always move us, our families and our communities away from self-referential care and concern. Our gaze and care will expand beyond ourselves. This is a healthy and exciting place for you to bring your family.

It is our number one priority as parents to raise our children to be able to live their lives fully as Catholics; which is to be missionary disciples. Yes, we want them to be successful and happy in all aspects of their lives but we believe their success and happiness will flow from living their faith dynamically, just as it was intended to be lived.

---

9.   Pope John II, *Redemptoris Missio*, 7 December 1990, 49.

How this Book Came to Be

As we travelled and continue to travel around the country and the world, one of our joys is to meet up with CCO alumni from across the span of our 30 years, many of whom are married. By and large, they are married to a fellow CCO alumnus and they have beautiful young (and large) families being raised in the faith. As we have watched them grow up, and as they have watched our family mature and expand, they have been turning to us in earnest, particularly over the past five years, asking us:

"How did you do it?!"

"How did you raise your kids to be so into their faith and happy about it?"

"How did you avoid major rebellion in the teenage years?"

"How did you raise your kids to have missionary hearts?"

"We want to know everything you did!"

At first we dismissed these as merely compliments and playful banter, but it never let up. It only intensified. These young parents were sincerely and desperately seeking best practices from role models of family life.

It really shouldn't be surprising. We've always had university students connected to our home life for all these 30+ years and we noticed even for these young people that they lacked family rootedness. Their family of origin, whether it was fragmented or not, often lacked tradition or meaningful spirituality. Even things as basic as regular family mealtimes in their growing up years were all but absent. If they lacked so much from their own family backgrounds, of course these young, faithful parents would be looking for role models of families where disciples are formed in the home from the earliest age.

So in response to these constant pleas, we chose to write our story *for them*. We initially felt uncomfortable about the idea of writing our witness and approach to parenting; as though we were proclaiming to be experts or something. But out of love for our alumni asking the questions, we humbly present this book—not as the be-all end-all about parenting, but simply to answer the question posed to us: "How *exactly* did you do it?" "How did you raise your kids to be missionary disciples?"

With the incessant CCO alumni plea for help, we felt we could no longer deny the promptings of the Holy Spirit. We approached our kids about the idea of writing a family book together. Yes, together! Why not write this book as a family? Let's have everyone in the family be the authors! After all, our kids have a unique perspective on how we raised them.

How this Book was Written

The whole family agreed to commit to this project. We started with a blank slate and a big question: "How did we raise our kids to be missionary disciples?"

We spent hours talking about it, generally in the living room from 1–4pm after Sunday brunch. What were the principles, stories and lessons that were most influential in our upbringing? Once key patterns started emerging, we defined our seven chapters. Then we began marching our way through the material, discussing it at length together and assigning each member of the family certain sections to write in each chapter. On and on this went for weeks and months.

Our primary concern was to communicate at a high level the principles at play in how we raised our family. Although we would have been content to stay at a philosophical level and not get prescriptive, we remembered the cry of those young CCO alumni families and the look in their eyes, "We want to know exactly how you did it!" So in each chapter we make an attempt to paint a clear picture of how we did what we did, but only for the sake of illustration. There are also additional 'how-tos' in the *Bonus Features* section at the back of the book for the curious of heart.

So as you read this book, please don't feel the need to latch onto our methods. We appreciate that you can't just cut and paste 'the how' for every family. And we also joyfully recognize that many families have seen success with raising their children in the faith in ways that are different than our own approach. Rather, we encourage you to focus on the principles. As it has been said, "Methods are many, principles are few; Methods always change, principles never do."[10] It has been said, "The man who grasps principles can successfully select his own methods. The man who tries methods, ignoring principles, is sure to have trouble."[11] Therefore, as you read this book, don't get caught up so much in the *hows*, but rather listen for the *whys*.

This book is simply a testimonial offering on how we did it, and we hope it helps others in raising children to be life-long disciples of Christ who live for his greater glory.

---

10. Warren W. Wiersbe, *The Wiersbe Bible Commentary: Old Testament* (Colorado Springs: David Cook, 2007), p.512.

11. This quote is attributed to Harrington Emerson, albeit unsourced.

Authors

This is certainly a unique project, having 10 authors including parents, children, married children, and in-laws—with each one contributing their unique perspectives, stories and writing styles. We wanted every chapter to contain at least a little something from everyone. Although this approach had its complexities, we felt it would result in a richer offering.

Bringing the pieces all together posed some challenges to ensuring that the final product gave one coherent message. This is why the family chose Mylène, our oldest, as the main author or, 'narrator' of the book. We chose her because she was in the unique position of being both a child and a mother. She is the firstborn, having lived under our parenting the longest (from our earliest colossal mistakes to our current ineffable wisdom). She is also a mother of two (and one on the way) and is therefore parenting her own little missionary disciples. Her voice as narrator speaks to what was lived and what is being lived.

And so, here it is. Our family reflection, guided by our eldest, Mylène, on how we raised our children to be missionary disciples. From here on in, we pass the baton to Mylène who will now introduce you to the whole family.

Meet the Regniers

Mylène

I am the eldest of the five Regnier kids. I married my husband, Marc, in July, 2013. We now have two kids: Max (4) and Audrey (2) as well as a boy on the way in June, 2019. I served for one year with NET Ministries of Canada in Yellowknife, Northwest Territories. Afterwards, I completed my degree at Carleton University, majoring in Political Sciences. I have since been devoting my time to my children as a stay-at-home mom. We currently live in Halifax, Nova Scotia where my husband leads a team of CCO missionaries at Dalhousie University. I love to bake, decorate, read, and do the occasional DIY project. I am an easy-going person, who equally thrives on being with people and being alone.

André

André (Dad) is from a family of eight kids and was raised in Prince Albert, Saskatchewan. He graduated from the University of Saskatchewan where he majored in Psychology and dominated on the varsity freestyle wrestling team. Dad is currently pursuing a Masters in Theology at the Augustine Institute. He and Mom co-founded Catholic Christian Outreach (described below). He is an ideas guy, a man who makes things happen and gets people moving. Dad has a passion for sharing Jesus with others and speaking into people's lives. An active person with a slight obsession with the weather forecast. He is an engaging international speaker and author of three books who is working on his Masters in Theology on the side.

Angèle

Angèle (Mom) grew up on a farm in North Central Saskatchewan with her parents and two younger brothers. She spent most of her time in the house with her nose in an encyclopedia. Mom is a convert to Catholicism from Lutheran and Evangelical churches. While Dad was the energy behind founding CCO, Mom was the practical strategist. She wrote all five books of the original CCO faith studies series, and established the foundation of the campus outreach strategies and training. She also wrote a book called *Forgiveness is Key*. Mom is laid back and fun, yet organized and responsible. She is intelligent, wise, funny, hard working, and is an engaging teacher. She is known to have a passion for the Saints, Ignatian spirituality and all things yellow.

Janna

Janna is the baby of the family and is very happy with that role— even if she's already in Grade 7. She's been swimming like a pro since the age of three and is content to spend her whole summer in the pool drinking the slushies that she whips up regularly. Janna loves to laugh and be with people, especially when she is the centre of attention. She gets along with everyone and is rarely upset. She is famous for her dark tans, 'white' blonde hair, and constant smile. Janna is easily the biggest extrovert of our family. She was named in honour of St. Gianna and St. Thérèse.

Natalie

Natalie is currently in Grade 10. She reads and plays guitar in her free time, and if you want to get her talking, mention Spiderman and she's all yours. Natalie is detail-oriented, independent, and responsible while also being very easy to get along with. She is known for walking on her tippy toes and running like a gazelle. She is proudly the only *lefty* in the family and biggest *frenchy* of us all (since she has only ever gone to Francophone schools). Natalie loves listening to praise and worship music and is very tight with St. Anthony, out of necessity, with St. Clare, out of nostalgia for her middle name, and St. Agnes, thanks to a prayer encounter at her church in Rome.

Caleb

Caleb will be married to his fiancée, Alana, in July, 2019. He has a Bachelor's degree in Communications from the University of Ottawa. Serving two years at his alma mater as a campus missionary, Caleb will continue his missionary work at Mount Royal University as he and Alana will be moving out to Calgary after their wedding. Caleb is a natural leader and has the ability to gain influence easily with the men around him. Caleb has a great capacity to be extremely funny one minute, and go deep the next. Caleb has a lot of natural talents and picks things up easily. He is a perfectionist, as well as being creative, intuitive, analytical, and stylish. If ever any of us want to know if what we are wearing or working on looks cool, Caleb is the first one we turn to.

Joel

Joel (Jo) has a Bachelor's degree from the University of Ottawa in History. He served as a campus missionary at Carleton University for two and half years and now works as a recruiter with CCO's Human Resources Department. He and Elizabeth got married in June of 2017 and are expecting a daughter in late Spring 2019. He is the family's resident smart guy who started reading at the age of four and loves history, philosophy, and theology. Jo is a talented cook and can often be found watching cooking videos or annoying Mom by adding ingredients to her dishes behind her back. Jo likes to be around people and is known to be passionate, opinionated, and strong-willed. He is an effective communicator—clever and quick-witted. He is always making people laugh, especially when in cahoots with Caleb. And finally, Jo insists that I point out that he has an impressive beard.

Elizabeth

Elizabeth (Lizz) married Jo in 2017 and comes from a family of eight kids who are all musically talented—basically they're the Von Trapp family singers. She has a love for coffee, wine, and the Theology of the Body, and shares Jo's love for cooking. Elizabeth is a real-life Disney princess who sings—usually while happily cleaning (no small animals included though). Elizabeth is sweet, kind, responsible, selfless, attentive to detail, and is always able to notice people, include them, and love them. She is easy to talk to, laughs at everyone's jokes, and gets along with everyone. Elizabeth served as a campus missionary at Carleton University and is now heading into the realm of full-time motherhood.

Marc

Marc married Mylène (me) in 2013. He grew up in Guelph, Ontario with his parents and older brother. Marc is the reigning tall guy and he has shown us parts of our cupboards that we never knew existed. He worked as a youth minister in Nunavut (in Canada's Arctic), served a year with NET Ministries and worked as co-ordinator of youth ministry at a parish for almost seven years before joining CCO staff. He impressively spent four years multitasking as a husband and father, working full-time at the parish, and studying full-time at Dominican College to obtain his Bachelor of Theology degree. He is a people person who is able to relate to young and old alike. He is an amazing dad and husband who serves others any chance he can. He is passionate and hardworking in all he does. And apparently, his wife is amazing.

Alana

Alana and Caleb are tying the knot in July, 2019. She grew up on a farm near Unity, Saskatchewan as the youngest of six kids. Alana, like Lizz, attended the St. Thérèse School of Faith and Mission. She later went on to earn her Bachelor of Education at the University of Saskatchewan. She is a CCO missionary (have you noticed a pattern, yet?) and apart from Mom and Dad, has been a missionary the longest. Alana has worked as a missionary at the University of Ottawa, the University of Saskatchewan, and most recently worked in ministry training, equipping our new missionaries. Next, Alana will be working at Mount Royal University as a campus Team Leader. Alana has natural teaching ability, she has a fun, friendly personality, and can keep up with Caleb and Jo's antics. She is wise, articulate, and influential to those around her.

Meet CCO

Although not a member of the family per se, you should probably understand a bit more about what Catholic Christian Outreach (CCO) is, since it will come up many times in this book.

Catholic Christian Outreach (CCO) is a university student movement dedicated to evangelization. It challenges students to live in the fullness of the Catholic faith with a strong emphasis on becoming leaders in the renewal of the world. CCO was founded by André and Angèle Regnier in 1988 at the University of Saskatchewan. From the humble beginnings of a handful of students, the movement now serves thousands of students across Canada and internationally.

Sadly, at university, most students stop practising the faith they were raised in. It is also at university that these young adults form their ideas about their identity, values, and future. This is a critical age and CCO wants to do something to stop the exodus from the Church through a clear proclamation of Jesus Christ, so as to elicit a conversion of heart. These newly converted and spiritually awakened young people quickly become disciples of Christ and leaders in the New Evangelization. They actively reach out to their peers through CCO's personal approach to campus outreach: small group faith studies, large group events, retreats, conferences, and summer missions.

CCO's goal is not just to share the message of Jesus, but to spread his mission. This mission is to form disciples who are also apostles—believers who, through the empowerment and inspiration of the Holy Spirit, send others to proclaim the message. You can read more about CCO at our website: *www.cco.ca*.

CHAPTER 1

It Takes a Village

*Raising Children Should Involve the
Whole Catholic Community*

MYLÈNE

When our family first gathered to discuss writing this book, we asked ourselves, "Why did we all grow up to be missionary disciples?" The initial answer was unanimous from us kids. It was the people around us that we looked up to. Our parents were certainly the primary influences in our formative years, but they weren't the only ones. Our parents purposely chose to bring people into our family life to enhance our family experience, to delight in us and serve as examples to us. Some were in our lives for just short visits, while others are close and familiar friends to this day. The influence of these wonderful people on my own life and my siblings' lives is more than they know. They became the safe, Christ-centred atmosphere that we would breathe.

I've always loved listening in on adults' conversations. As a kid, I have memories of leaving the company of my cousins playing to go sit in my grandparents' living room and be entertained by my aunts and uncles talking and laughing. Other times, while with our group of family friends, I would initiate that all of us kids play 'spies' and sneak into the living room to try to listen to what the parents were saying. I have fond memories of having CCO staff members at our house, laughing, talking and goofing around. Some of the topics that I heard went over my head, but most of the time, I just loved listening, learning, and absorbing everything that was being said. Yes, I admit, this is just a nice way of saying that I was a nosy kid. But without my being aware of it, the chances I had just to be in the presence of these individuals and listen to the way that they spoke was ever so softly shaping my perspective on life. They say it takes a village to raise a child; I would agree because that was how I was raised.

ANDRÉ

I remember when Mylène was a newborn; there were so many people there to help us out. Both sets of our parents were there to hold Mylène and to give us some rest. People brought food over (mostly so that I would not starve). There were gifts, congratulations, 'oohing' and 'awwing' all around us. There was the presence of experienced mothers who assured Angèle that Mylène's little cough was nothing to worry about. What struck me was that we were not alone; there were people who loved and cared for Angèle, Mylène, and I. We could count on them.

Our family has grown in number and in age since then. I am so proud of my children. They love to have fun, they are intelligent, confident, and socially mature and, to top it off, they have faith that is real and dynamic. I could not be happier. I am not alone in my observation and delight in my children either. I have had their teachers and ladies after Mass come up to me and gush with praise of our children. After Holy Thursday Mass, where I sat for one hour in front of the Blessed Sacrament with an eleven-year-old Janna, I had a parishioner come to me with tears in her eyes and asked me, "How did you raise such beautiful children that have faith?" At that moment I was feeling pretty good as a father. However, I knew that she was asking with the knowledge that her kids had walked away from the Church a long time ago. I could have spent a long time sharing with her the content of this book, but instead I simply said, "I can't take all the credit; there are a lot of people who have influenced my children."

As I look back at the last twenty-five years, we have had many friends and family who have been there for us and our kids. These people in our "village" reinforced what we, as parents, tried to impart to them. Children may not always listen to their parents, but there is usually someone in the village who can get through to them. Our job as parents is to surround them with villagers who share our values.

My parents knew that children sense and absorb more than adults often realize. Kids see everything. The people around us would be influencing us, whether they liked it or not. As my dad said, the trick that they discovered for creating a village of individuals around us was to choose people who would reinforce the beliefs and culture they were trying to raise us in. They also wanted these people to be contagious. (And I do not mean they had to have leprosy.) They were contagious in that they were attractive, relatable individuals who we liked, looked up to, and had fun with. Ultimately, our village provided us with a preferred vision for the future. Mom and Dad wanted us to see these people and aspire to live like them, as a positive alternative to what the world offered.

In our family discussion, we narrowed down three distinct but equally important groups of people who formed our village. First, role models—particularly ones who were just older than us. Second, faith-filled families. And third, a youth group environment. Let's check out the village scene, shall we?

Young Role Models

Kids and teenagers often look to people slightly older than them as role models. This category of people wove quite naturally into our daily family life with my parents being founders of a university student movement and all. We had certain periods of time when CCO people lived with us too. But besides that, it was just normal for us to have 18–30 year olds over at our house on Saturday nights, gathered around the living room laughing, playing games, and having wrestling matches on the living room floor.

Yes, wrestling. Dad was an accomplished varsity wrestler in the day, something we as children were always proud to announce whenever the opportunity arose. And that's why wrestling was often a party game when people came over. Wrestling is actually an ingenious way to engage both young adults and children alike! I doubt that any strategic thought was put into it though—it's just the organic result of having André Regnier as a father and party host.

I am so grateful for all of these individuals who spent time with us as children and the way they invested in us. They didn't treat us as 'just kids'. They gave us their loving attention and made us feel valued. Whether their interaction with us was big or small, they were individuals whom we watched and aspired to imitate. I would go so far as to say that their influence was one of the biggest factors that fuelled our desire to live faith-filled lives. Who they were deeply attracted us. We wanted to be like them. Their example brought to life St. John Paul II's words: "Life with Christ is a wonderful adventure."[12] Adventure! What more could a child ask for?

---

12. Pope John Paul II, Homily of the *Holy Father During Mass with Young People, 26 April 1997, Czech Republic*

JO

In elementary school, we always had to write at least one entry in our creative writing journals about our hero or role models. My friends would write about their favourite hockey player, actor, or superhero. For me, this was always a really hard question to answer. The issue wasn't that I had no one to look up to; it was that I had so many. Also, how do I explain why Lee, Cary, Jeremy, and Eric were my heroes rather than a typical celebrity or athlete? These individuals were CCO staff members and students who impacted me as I grew up. They weren't famous, rich, or anything that a kid would typically look for in a hero. They were just regular folks. What made them extraordinary was their faith.

I have so many great memories growing up around these role models. These people were older than me but still young, so they were people I could relate to and strive to be like. But I did not just look up to them solely because they were fun. They truly were men and women of God. They lived the joy of the Gospel every single day, and everyone knows how contagious joy is. What made them effective role models was that there was no distinction between their spiritual lives and their 'normal lives'. I looked at these people and thought, "One day I will be like them." One minute they were having an intense spiritual conversation with my parents and the next they were chowing down on chips and playing frisbee with me. They lived seamless lives and were authentic witnesses of Christ in my life. Faith wasn't something they did; it was central to who they were.

It may seem like nothing, but I believe this was one of the key things that encouraged us kids to pursue holiness in our lives. Growing up, what did I think was cool? Who did I want to be like? What did I want my life to look like? I wanted to be like the young adults I was surrounded by. While my friends were being formed by the lives and messages of the 'world', I was looking to young people of faith. In my eyes, in order to be cool, you had to have faith and Jesus had to be at the centre of your life. There was no contradiction between being fun and being holy.

In order to further prove the importance of role models, I think it is significant that all of us kids chose CCO staff as our Confirmation sponsors. These were the people we looked up to. Our role models. We wanted to be just like them.

Mom and Dad have had countless parents approach them to lament the fact that when it came to faith, they had little to no influence on their older children. "As soon as I bring up faith, Church, or God they roll their eyes and shut down." Sadly, parents often will not be the one to bring their older children into the faith. These children need someone who has the 'cool' factor to do that for them. I know what you're thinking. "Hey! I am a cool parent! I'm still hip!" Granted, but while you may be a cool parent (mine definitely were), young role models will have a special appeal that children will be drawn to follow. Who will be the young person that your child will look to?

Our family had it easy since my parent's job involved working with young people. So for other families, it might take some digging and searching. Here's some ideas:

- Seek out some young people at your parish or in your city and invite them for supper regularly. Your family's example will be just as much of a blessing to them as theirs is to your family.
- If you're so lucky, integrate young seminarians or religious or priests into your family social life.
- Maybe you can find babysitters who are young, faithful, and cool.
- Is there a fantastic young person who could live with your family? (i.e. home-cooked meals and cheap rent in exchange for being naturally awesome and engaged with the family).
- Host NET missionaries at your home as much as possible so that your children can see their authentic witness.

Another lovely option is to have a large family! Natalie and Janna are quite a bit younger than my brothers and me, so in addition to the other young adults that frequented our home, they have also had the constant example of their older siblings to look to.

NATALIE

My siblings are some of the most influential role models for me. I watch how they act and how they live their Catholic lives. I look up to them. I ask them for advice in different aspects of my life that I struggle with, and they often tell me that they've experienced the same thing. They tell me how they got through it and what positive or negative consequences came from their decisions. They help me get through the tough times. I look up to their relationship with Christ and desire to be as cool as them and have a better and stronger relationship with Jesus as well.

When we were young, obviously we as kids could not really be role models for each other (except when it came to getting into trouble). That's why my parents made sure we had a large amount of Catholic young people who surrounded us. The ways in which modern culture draws kids and teens in were practically ineffective on us. Drugs, alcohol, and pop culture held little influence when the lifestyles of these faithful young people had so captured our minds and hearts. No matter how 'cool' the most popular kid in school was, we honestly felt that the young adults that we were friends with were way cooler. Thanks to these solid, faith-filled role models, the glamours of the world did not capture our hearts.

Family Community

Most families naturally gravitate towards other like-minded families. Sometimes they find them in the wider social community and sometimes it's found in staying close to their extended family. Some families are blessed to have both of these groups of people to support and bless them. How rich is that? We had that for only a few short years before we moved to Ottawa. I have fond, yet faint memories of living in Saskatoon and running around with kids my age in the church hall, and playing imaginary games with my many cousins.

ANGÈLE

A watershed moment in our life was when CCO posted our family in Ottawa. It was a big move for us simple prairie folks to move to the nation's capital—a city of a million people. All of our family and friends would be a 34-hour drive away.

On the morning of our move, we stopped at the CCO headquarters in Saskatoon to say goodbye and celebrate a travellers' Mass before heading off. André's relative, Fr. Yves Marchildon, was road tripping it with us. He also served as good spiritual insurance for a trip like this.

I will never forget the Gospel reading for the day; it moved me to tears.

> Then Peter said, "Look, we have left our homes and followed you." And he said to them, "Truly I tell you, there is no one who has left house or wife or brothers or parents or children, for the sake of the kingdom of God, who will not get back very much more in this age, and in the age to come eternal life." Luke 18: 28-30

In truth, we were leaving everything behind for the mission. We felt it, believe me. It was a grand 'yes' we were making, and it was a lonely 'yes' too. But there was a promise to us in this Gospel narrative and I can testify that we have experienced it during our 20+ years here in Ottawa. Even though we left our families, we were given a community of families who enriched our lives.

Originally, we knew only five people in Ottawa—three priests and one couple who had a brother who was a CCO missionary. Lorie and Richard O'Reilly took us under their wings. They were friends with other families who all went to the same parish and in short time, all our families became close friends. We had to work for these relationships. You see, we weren't living anywhere remotely close to these people. They all lived on the east end of Ottawa while we were downtown (living at Notre Dame Cathedral). We were parishioners at St. Margaret Mary Parish—the parish closest to Carleton University where we were establishing CCO.

We would go to Mass at St. Margaret Mary, being sure to linger and visit there, and then pack the kids up in the van and drive down the Queensway to get to Annunciation Parish just in time for the end of 9:45 am Mass, which our friends were just coming out of. This was not an easy thing to do with three little ones; it was often stressful, hectic and frustrating. It would have been way easier to go to Mass and then head home, rather than throw the whole family into our old minivan and rush to the other side of the city. We were willing to make the trek week in and week out because we knew the long-term benefits would be worth it for the family. We would waltz in to Annunciation Parish Hall just in time for cookies and coffee! What mooches we were. But of course it wasn't about the cookies. It was about the community and friendships for us and for the kids. Out of these friendships grew faith-sharing small groups, opportunities to serve in parish ministry together, travel, and family get-togethers that continue to this day. The small group faith-sharing in particular was a huge blessing and support for us in raising our children. With my sisters in Christ, I had good listeners and received advice on things I was going through personally, or with family dynamics I was dealing with. I needed this. But mostly, the small group was a place of spiritual accountability, encouragement, and challenge. When I am spiritually supported and healthy, my family gets the best version of me and that is a strategic advantage for parenting.

Eventually we moved into a home closer to Annunciation and where these other families lived. We became active in the parish. Every Sunday, we would attend the 9:45 am Mass that, as my mom mentioned, offered cookies and coffee in the hall after Mass. There we would feast on mouth-watering goodies and, as kids, it was always exciting when a new type of cookie was on the roster. To this day, if one of our parish's classic closing songs is sung (does any other church sing 'Jerusalem my Destiny'?), my brothers and I notice that our mouths immediately begin to water with a strange yearning for church cookies and apple juice.

Due to the large age gap, my brothers and I have different childhood memories than my sisters would. Natalie was born when I was 11 and Janna when I was 14, so their childhood memories would have been in my teen years. None of our family friends had children their age and so my parents sought out friendships with CCO families who had girls the same age as my sisters. This community of CCO families has been such a blessing, especially to my sisters.

JANNA – Friends with Faith

I like my CCO friends (Elizabeth and Bridget) because they love God like I do. They are very supportive. Once I got a C– on my test and I was really bummed out. I told them about it and they told me, "Don't worry, that happens to everybody". They made me feel like it was no big deal so that I didn't feel judged. Another reason why they are good friends is because they keep their word. If I tell them a secret, I know they would never tell anyone. Whenever I'm at their house or having a sleepover with them, I always feel safe but when I'm visiting another person's house who isn't into their Catholic faith, I don't feel as comfortable. Elizabeth and Bridget don't make bad decisions and I can be comfortable around them with my faith. Honestly, I have never gotten into a fight with Elizabeth and Bridget because we're always kind to each other and respect each other, but I find with other friends, we fight sometimes because we don't show as much respect to each other.

It's beautiful for me to read Janna's description of her relationship with her Catholic friends. She put into words the same experience I would have had with my friends at that age. These communities of families created an environment of comfort, love and safety. Not simply in the physical sense but in the emotional sense. In these familial communities, it feels as if the other parents are your aunts and uncles. You know that they care for you and you trust them. I think that this is extremely important for kids in these sensitive years.

In addition to the comfort, safety, trust, and joy that come out of these relationships with family friends, it was also an invaluable source of support for encouraging our Christian values. Being around other families who had the same values encouraged Mom and Dad in their parenting and showed us that there are other families who lived out of the same moral framework and lifestyle.

Growing up, we were continually seeing the same values from our home life being lived in the other families in our Catholic community. Of course, the other families in our community had slightly different ways of parenting as well. For example, there were some movies that our friends were allowed to watch that we weren't, but we always took these differences lightly. We were able to grow in our childlike love for Christ and his Church through our experience of the Body of Christ in these families. We were faced with a drastic difference in parenting when with many of our school friends – not that it was all bad – but it can be difficult to navigate these things as a kid. And for myself now as a parent, I know how much anxiety it causes me when I think of how other kids and parents can influence my own children. That motivates me to build a village for my family that is solid.

The kids in 'the village' we grew up in would play Mass, watch Veggie Tales, or make a Christian-themed skit for the parents—and we made many of these skits. I want to acknowledge the superhuman patience of the parents who had to sit and watch these painful productions, all the while making us kids think that our performance was worthy of Broadway. Overall, there was a common sense of morality among the adults and the children alike.

In fact, the friendships I formed as a kid have lasted my whole life. My childhood group of Catholic friends has grown up; many of us are now married and having kids and even our children are all friends now. In the summer of 2018 though, Marc and I, like my mom and dad, responded to the Lord's call to move across the country for the sake of the Gospel. It was hard; it was scary. It was unimaginable for me to leave behind my whole life, all my family, friends and support systems. We weren't just leaving our city, we were leaving our village. In those last weeks together as a family, we had been working full-time on this very book. Eventually the day came when it was time to leave everyone and everything behind.

We went to my parents' place for our 'last brunch' as a family. We talked, we laughed, we ate. And then someone had the idea to read the daily readings aloud. As soon as it began, I was dumbfounded. It read:

> Then Peter said, "Look, we have left our homes and followed you." And he said to them, "Truly I tell you, there is no one who has left house or wife or brothers or parents or children, for the sake of the kingdom of God, who will not get back very much more in this age, and in the age to come eternal life." Luke 18: 28-30

Tears filled my eyes. It was the same exact reading Mom and Dad had read when they left for Ottawa from Saskatoon many years prior. The Lord works in the details! It was a profound moment for our family. We all sat in a few moments of silence, aware that this was holy ground. It was a 'coming full circle' experience. Now Marc and I were in my parents' shoes. We knew what we had to do once we got to Halifax. We hugged, we cried, we got in our van and drove across the country, all for the sake of souls.

Once in Halifax, we did what my parents had done years earlier. We connected with other young Catholics, mainly CCO staff families (a double whammy of role models and community). We made sure to attend a vibrant parish with lots of young families, all so that our kids could be nourished like I had been growing up.

Relationships with priests and nuns should also be mentioned. We had the blessing of having several seminarians, priests, and bishops (and a papal nuncio!) in our home. My parents' friendship with clergy offered us kids an authentic witness of our parents' faith. It showed us that the priest is not just someone who says Mass on Sundays but someone who would play sports and eat deep-fried chicken wings with us. Having priests and other religious as a part of our community, in a fun setting, created a healthy relationship with the Church. It helped me to see God the Father as more approachable, because 'Father' was someone that I felt close to. Church became all the more a 'home'—somewhere I felt delight and somewhere I belonged. I am blessed to even have a priest and a nun as my godparents. This always gave me an especially close connection to the clergy.

ANGÈLE – Fostering Vocations

The presence of seminarians, sisters, priests and bishops in our home was a natural catechesis for vocational discernment as the children saw healthy and attractive vocations regularly. I believes the fruit of their presence in our home was that the kids never indicated the typical fear young people have, that God might call them to be a priest or a nun. I'm not saying they didn't experience it, but I can tell you, we never had to talk them through it. What we did talk about though, was how they admired or were attracted to the priesthood or becoming a sister.

Our approach in all of this, even their interest, was to play it cool. We followed their lead. We gave them lots of opportunity and room to see the beauty of these vocations and to talk about it or not talk about it. When we saw an attraction, we increased our prayer and gave God permission to call our child to whatever vocation he wanted them in.

The reason we played it cool was that we have seen the problem that happens to a young person's freedom when an enthusiastic parent or grandparent proudly announces to their friends that their daughter aspires to be a nun, or their grandson wants to be a priest. This cheerleading approach does something to rob the child from being able to grow up and discern in full freedom and privacy. They can feel pigeon-holed and trapped by innocent attractions to the beauty of a holy life. Safeguarding that personal freedom was paramount to André and I. As much as we would love to have one of our children be a priest or a nun, this vocational calling is between them and God. We did not want to sabotage what the Holy Spirit was doing through lack of support or a deluge of support.

And so what we pass on to you, is to encourage vocations in an atmosphere of gentle freedom through natural, healthy conversations and with the real-life friendship of priests and nuns. If your teenage child or even college-aged child is more seriously discerning a vocation, we still recommend to you, dear parents and grandparents, that you keep their discernment confidential. It is a very personal and weighty decision and it can be really hard on a young man in particular to see the glowing face of his mother, grandmother and every little old lady at Church who is eagerly awaiting his ordination (but he's only 15 years old). Talk about pressure! Parents, please protect your child's heart and give room for these aspiring young people to clearly hear the Lord's call without pressure.

As you can see, community is such an important part of the faith journey. It is something that equally benefits both parents and children. It was truly invaluable to our family to have people who helped us to be stronger in our faith. These friendships encouraged our family in our faith and values and offered a safe place for fun.

ANGÈLE

Raising our children in the village meant that we as parents were a big part of creating environments for the kids to grow spiritually together. So that meant being a volunteer, leader, or all-out organizer of: children's liturgy, Kids4Jesus clubs, Vacation Bible School, All Saints Day parties, sacramental preparation classes, or Mom and Tots groups. These wonderful ministries for kids really don't happen unless moms make it happen.

My kids have awesome memories of these experiences and they were truly positive sources of evangelization and formation for them. Praise God. But just to get real for a few moments; for me it was a struggle. Frankly, the last thing I wanted to do was lead these programs. It was like executing a birthday party every single week. We all know that a glass of wine is the required decompression strategy for post-birthday party syndrome, and maybe if I had had a glass of wine after every children's program I organized and delivered, I would have been more motivated … I should have thought of that before!

But honestly, I dreaded every single week. It was so hard to give myself to it. It would have been awesome if there had been motivated, altruistic, gifted people who offered these programs for the kids so I could just head on over to Starbucks and enjoy a cappuccino while glancing over home decor magazines. How awesome would that be? Too good to be true—that's how awesome. I knew if my kids were going to get these experiences, they would have to be initiated by me and the other moms. And I think you need to know that too. Your personal investment for love of your kids and your friends' kids is going to make these village moments happen. No one is as motivated as you are for your own kids. And as exhausted as you are my dear young parents, you actually have more energy than 50+ year olds to deliver these kid programs. Believe me!

My kids have great memories of those experiences, but do you know what? Often my friends now happily reminisce over them too. Even for me in the moment, as unmotivated as I was, there was always something very satisfying once it was done. I knew it was good and that positive things were happening for the kids (even with assorted behavioural nonsense that inevitably ensued). What I'm saying is, it was all worth it. It was hard, it was work, it was brutal, it took my energy, *but* it bore good fruit and was an opportunity for self-gift in my parenting. It was a decision us moms made to do something for the good of the children in our village.

Youth Group

The third major influence in our village was youth groups. Our family was blessed to be a part of a parish with an amazing youth group. As kids, we were ministered to by solid, faithful, and influential youth ministers and volunteers. The youth programs were an essential part of our formation as teenagers. In youth group, we were taught catechesis, how to develop a personal relationship with God, and how to live out the faith *at our level*. We were able to develop close friendships with people our age who were also wanting faith in their lives. When we became leaders for the junior youth group, we learned how to share our faith with others and it really formed our missionary hearts and increased our desire to lead people to Christ. Youth group was where all of us took the faith that we had grown up in, and truly made it our own. Our faith identity was no longer contingent on our parents. It became our lived relationship with God and his Church.

There are some barriers that can come up when trying to get your child involved in youth group, however. We want to address three common barriers to entry:

1. Fear of Cliques

I remember the first time I went to youth group in Grade 7. I walked into the hall of our parish—the same hall I had spent countless hours in as a kid, running around with my friends after Mass, eating cookies, and drinking apple juice. This time though, I was terrified. I opened those big white doors to a group of pre-teens I barely recognized. As I looked around, I felt completely alone. Everyone was having fun talking to someone while I stood there awkwardly by myself, practically with a sign over my head flashing 'loner' or 'loser'. In the world of a teenager, this is pretty much as bad as it gets. As soon as everyone was called to sit down for the night, I found myself alone with no one to sit with. I ran out of the room, grabbed the church phone, and dialed my parents. I sat in that little hallway crying and begging my parents to come and take me home.

I am telling this story because I suspect many teens out there can relate. Unfortunately for many kids, this marks the end of their youth group experience and they never come back again. Many parents approached my husband when he was youth minister complaining that the group was too 'cliquey' and that their child was not properly welcomed.

Even though I felt like this too when I was 13, my parents decided to encourage me to just keep going, and I did. In fact, while discussing this book, I found out for the first time that my mom had approached one of the leaders and asked her to 'have my back' and make sure I was comfortable and making friends. Mom confessed that she had been really worried for me, and all my siblings, during this stage of integrating into youth group. She struggled with fears that we wouldn't fit in, we wouldn't like it, we wouldn't want to go and that our young lives of faith would begin to unravel. She told me how she had to push beyond the anxiety and make sure it didn't come out in how she related to us about youth group—like slipping into a forceful approach, or being too excited about it. She said she tried to play it cool so as not to set us off with any weird vibes on her part. Wow, I had had no idea this was all going on for her then, although I did see some of it play out with Natalie and Janna at times.

Thanks to the support of my parents, I pushed past the awkwardness of not having friends in that moment and came to a point where I made great friends, some of whom remained in my life throughout high school and are still some of my closest friends today.

A year later, if you had looked into the parish hall, you would have seen a crowd of teenagers who all seem to be having fun talking to someone. And this time, *I* was one of them. This is the reality of youth group; every single teen needs to start somewhere. The awkward beginning is just a normal part of the journey, but eventually those who come weekly and engage fully will make great friends. The accusation of cliques in youth group is a bit tricky, I find.

Cliques are exclusive and destructive to teens who want to form friendships. But I think that often what many people perceive as cliques are actually just healthy fellowship. In any group of people, conversations naturally flow among people who already know each other. This does not mean that exclusions are taking place. I perceived on my first day of youth group that cliques were everywhere. The truth is that conversations were happening everywhere and I just had to meet some people to be a part of them. Looking back, I see that it was a normal life lesson that I was fortunate to learn early on. I am sure my parents were heartbroken to hear their daughter on the phone crying because she felt like she did not fit in. But instead of taking this personally and feeling resentment against the whole youth group environment, they encouraged me to keep going, suggested friends that I could invite to go with me, and kept bringing me every single week—even when it was difficult—because they knew that eventually, it would become familiar and easy.

Caleb had to overcome a different struggle when it came to youth group.

2. "Too Cool for School" Attitude

CALEB

Even with a family as invested in faith as mine, I needed to go outside of the home to grow spiritually. I see now that it was really important for me to be able to make a personal decision to follow Christ in a context that was away from my family. It can be very easy for children to reject their Catholic faith. But I feel like it is not any better when someone just slides into a 'cultural Catholicism' which reduces their Catholic identity to the fact that their parents are Catholic.

Teenage years are almost inevitably filled with rebellion. I thought I was way too cool for youth group—it just seemed nerdy to me. From the outside, the idea of youth group did not seem like entering into this exciting adventure with Jesus. It seemed like awkward icebreakers and subpar potlucks with people I didn't even know. This 'too cool for school' mentality could have been detrimental to my spiritual growth. My parents saw it right away. One of the first youth group events that I was invited to was a weekend retreat. "Count me out," I thought. I remember Dad sitting me down before the weekend and practically giving me no other choice. He approached youth group the same way my parents approached Mass: "This is just what we do and there is no other option." In other words, he forced me to go that weekend. I remember sulking in the car the whole ride up. And I pouted for the first couple of hours of the retreat too. But slowly, I started to open up. Of course, just as my dad had assured me, I really enjoyed the weekend. It was in fact a time where I encountered God the Father's love for me.

I'm pretty sure that if Dad had given me any other option to get out of this retreat, I would have taken it. And that would have set a precedent for every youth group night thereafter. Dad standing his ground that day was so important for my future journey to Christ. If I'm being honest, even after this positive experience at the retreat, it was still a battle (albeit a much smaller battle) to get me to go. Regardless, I was thrown in the family van week after week, and sooner than you could cry out "God is good, all the time—all the time, God is good," I was begging Dad to hurry up so that I could get to youth group faster and hang out with my friends.

3. Lack of Opportunity

We know that not everyone will have access to a youth group. Or, if they do, their youth group may be weakly executed (to put it nicely). If your parish does not have a youth group (or a good one), then we would advise doing whatever you have to do in order to get to one. Elizabeth's family is a prime example of this commitment to ensuring that teenagers have access to youth group.

ELIZABETH – Make the Effort

In my own family, I am the fifth of eight children, so I had many older siblings to look up to and few things looked more attractive to me than the excitement of youth group. When my two older brothers were old enough for youth group, there was actually nothing for them at our country parish. So my parents would take most of the family to Mass at the local parish Sunday morning, then drive my brothers 45 minutes away so they could go to Sunday night youth Mass at Annunciation (in the city). When I became a teenager, I begged my parents to move parishes completely so that we could go to youth group and worship at Mass as a whole family every week. I needed to be supported by people who were my age and who were into their faith. I could not find that anywhere else (other than at a Catholic summer camp for two weeks of the year). My parents heard my cry and realized that they couldn't sustain keeping their feet in two parishes; they committed to the further one with the youth program. I was so happy!

I recognize that this took serious sacrifice from my parents but it was so necessary. In fact, they were driving twice a week to the parish (some of us were at the junior youth group, some at the senior one). My parents sacrificed time, money, and even preferred vacation opportunities to form a village around our family.

If having a village surrounding your children is so important, yet you live far away from opportunities such as youth groups, family retreats, or even youth conferences, what then? Well, I think my parents were on to something: do whatever you need to do to get them there—even if it requires you to make sacrifices.

As Elizabeth emphasizes: do *whatever* it takes! We are aware that many faithful teenagers have been formed without the influence of a youth group. So yes, it is not a necessary prerequisite to becoming a faithful person. But we would argue that it is not worth the risk.

If a regular youth group is not offered, we suggest you send your kid to a conference or retreat, whether it is near or far. Alana, as an example, never went to youth group growing up. Her hometown did not have a dynamic youth group, and there were no other options nearby. But, she had a major conversion after travelling long-distance to attend a retreat:

ALANA – Retreats

I can stand by Elizabeth with her sentiment of doing whatever it takes. Growing up in a small town in Saskatchewan, there were not many opportunities for young Catholic role models in town, let alone a vibrant youth group. Finding my village consisted of travelling to weekend 'Face to Face' retreats to find a sense of community. My mom would often drive me to other small towns in western Canada for these retreats, sometimes traveling up to eight hours. Not to one-up Lizz, but it was usually uphill, both ways … in the middle of winter. Did I mention barefoot?

All jokes aside, these weekend retreats were like an oasis for me during those pivotal high school years. It was at one of these retreats that I first made the decision to invite Jesus to be at the centre of my life. It pains me to say that out of six kids in my family, I am the only one who is still practising the faith. We all had the same upbringing. Sunday Mass was not a question and family prayer was common. So what made the difference? The one and only difference was that I was given the opportunity to attend Catholic retreats—retreats where I had the opportunity to hear the Gospel in a clear and simple way and was invited to respond. My mom often shares that she wishes the same opportunities were given to my older siblings because she saw the impact it made on my life. My mom could have said "that retreat is too far" or "this is getting expensive" but she saw the value of it and was willing to sacrifice, and her sacrifice had eternal consequences in my life. If the opportunities are not present to form your village close to home, take that bus uphill both ways. You will find it is so worth it. For me, it meant the difference between faith and falling away!

As a family, we have seen that conferences, retreats, youth events, and parish youth groups are all valuable ways for teenagers to engage with the faith on their own terms and in a way that appeals to them. Our parents saw the importance of this and they tried to co-operate with the work that these ministries sought to fulfill in the lives of the teens that they reach out to. Marc, has a few words of advice to share from his perspective as our parish's friendly neighbourhood youth minister emeritus.

MARC – Youth Minister's Advice for Parents

When you think of youth group, do you imagine a group of perfectly pious children devoted wholeheartedly to their faith, who can list Latin as their second language, go to Church every day, and are regularly levitating when they're not bilocating? In most realities, it is a place where kids get messy, run wild, and have one volume: LOUD. This is not to say that youth groups don't encourage spiritual growth, because they absolutely do. All the games, chaos, laughter, and yelling are crucial to reaching teens at their level. And that connection and comfort builds a platform of trust from which we can speak to the youth about making a commitment to follow Christ.

In my eight years of experience as a youth minister, I have seen that parents can play a big role in co-operating with the work of youth ministry. Here are some strategies I offer from experience to ensure that your child is getting the most out of youth group:

1. In my own estimation, I would say 70 percent of youth group kids do not return if their parents are not invested in their own spiritual journey. Young people are like sponges; they absorb far more than we realize. I found that they were really open to the teachings we gave at youth group, but I also noticed that if the youth didn't see those same Catholic discipleship practices modelled at home, the seed of formation we gave them rarely grew.

   Youth who are learning that Jesus is the most important thing at youth group should be able to recognize this priority in their own parents' lifestyles. If teens are told at a youth group talk to strive for a daily prayer life or to go to Mass on Sundays, but the parents are not doing it themselves, the teens won't bother. So my advice to parents is to be those living role models. You don't have to give the talks to youth, you just have to walk the talk.

2. If your child is really enjoying youth group, they may end up pushing their limits with curfew and not let you know exactly what they are doing at all times. That is, they get home a little later because they were hanging out after youth group to go grab ice cream or a burger. As a parent, give your child space and freedom to rebel in a healthy way. Don't smother them. Instead, be a parent who encourages them to have fun with their friends. Why not? They are hanging out with the crowd you most likely want them to be with and in a safe environment. Far too often, I have seen parents smother their teens with the good intention of being diligent parents. The repercussion is that the teens miss out on opportunities to bond deeply with their youth group friends— *something which often occurs beyond youth group hours.*

3. This is a little thing I used to say to parents. If you want to know what's on your child's heart and how to encourage them spiritually, you need to P.A.Y. them.

   ■ **Praise** them often for making a holy decision to go to youth group.

   ■ **Ask** about what happened with follow-up questions, always being attentive and truly listening to them. And then,

   ■ **Yield**. Children do not necessarily want to be given the answers for how to fix their problems. It is part of their growth as an individual to work through life. This means parents must learn the skill of biting their tongue at times. This also means not being afraid of silence with a teenager. Just because there is silence does not mean they do not want to talk to you. Be patient for them to open up, for the courage to well up inside of them. Every child is different in the way that they communicate. Some may not want to share anything at all, while others may just need to be asked. Your patience and kindness will pay off. Believe me.

Conclusion

As we said from the outset, our great hope is that by reading this book, you will be able to look at its principles and adopt some of the methods we used in order to help you raise your children to have a personal relationship with Jesus, live their faith dynamically, and have an evangelistic heart. As you can see, my parents cannot take credit as the only vessels that God used to teach and show us how to be disciples. The 'village' that we grew up in was an essential aspect in achieving this goal. We are who we are thanks to many beautiful, faithful people. So to close this chapter, we would urge you to establish your village:

- A village with youthful role models who children can look up to and aspire to be, whose relationship with the Lord is alive and attractive.

- A village with faith-filled families who can act as a community for yourselves and your children, walking with you on your family's faith journey.

- A village with a youth group where your children can go to belong, encounter Jesus, claim their faith as their own and grow in Catholic leadership.

Reflection / Action Points

1. How is your family's village looking right now? Who are the people influencing your children? Do they confirm and affirm your family values?

2. Which of the three parts of the Catholic village is your family strongest in (young role models, family community, or youth group)? Which of the three is your family the weakest in?

3. How can you seek out relationships with people who could become part of your Catholic village?

4. Where is the best youth group or youth conferences in your area? What is your resolve to get your kids there?

5. How can you P.A.Y. (Praise, Ask, Yield) more for your teenage child?

6. Are you part of the village for other families? How are you influencing them, and how can you continue to do so?

CHAPTER 2

In The World Not Of The World

Being Missionary as a Family

MYLÈNE

The world we live in is becoming more and more secular. Our society has largely rejected God and we are seeing the devastating consequences of that. It is all over the news, it's in our social media, our schools, and even our Church. Young Catholic families struggle and strive to raise children who will be able to weather the storms of this world and come out the other side with their faith intact. What if this is the wrong goal though? What if we aimed not just to *survive* the storm but to actually fight against it? Why not aim higher than just hoping your kids will go to Mass when they grow up? Why not aspire to raise children who have a dynamic faith animated by a lived relationship with Jesus? Raising children for holiness is essential, but even this is incomplete. The Church's missionary mandate begs us to look outward. Holiness and mission go hand in hand. As Pope Benedict XVI said in his homily at Santa Maria di Leuca and Brindisi:

> *"It is clear that the Church's holiness and missionary character are two sides of the same coin: only because she is holy, that is, filled with divine love, can the Church carry out her mission, and it is precisely in terms of this task that God chose her and sanctified her as his property."*[13]

Pope Benedict emphasizes here that holiness and mission are two sides of the same coin; you cannot have one without the other. That is the paradigm my parents had in raising us. They wanted to nurture our love for Jesus *and*

---

13. Pope Benedict XVI, *Homily in St Apollinaris Wharf, Port of Brindisi*, Sunday, 15 June 2008.

his mission. Many Catholic families naturally understand that passing on the faith is necessary. But passing on the mission doesn't come as naturally. It feels too forceful, perhaps. What we hope you come to understand is that holiness and mission must come hand in hand. If our faith is presented as something that needs to be shared rather than an insular personal good, then the value and importance of it becomes universal. It becomes bigger than our little world. Showing the importance of mission in tandem with holiness gives our kids a higher understanding of the faith, an understanding that it is something *so* important, that the whole world needs to know.

Our parents grounded us spiritually, thanks in large part to our community of faith. But they also prepared us to care about those in the world *outside* our village. As missionaries, they are keenly aware that for every one person we know who is faithful, hundreds of thousands more are out there who are lost. Disciples live in a world where they are a minority, and this requires a tricky balance between living defensively (to remain faithful) and offensively (to evangelize). My parents tried to find this balance for our family and for us kids. Our parents wanted us to be in the world but not of the world; to be the salt of the earth and the light of the world. They knew that our family in itself is called to be a powerful agent for evangelization in society, and that each of us children in our own relationships and circumstances would be a powerful army of authentic, albeit mini-witnesses so desperately needed in our culture. They were concerned about the impact on souls and society if all the good families retreated into hiding. Their perspective was surely formed by the Church herself:

> *"One cannot fail to stress the evangelizing action of the family in the evangelization apostolate of the laity. At different moments in the Church's history and also in the Second Vatican Council, the family has well deserved the beautiful name of "domestic Church." This means that there should be found in every Christian family the various aspects of the entire Church. Furthermore, the family, like the Church, ought to be a place where the Gospel is transmitted and from which the Gospel radiates. In a family which is conscious of this mission, all the members evangelize and are evangelized. The parents not only communicate the Gospel to their children, but from their children they can themselves receive the same Gospel as deeply lived by them. And such a family becomes the evangelizer of many other families, and of the neighborhood of which it forms part."* [14]

---

14. Pope Paul VI, *Evangelii Nuntiandi*, December 8, 1971, 71.

How Our Family Evangelized in the World

ANGÈLE

A challenging question was raised by my daughter-in-law as we gathered for our chapter preparation discussion one Sunday after brunch. Elizabeth asked, "So when the kids were little, were you missionary as a family in your home?" In other words, did we intentionally invite people into our homes whom we sought to evangelize? To be honest, she had me a little stumped. Much of the context of which we had been discussing was sounding more protective and insular than outreaching and evangelistic. Hmm. Maybe we did only have 'churchy families' over to our house. This was a sobering thought, since I so passionately believe God calls us to be a missionary family engaged in the world. I had to do a bit more analysis and reflection on how we did it and how we are doing things these days. Did we largely raise our family in a community of faithful people or were we more open, bringing others (who are not practising their faith) into our home as a means of outreach?

On one side, our family can be a positive witness and influence, and we want to do that because we desire for these people to know the Lord.

On the other side, in many ways, we are still evangelizing our own children until they make their own 'adult, informed decision' to be a disciple of Christ.

As missionaries, you would think that we focused on the former, but we actually were more conscious of the latter. Let me explain. Indeed, we do see ourselves as a missionary family with a heart to evangelize others, and we did that in a variety of ways and touchpoints which you will read about in this chapter. But when it came to our social life in the home, we found we needed to guard that in a particular way to be a safe and good place to raise our kids.

We kind of learned that lesson through experience. I remember a season in our life when we were getting chummy with a particular secular family. For André and I, we had no desire to judge them for their moral parenting compass. We weren't scandalized that they didn't see things the way we saw them through our Catholic Christian lens. We hoped that someday, in the light of God's grace, they could come to understand. The problem for us wasn't if André and I could be understanding, it was *if our kids could understand*.

Over the months of family social time with them, we consistently got into confusing situations for our children. The kinds of activities their kids were trying to get our kids into were super uncomfortable for me: certain movies, music, and games. It got awkward for our kids who often instinctively knew we wouldn't approve of the stuff these kids were doing. They didn't understand the way the other family acted. The kids were either scandalized by their behaviours or jealous of what the other children were allowed to do: "Why does her mom let her dress like that?" "Why does he get to talk back like that to his parents?" "Why are they allowed to have that technology?" When those questions are just occasional occurrences, they can provide teachable moments to form their young consciences. But too much opposition, too often—at school, after school, on the weekend, everywhere—risks crushing these seedlings' sprouting faith. Luckily for us, they moved to another city and that solved the situation. Otherwise, we would have had to find excuses to dial back the relationship for the sake of our kids' hearts.

So how then am I actually answering Elizabeth's question? We largely guarded our family social life, weekends and vacations to be with our 'village.' Our family's missionary interactions happened, but in other spheres. For example, being a witness in our school community.

Our decision to have our kids in the Catholic public system is an intentional way to live out our call to be a missionary family. I feel like we've tried it all when it comes to schooling. I homeschooled for two years, and we also had Mylène in private Catholic school for a year. But the conclusion that we have come to is that, as CCO missionaries, our family needs to be missionary and we cannot hide our children from the world. They must engage with the people living in the world. The presence of our children and family has been a good thing to boost both the Catholic identity in the school as well as our kids' development so as to learn how to make the right decisions in the midst of their peers. This learning in a classroom is timely and age-appropriate. Teaching our little kindergarteners how to mind their manners when others were not or instructing our nine-year-olds to walk away from inappropriate language and games were powerful real-time opportunities to help our kids discern what is wrong and to have the courage to be their own person and do the right thing. It would make me nervous, at times, knowing that my children might be exposed to things that I didn't want them to see or hear yet, but I was convicted that we were building their formation muscles to strengthen them in the seemingly small moral choices so they can have the self-confidence to act according to their consciences in the weightier ones.

We also encourage our kids to choose friends who make good choices. Even if they aren't particularly practising, the moral compasses of these friends can be pretty tuned. In these little friendships, we use any incongruence as a teachable moment to help our children choose the right thing to do. For example, a friend they have in school might enjoy a particular TV show, or music artist, or fashion style. These engagements 'with the world' are opportunities for conversation with our children to determine if it is okay or harmful for them. These conversations tend to turn into a missionary training lesson as we talk the situation through, helping the kids determine how to navigate conversations with their friend regarding that thing their friend is into and they are not. We want to help them find a way to perhaps avoid the topic, or how to explain their lack of interest without sounding judgmental. Sometimes it is necessary to equip our child to explain why it isn't right to do the things their friend wants to do. These interactions with good school friends provide many teachable moments for the children to learn how to be a witness to their peers in real life situations.

There are other opportunities for kids to be witnesses to their classmates and even to their Catholic school teachers. I recall situations where the kids spoke up in class to say things like, "Umm, actually, just because Jesus became human doesn't mean he sinned," or, "Actually, Mary was without sin too. This is why she is called the Immaculate Conception." The stories go on and on. It definitely takes courage for a young person to speak about the faith in front of their whole class, but what we feel is more important is the manner in which it is said. We've taught our children to always answer respectfully and to avoid any air of arrogance when they speak up. Speaking in a haughty way only discredits the truth they are trying to communicate. I have to admit, most of the time Mylène, Jo and Caleb did a great job of speaking respectfully, something that Natalie and Janna now get to wade into.

That respectful approach interacting with Catholic teachers goes for us as parents too. A fellow CCO missionary composed a carefully worded email to gently point her son's teachers to the truth that Jesus was indeed God, even though she had taught the class that he was not. Later, her son came home and told his mom that his teacher told the class "that she was mistaken, and that they needed to know that Jesus was in fact truly God, second Person of the Trinity—and she said it was because you taught that to her." Can you imagine the emotion for this mom of knowing that her clarity and charity had won the day?

Sports teams or other such community activities are another arena for evangelization (pun intended). Witness in this sphere of influence comes largely through our child's behaviour as well as our own. *How* our family interacts with other children, parents, and coaches is subtle but powerful. How do we speak to or about the coach? Other parents? Our spouses?

When we don't get into gossip but instead speak in a tone that is positive, joyful, and sincere, it stands out. When they don't hear bad language or criticism coming out of our mouths, they notice that something is different.

And then there are Sundays and sports. It doesn't get more obvious that you are a practising Catholic when you make sure your children get to Mass despite tournaments and the like. (How times have changed—sports on Sunday never used to be a thing so much.) But this is where the culture is at and the contrast of values provides an opportunity to witness to our faith. This can be done in a beautiful way as long as you don't get preachy or weird about it. For us, we just find a way to get to Mass without making a stink about the schedule. And if that means we have no alternative but to miss out on a game or a team breakfast, we just matter-of-factly let some people know we will meet up with them later after we've gone to Mass. We aim to have no snarkiness of voice, no judgements of the fact that they are not going to Mass. But we also try not to have any sheepish awkwardness about it either. We try just to keep it natural, chill, and confident— not holier-than-thou.

There are also those neighbourly interactions with the people on your street with whom to be friendly, kind, and helpful. Keep in mind that they see how you act, and interact. They see how you live your life and how you and your children are in the car heading for Mass every Sunday morning.

So in all of this, I think you can see that we didn't hide our family in a monastery on top of a remote mountain in order to keep their little hearts pure and guarded for God. We are a missionary family in the world and we know that everyone we encounter each day is loved by the Father and that Jesus died for them.

Certainly we are in the world, but we are also not *of* the world, and that's where the community—the village—comes in. Our life and interaction in the world does need that community of believers to protect, form, inspire, and model the kind of person of faith we desire our child to be. We can't do it alone in our mountain monastery. We do need that community to help us grow our children in a holistic and healthy way. We also need the world with, dare I say, some of that worldliness to be a practice ground for building our children's consciences and giving them real experiences of witnessing to their faith as missionary disciples.

Being placed in scenarios where we were 'in the world' obviously had its difficulties. Being Christians in a world that hates or opposes what we stand for is definitely hard, even scary, at times. But it is a growing process. The time in my life when I most struggled with standing firm in my faith was my high school years. Sadly, even in this Catholic school environment, I was constantly surrounded by non-practising people. I witnessed Jesus being discussed irreverently in religion class by students and teachers alike and heard morally objectionable conversations all around.

John 15:18-19 says: "If the world hates you, keep in mind that it hated me first. If you belonged to the world, it would love you as its own. As it is, you do not belong to the world, but I have chosen you out of the world. That is why the world hates you." Being judged or laughed at for your Catholic beliefs is something that every faithful child in a school setting inevitably faces. As Christians, hope and strength comes out of our knowledge that, yes, we are in the world but we do not 'belong to the world'. We belong to something; that is, *Someone* far greater than this world. Battling through the difficult conversations and mocking comments, I was drawn closer to the Father in my acknowledgement of him before others. I was able to remain strong and hopeful because I knew deep inside that my identity was rooted in him who is the way, the truth, and the life.[15]

I, of course, am no longer a high school student, so let's hear from Natalie about being a witness in the current school scene.

NATALIE – Friends at School

It's true; not everyone is as into their faith as I am. I learned this at a very young age and, although it was hard, I learned to accept it. Because of this, it has been hard for me to find *good* friends. I have learned that I need to become a leader, someone who accepts my non-Catholic friends and tries to bring them closer to Jesus. An example of this is that instead of judging my friends for their behaviours, I regularly invite them to come with me to youth group.

Sometimes people notice that there is something different about me. Some kids come up to me and ask why I'm constantly smiling and happy. Some people tease me and call me 'goody two-shoes'. Even though they joke with me like that, I know they still like me and find me cool. I don't get into people's faces about Catholic stuff, but I also don't hide my faith either—be it my crucifix on my neck, the songs on my playlist, my regular involvement at the parish, how I talk, or how I treat people at school.

My friends sometimes talk about stuff I'm not comfortable with. This is really hard for me. I'm not always sure about what I should do or say. I can't just tell them that what they're talking about is wrong or bad. They wouldn't want to talk to me; they would think all I do is get mad at everything they say. So I try to respond by not laughing or by silently standing there so they get the impression that I'm not enjoying the topic in hopes they will change it. But there was one time in particular where it went too far.

I was talking with my friends about Jo and Lizz when they got engaged. They asked if they slept together. I told them "no" and they were surprised. They asked me why and I told them that it's because our family believes that sex should only follow the lifelong commitment of marriage. They started arguing with me and

---

15. cf John 14:6.

telling me that it's okay if couples sleep together before getting married. But again I told them, "that's what my family believes." They continued to talk about this subject and I became uncomfortable. I mean, who wouldn't feel weird if their friends were talking about their siblings like that? I asked to change the subject and they simply told me "No. If you want us to stop, then leave. Because we won't." So I left.

Being in the world but not of the world is challenging. It's hard to swim against the current while still trying to remain relatable to those around you, especially when you're only in early high school.

When I was about to enter Grade 8, a family from 'our village' told my parents about a private Catholic school that they were planning on sending their daughter to. I had never been in the same school with either of my best friends so the prospect of going to school with one of them was a dream. My parents registered me to go to this small, unabashedly Catholic private school. That year was probably the best school year of my life. I woke up every morning without dread. Maybe it was because I wore a uniform and did not have to decide what to wear every day. But what made it so fun for me was the fact that I could fully be myself. The friends and the Catholic atmosphere made me comfortable. I was able to be me—the real me.

Then the year ended and I had a decision to make. Should I remain in this place of Catholic comfort or do I go back to the public Catholic high school for Grade 9? This was the first time I had to discern something big by myself. My parents suggested I take a Bible and set aside some time to pray about the decision. That was a big assignment to give a 14-year-old, but they knew the Lord would speak to me and I would listen.

I remember it well. I was sitting on the rocking chair in the living room. The house was silent. Clearly everyone must have been gone. I'm sure Mom and Dad took the other kids out shopping or something to give me space to pray. I was in great emotional distress. Making this decision was extremely daunting for me. I thought through every single possibility. I went over the pros and cons repeatedly. I was making no progress in either direction.

I sat there, closed my eyes, and lifted a prayer to God, abandoning the following year to him so that his will would be done, not mine. As soon as I sat in silence, the words John 16:20 came into my mind and wouldn't leave. I grabbed my dad's worn leather Bible and looked it up:

"Very truly, I tell you, you will weep and mourn, but the world will rejoice; you will have pain, but your pain will turn into joy. When a woman is in labor, she has pain, because her hour has come. But when her child is born, she no longer remembers the anguish because of the joy of having brought a human being into the world." John 16:20

I read this verse over and over again in awe. I knew in my heart what the Lord was asking me to do. You see, I had a specific friend in the Catholic public school system that I really felt the need to witness to and share Christ with and this was one of the pros of going to public school. I knew, in reading this passage, that God was asking me to make the hard decision in order to lead others to him. He was calling me to discomfort in that moment, for the promise of joy in him, and for the purpose of glorifying him to those I encountered.

After speaking to my parents years later, they confirmed that this call I received was as much a call for them as it was for me. Obviously, they also struggled with the decision between placing their children in a sheltered, comfortable situation or to place them in the world. In Christ's beckoning to me as a 14-year-old, he was confirming to my parents that our family was called to be missionary. To live in the world but not be of the world.

I am thankful for my experiences in both homeschooling and Catholic private schools. Our family has been in both, and I think that we were where we were supposed to be in each of those times. We recognize that God calls every child and family to something different. It is the role of parents to discern this and to empower their children's discernment when they are ready.

Learning to live out the mission in my daily life was a real learning curve. But I persevered because my little missionary heart was stronger than my fear and uncertainty. Of course my parents, being quite literally professional evangelists, knew what they were doing. (One might assume that my parents trained us in the matter of evangelization, but I really have little recollection of them ever doing that unless we asked for advice.) What I do know is that a missionary heart was instilled into me by the example of my parents and in the way that they spoke about those who were far from the faith. The key to reaching out to people is not to tell them how they should be living but to introduce them to him who offers them eternal life.

Relationship Before Doctrine and Devotion

ANDRÉ

As we have explained, the current state of the world can provoke two extremes. First, to succumb to the pressure, embrace the world, and become lax in the practice of the faith. This is the prevalent behaviour of Catholics today. The other extreme is to become insular in our faith and hostile to the outside world, seeing them as the enemy. Neither of these approaches make for compelling witnesses to the faith. The former being 'in the world, of the world'; the latter being 'not in the world, against the world'. If we want to reach the whole world for Christ, we need to learn to be 'in the world' so that we can reach people. However, in order to actually reach them with the Gospel, we need to be 'not of the world' because we belong to Christ.

Now, if we are going to reach out to 'the world', we need to know how best to engage with people who do not know God or do not know him well enough. For the most part I would say that we, the modern Church, have missed the mark in our approach. Our message of first importance leans towards promoting doctrines, observances, and regulations of the faith. This backfires and comes across as preachy and judgmental. We think we're promoting the practice of the faith but we fail to see that people really need to have a living faith first. From the hundreds of conversations I have had with university students, I can tell that young people are resistant to faith because they see it as a series of rules they must follow and a restriction to their freedom.

If someone were to slap down a big book in front of you filled with rules and regulations on how to live a married life, but you were still single, and told you that you must follow every rule, you would immediately reject it. "What do you mean I am not allowed to date other people anymore?", "Why would I want to share my belongings?", "No, I don't want to have to run all my decisions past someone else!" Outside of a marriage relationship these rules seem arbitrary, restrictive, and undesirable. I believe we have been explaining the faith like a marriage without a spouse. In order to reach the world we need first to propose a relationship, not impose a set of doctrines. In making the relationship our message of first importance, we make faith attractive. Pope Benedict said in an interview, "Christianity, Catholicism, isn't a collection of prohibitions: it's a positive option. It is very important that we look at it again because this idea has almost completely disappeared today. We have heard so much about what is not allowed that now it is time to say, 'We have a positive idea to offer.'"[16] That positive idea is that God invites us to enter into a loving relationship with him now and forever.

16. Pope Benedict XVI, *Interview of the Holy Father Benedict XVI in Preparation for the Upcoming Journey to Bavaria.* 05 August 2006.

When we were evangelizing our children, we started by communicating the message of first importance: that our faith in God is a matter of a personal relationship with him. This personal and intimate relationship changes the way you live your life and how you relate to God, his Church, and the world around you. Once people have encountered and responded to God's invitation to relationship, they have a desire and understanding to conform their lives to that relationship, which is where doctrine and devotion become essential.

We spoke to our children about how God, in his love for them, was inviting them to enter into a personal relationship and that it was their decision to allow him to be at the centre of their lives or not. Honestly, this decision changes everything. Each of our children personally moved from just knowing about Jesus to encountering him and being in a living relationship with him. Thus, in a certain way, you could say that each of our kids had a sense that they were lost and needed to be found. This realization was important because it helped them to see that the people in the world around them are lost from God, just like they themselves had been once. They also appreciated how the relationship they were encountering with Jesus that now animated the doctrine and devotions in their life, was the missing piece that held so many people back from the Church. With this understanding, we can look at friends and family who are not practising and not consider them to be bad people, but rather look at them with compassion and patience as people who do not yet have this relationship. The world is not the enemy; the world is the mission field.

While this mentality was something that we were taught our whole lives, it was still painful for me to watch my friends turn to sinful lifestyles. Unfortunately, a close friend of mine whom I felt called to evangelize in my high school years struggled with bad decisions. It was a teeter totter between her coming to love and believe in God and her suddenly giving it all up in favour of lesser, worldly things. This is a struggle that is often seen in high school students who haven't learned how to make tough decisions. This was a source of much frustration for me. I remember one day writing in my prayer journal and ranting to God about this issue. I had just learned through another friend that she had been into some pretty deep stuff on the weekend. I was so angry at the sin in her life and the doctrine that she failed to live by that I fiercely scribbled over and over again, "I'm just so MAD" over a quarter of the page. The Lord let me do my little rant (as he does) and then gently spoke words to me that I have never forgotten. I felt him say to me, "Bring her to me first, then all of her sins will fall away." I had become so focused on the way she was acting and how she wasn't living the 'right way' that I forgot the message of first importance: Jesus. My heart was filled with judgment rather than love and, as a result, I failed to convince her to change her ways. The only way to change her was to let Jesus change her. Genuine and sincere obedience to doctrine can only flow out of a real commitment and love for God.

JO

Growing up, my nickname in the family was 'FS: Fight-Starter'. I was always the first to start a fight and I wouldn't drop the bone until I had proven to everyone that I was right. And I didn't want them just to admit I was right; they had to understand why I was right and they were wrong. This was a major character flaw that caused more conflict and yelling in our family than I would like to admit. But I believe it came out of deep convictions. Truth matters to me. In our relativistic society, truth is becoming more and more obscured, and feelings are becoming more important than facts. I am not one of those people. I am a passionate person and I am not afraid to express what I believe to be true, even when people disagree—I would even say especially when people disagree.

The 'truth' that I am the most passionate about is my Catholic faith. I would consider myself a knowledgeable Catholic. I love to read articles and books, listen to podcasts, and ask questions—all in order to have a better grasp of my faith. I want to drive headlong into its mysteries. I love those AHA! moments when something clicks and I realize a truth in a deeper way. Behind this deep passion for the faith lies that young boy nicknamed FS, who is also gathering information as ammunition for his next debate or discussion. I have had to learn over the years to curb my adversarial spirit, not to hide the truth but, rather, so that the truth might be effectively proclaimed. As St. Augustine so eloquently put it, "The truth is like a lion; you don't have to defend it. Let it loose; it will defend itself." [17]

Our family has been effective at sharing our faith because we try not to impose the faith, but propose it. I, FS, however, had a hard time wrapping my mind around this concept.

In high school, I was known as the 'Catholic guy'. This didn't mean I was a nerd or a social outcast. I was actually part of one of the popular groups in my school. I was the Catholic guy, Steve was the guy who always gave out gum, and James was the guy with a car. Being Catholic was my thing, and people knew it. When people had questions about faith, they came to me. I was often the centre of the conversation in religion class. I practically lived for the contentious debates we would have in class over some of the hot button issues, such as abortion or

---

17. Attributed to St. Augustine of Hippo.

same-sex marriage. I relished the opportunity to show everyone just how much I knew and to get people to see the truth. In doing this, I started many a fight, and this left a sour taste in the mouths of my peers towards the faith. I was more concerned with winning the argument than I was with winning their hearts.

On Facebook, in my quest to be a warrior for the truth, I would post controversial statuses, and join in debates on other people's pages. I remember spending whole evenings on my phone, responding to comment after comment, allowing anger, frustration, and judgment to grow in my heart: "Why don't they understand?!"

After high school, I realized how flawed my approach had been, and I regretted how many opportunities I had missed in my blind desire to bring people to the truth. The reason I wanted them to understand so badly was because Jesus had changed my life. When I was in middle school, I went to a retreat put on by my parish. During a night of Eucharistic Adoration, I had a powerful encounter with the personal love of God. I met Jesus in a real and tangible way. That weekend was when I chose to place Jesus at the centre of my life and that decision changed everything. I knew he was The Way, The Truth, and The Life.[18] I saw the beauty of the Church, her traditions, and the truth she protects, but again, this flowed from my relationship with Christ. I desired to bring people to Jesus, but it was not until university that I realized what the proper approach was.

I was leading a CCO faith study, and a guy I know from high school joined it. (To respect his privacy, let's call him Dan.) Back in high school, Dan was an atheist. I remember him approaching me in the hallway after class and asking me why we believe in original sin. For me, this was an easy question and proving the truth to him would be like stealing candy from a baby. I gave him my most impressive arguments but was met by a straight face, rolled eyes, and a "Yeah. . . Thanks." He was not buying it and I had no idea why. Fast forward to the following year. In the *Discovery* faith study, we look at the basic message of Christianity: the identity, life, and death of Jesus Christ—inviting people to respond to his invitation to relationship. In the study we are not meant to debate, argue, or impose the faith. Rather, we propose the truth and invite people to respond to God's call. That's exactly what I did with Dan. With this non-confrontational approach, he was able to grasp the truths I was explaining. By the fifth week of the study, Dan acknowledged Jesus as God and chose to place him at the centre of his life!

This conversion was so sudden and amazing, I even had a hard time believing it had happened. I remember a conversation we had a few weeks later. Dan explained how he believed the Church was true, but he could never come to

---

18. cf. John 14:6 (emphasis added).

accept the Church's teachings on marriage, especially same-sex marriages. Again, I gave him my best answer; I proclaimed the truth simply and clearly to him. But this time my goal was not to win the argument but to win over his soul. So after I presented what I believed, I told him, "Honestly Dan, the more you come to know Jesus in your life, the more this will all begin to make sense." With that, he had to go off to class and we didn't speak about it for a while.

I want you to realize how radically different this approach was. I was not trying to force the truth on someone; I was allowing the truth to move his heart. This doesn't mean we shouldn't have these tough discussions, but we shouldn't unleash the Lion of truth in order to have it tear people to shreds. We need to remember this Lion is Jesus, who is also the Lamb. And I think people need to know the Lamb before they meet the Lion. Many of the truths of our faith don't make sense to people unless they have encountered Jesus in their lives. That was the missing key, and the reason why nothing I said in high school had an impact.

A few months later, Dan was speaking with Elizabeth after Mass. He was explaining to her the Church's teaching on marriage and same-sex attraction. He passionately shared with her that what the Church taught made so much sense. He came to this realization simply through prayer and his own research into the subject. As he drew closer to Jesus and gave him more permission in his life, the truth became self-evident.

> *"Always be ready to make your defense to anyone who demands from you an accounting for the hope that is in you; yet do it with gentleness and reverence." 1 Peter 3:15-16*

Ambassadors for Christ

The way that we present the faith to everyone we encounter is important. People's conceptions of the faith can only be formed by the way that the faith is presented to them. Often times, they have only very few people who display Catholicism to them in an authentic and captivating way. Faith needs to become a 'positive option.' As witnesses we need to live under the assumption that we may be the only faithful Catholic others will *ever* encounter. This means we must behave in a way that makes Christ and his Church attractive. Growing up, my siblings and I were all quite conscious of this. We were often trying to present ourselves in a way that was appealing, virtuous, and inspirational to our friends.

"So we are ambassadors for Christ, since God is making his appeal through us; we entreat you on behalf of Christ, be reconciled to God." (2 Corinthians 5:20) What is the role of an ambassador? An ambassador is the representative of a country's supreme leader. Their role is to develop positive relationships with those in their vicinity, and ultimately to do all that needs to be done for their own country. As ambassadors for Christ, we do not belong to this world. We are living our lives for Christ. We are representing him to others through our interactions with them. Being an ambassador for Christ is a real role that even children can play in their everyday lives. Children can do this so simply and authentically by being good, kind, and loving to others. When children talk about their faith, who can resist the charm of their innocent, believing hearts? They are able to have a real influence on people's lives.

JANNA – Being a Witness in Elementary School

There was this time at school when I was in Grade 5 and there was a kid in my class who was telling a story about someone who died flying a helicopter. Another boy in the class got really upset after listening to the story and the whole class could tell. He went up to our teacher and was kind of worked up about it; feeling really scared about dying. He already was the kind of kid that had emotional issues, so sometimes our teacher would let him pick a classmate to talk things through with. That's when my teacher told him that he might want to think about talking to me. So they both came up to me and asked me to talk with him.

He told me he was scared that, when he died, he might not get to go heaven. "What if heaven isn't real?" I could relate to what he was saying because I had similar questions in the past. Then I told him that if you believe in God and follow him, you will go to heaven. Even though you will die here on earth, in heaven you will live and there will be no more pain, or sins, or sad stuff. We will live with God forever.

He was very happy with our chat. He told me that if he ever got scared again, he would come back to talk to me.

A few weeks later we did a secret Christmas card exchange. What happens is you draw the name of someone in the class and then you write something really nice about the person. Then on the last day of school we read them aloud and we all try to guess which person they are writing about. It's really nice and really fun.

So this classmate who had been scared was reading his description: "There's a girl who is really Catholic. She helped me when I was really scared. When I think of her, she reminds me of Jesus." He was talking about me, and I think all my classmates knew it. It was a very little card, some of the other cards kids made were much fancier with decorations and sparkles and stuff. But his card was the most special card I have ever received. I was so happy to be 'Jesus' to him in my small way.

This is such a beautiful story, and it just shows how Christ can and will work through children to lead others to himself. Let us not diminish the way God can work through his little ones! Being an ambassador for Christ is something that teenagers can particularly take on with vigour.

MARC – Being a Witness in High School

Working in youth ministry, I have seen that within Catholic families there sometimes can be a tendency of being inward focused. In our world, we have lost a sense of responsibility for our brothers and sisters. St. Augustine said: "My heart is restless O Lord until it rests in you."[19] Well, evangelization is really taking on the ownership of the world; it is exclaiming: "My heart is restless O Lord until ALL of my brothers and sisters rest in you." In actuality, the Church needs young people, your children, to be like the Good Samaritan and go to extraordinary lengths to ensure that their friends, family, and, ultimately, the world step away from the culture of death into the light of Christ.

Evangelizing teens is hard. It often feels like an uphill battle marked by small victories that can so often wither away. Today's teens grow up in a culture of comfort. It is easier to play video games than pray, easier to sleep in than wake up and go to Mass. So often for teenagers, I see how "the spirit is willing but the flesh is weak" (Matthew 26:41). However, in teens who had a real conversion, I saw an authentic enthusiasm that was contagious. They simply couldn't help but share the joy of the Gospel and, in doing so, they became huge influencers in their sphere of friends, school, or church.

Victoria, a youth I had the privilege of journeying with for six years, recognized her potential to influence her peers. She understood that the most important thing she could ever do for them was to help them encounter Christ. This encounter drastically changed the lives of so many of her friends, and her spiritual legacy is vast because of it.

I believe my children have the potential to impact the world. I encourage you as parents to also have great expectations for what your children can do in the world, even at a young age! This is not to say that you should be pressuring your children to evangelize their peers. What is important here is to gently encourage your children to 'go out,' to affirm their potential for leadership, and to believe that your children can do great things by God's grace. The world needs the witness and influence of your children. I have seen teens do amazing things in the lives of their peers and I believe that if all Catholic families encourage this in their children, many lives will be changed.

---

19. Saint. Augustine (translated by Henry Chadwick), *The Confessions, Oxford World Classics*, (OUP Oxford, 2008). (paraphrased).

One way that our parents taught us to be ambassadors of Christ is by teaching us to have 'holy goofiness'. Alana explains her experience of coming into our family and learning how to do this.

ALANA – The Joy of the Gospel

Coming into CCO four years ago as a fresh little intern, I saw the amazing missionary disciples around me. They were true ambassadors for Christ and I wanted to be just like them, but how could I practically do this? Thankfully, there are so many teachings, core values and tenets central to the spirituality of CCO that guided me on the journey. The same secret sauce found in the Regnier family, influences CCO's spirituality—and vice versa—which is why I feel I can pull teachings from CCO here. In CCO we have three Core Values: Holy Goofiness, See and Seize Opportunities, and Abandonment and Reliance on God's Providence. I want to highlight how I see holy goofiness played out in the family, especially as a means of being an attractive ambassador of Christ.

Holy goofiness means taking God seriously, but not taking yourself too seriously. It isn't being childish, but it is about having a childlike heart. You don't have to be the most hilarious; you can be 'holy goofy' by enjoying and delighting in the people around you. I think this core value is so important because often the world views practising Catholics as being 'sticks-in-the-mud' who don't know how to have fun. Holy goofiness is a good remedy to this misconception (and sometimes reality). It is our joy that attracts the lost, that pulls them in and makes them curious as to why we are different.

As much as I knew Jesus coming into the family, I also had a lot to learn from them about living in the freedom of being his child and not fearing what others may think, which is at the heart of holy goofiness. In 2016, I had the chance to go to World Youth Day in Krakow, Poland with the Regniers and it was there that I grew in taking God more seriously than myself.

Our mission team had the immense task of dispersing and sharing the kerygma (the basic Gospel message[20]) with millions of young pilgrims. One of the ways we were asked to do this was to present the kerygma on large stages dispersed across Krakow. On the very first day we were going to make this kerygmatic presentation, we were on one of the largest stages in downtown Krakow. We were ready to share the *Ultimate Relationship* (CCO's kerygmatic booklet) in the crowds and hundreds were expected to be there. We were trained, prepped, and ready to go! We prayed together in preparation for the event. André was

---

20. See Bonus Features for more info on the 'kerygma'.

going to give a kerygmatic presentation followed by another team leading some music ministry on stage. With great expectation and great anticipation we hit the stage, only to realize we were the only ones there. André had no choice but to give his talk to our group of five to 15 people. Not only were there only a few people in the crowd, but to top it off, they didn't speak English and we had no translator. It was such a ridiculous experience. Halfway through, he broke into laughter and so did we. What an embarrassment! In this moment, we could have been struck with discouragement, but it was our ability and choice not to take ourselves too seriously that made this a joy-filled experience that we continue to laugh at to this day. But, still taking God and the mission seriously, we headed out into the streets, doing skits for the sake of attracting curious bystanders to share the Gospel with them. We had to leave the safety and security of the stage to reach the lost. We had to go to the sheep and smell like them so they would come close to us, even though many walked past us rolling their eyes. Holy goofiness helped us to be attractive ambassadors of the Lord and not allow this embarrassment to bring us down in the slightest.

Loving the Lost

As the faithful, we are called to be 'the aroma of Christ' to all we encounter. This is an immense responsibility as well as a humbling honour. In order to give off the aroma of Christ, we need to view his lost children as he does.

> *"The Pharisees and the teachers of the law muttered, 'This man welcomes sinners and eats with them.' Then Jesus told them this parable: 'Suppose one of you has a hundred sheep and loses one of them. Doesn't he leave the ninety-nine in the open country and go after the lost sheep until he finds it?"* Luke 15: 2-4

Christ sees sinners through a lens of love. This is something that our parents were careful to cultivate in us from a very young age. We would regularly come home from school and complain to our parents about something that someone in our class did that was 'bad,' whether it was directed towards us or not. We would immediately roll our eyes as our mom gave her classic response: that we should pray for that classmate, and empathize with them. "What if their parents aren't loving towards them, or they have a difficult family life? These kids often do not have the loving home life that we do because they don't have faith in the picture." While this response from our mom was irritating to receive at the time, our attitude eventually shifted. She was showing us that 'the lost' were simply just that: lost. And how sad is it to be lost. Through her conversations with us, she was forming us to have a *missionary gaze*—to look at others through God's eyes of compassion, mercy and love.

Through the way our parents encouraged us to speak about 'the lost' and have compassion towards them, we were able to engage with difficult people in a kind way and not feel 'righteously separate.'

While our weak nature often leads us to look to people of the world with bitterness and annoyance, Christ is calling us to love, to spend our time with the tax collectors and sinners. This particular fact has always struck me. When Jesus began his public ministry, everyone was drawn to him— even sinners. To draw people to himself, he would have had to be more than simply a miracle worker who spoke inspiring words. He would have had to be immensely dynamic, engaging, and attractive—so much so that prostitutes and tax collectors, who would have previously been self-absorbed and anything but religious, *wanted* to spend time with him and eventually changed their lives because of him. We are called to imitate this. Are sinners drawn to us? Is the way we live our lives contagious?

CALEB

Even at a young age, I recognized that I wanted my friends to know and understand the truth that I knew was the Catholic faith. I was able to see and recognize that these friends were lacking something so beautiful that my family had. This realization did not come out of a spirit of judgement, which might say things like, "What's with the Johnson family? Don't they know they should be going to Mass on Sundays?" Rather, it came out of a spirit of love which says, "Could you imagine how great it would be if the Johnsons began coming to Mass with us on Sundays?" I always understood that people who didn't follow Church teaching or recognize Jesus as Lord were not bad or foolish. Rather, they were the mission field. They were those living in spiritual poverty.

So how can a young boy begin to see the world, his little friends, and their families from such a perspective? Well, put simply, more is caught than taught. It was modelled in the behaviours of my parents. It was maybe not anything they verbally explained or taught me, but behaviours I saw which communicated these realities to me. I can remember having friends over often on Saturday nights for sleepovers. On Sunday mornings, my family would go to the 9:45 am Mass at our parish. This meant that my friends would either come to Mass with me and the family, or they would have to get picked up early before we packed the van full of kids and left. I can remember one Sunday hearing my mom on the phone with my friend's mom, offering to bring him to Mass with us and then drop him off at home afterwards. His mom quickly declined and said she would pick him up at 9:30. My mom got off the phone and was not discouraged or angry, but seemed to be filled with sadness that this mother did not want her boy going to Sunday Mass. He was a baptised Catholic but his mom still preferred that he go home rather than go to Mass. My mom could have easily whispered under her breath something like, "He's baptised. He should be going to Mass anyways. I'd be doing your kid a favour." Now, what would a statement like this have communicated to me? In my little brain I would have extrapolated that these people are bad, that they are not to be loved, but rather seen as bad people. My mom's response communicated love and compassion to me. I understood that she saw my friend's family as the 'lost', and that the Father wanted them home. You would be surprised at how much is caught by your children from such small interactions as this one.

It is this love and compassion towards the 'lost' that compelled me to want to witness to my friends as a teenager and young adult. Being 'in the world, but not of the world' was certainly the main way I witnessed to my friends. This phrase has become a sort of cliché within Christian circles but I believe it is essential if we desire to witness and to see young people witness.

The perspective of an overwhelming amount of young people today is that to be Catholic is to be missing out on what makes life fun and great. They perceive that living their lives the way God wants them to be living would be boring and miserable. Pull any 15-year-old out of his Grade 10 religion class and he would tell you, "following God would make my life suck!". I know this because I've asked many young men this same question. The remedy for this is vibrant Catholics who are able and willing to be in the world but not of the world.

To be 'in the world' means that you can be eating with a friend and have a discussion why Terminator 2: Judgement Day[21] is the best of all the Terminator films, why Lebron James is the 'GOAT', or chatting about the newest TV series on Netflix. This friend has now seen that: "This guy is Catholic but he is normal; he does the things that I enjoy doing, like watching movies. This guy takes his faith seriously but that doesn't mean that he can't do anything fun." Of course, we know that to follow Jesus means that, yes, we will have to give up certain things in the world which pull us farther from Jesus. This is where being 'not of the world' comes in.

Not being of the world means first of all, that we are mindful of the types of media and worldly stimuli that we consume. The types of movies I watch don't go outside of moral restrictions, this requires a discerning heart and common

---

21. Terminator 2: Judgement Day. Directed by James Cameron. Tristar Pictures. 2011.

sense. It means that I shouldn't listen to music that makes me feel ashamed or guilty. It means the types of conversations I have shouldn't make me feel like I need to go to Confession afterwards. The list goes on. Apart from these aspects, being 'not of the world' means understanding that you are a part of something *greater* than what the world has to offer. It is recognizing the adventure that the Lord has for you, and knowing that you are a son or daughter of God above all. Even as a little boy, I always felt like I was part of something bigger, bigger than my desk and my school yard. I knew there was an adventure for me. So being not of the world meant I lived and acted differently than my peers.

So how does being in the world but not of the world co-exist and work in tandem? Well, through being in the world, I can witness to my friends by showing them that there is still joy, familiarity and adventure in the Catholic life and, with this, I am able to build basic trust and rapport. By being not of the world, I can show them that there is more. There is more fulfillment, more joy, and more freedom that comes from being part of something greater than this world.

Being *in the world* acts as a bridge to invite people to be *not of the world*. This was a practice which I used all throughout my teenage years onwards. Even in sports, it was important to me that my teammates could see that I could dominate on the field, court, or ice, but that I had something deeper and more significant that made me who I was; Jesus. I can confidently say that living my life in this manner enabled people who were close to me to have a different perception of Catholicism. In campus ministry, I have seen how something as simple as spending an hour at the gym with an unconverted faith study participant can move *mountains* in their life. Something about the grittiness of sweating and pumping iron together breaks down countless barriers for them. Through being in the world but not of it, people can see that a life with Christ does not mean a life of boredom. Rather they saw a life of adventure which leads to ultimate fulfillment.

Being missionary was not simply something that we did. It became part of our identity. Like the good ol' evangelists we are, we dragged someone else along into claiming this 'missionary identity.' We also managed to get her to become a Regnier as well. Double win! Here's her story:

ELIZABETH – 'Missionary Conversion'

When I was in Grade 7, I made the decision to seriously commit to a relationship with Jesus. This decision changed a lot in my life, particularly the people I hung out with and the way I spent my time. A flame started to burn in my heart and all I wanted was to live for Jesus. This flame grew and consumed me so that everything I thought, said, and did was analyzed so that I could learn how to follow Jesus better and better. I think the love that I had for Christ in that period of my life was beautiful. I also realize, in retrospect, that this time was quite self-focused which made me lack in reliance on God and the consideration of others. I tried to become holy on my own and I thought I was pretty good at it, while also noticing that the people around me weren't. Rather than loving them and desiring for them to know Christ, I would judge and ignore them while I focused on my own spiritual journey.

This situation (bittersweet when I look back on it now) lasted up until Grade 12. At the end of Grade 11, I had the opportunity to spend time with Jo, and we grew from acquaintances to being friends, eventually to becoming best friends. Being around the Regnier family and hearing how they spoke and acted was weird for me. Yes, they're weird as it is, but what I thought particularly odd was the way they lived their Catholic faith. They were missionary and made choices in their faith not only for themselves, but for others. It boggled my mind!

I remember one time walking with Jo from his house to the park. He told me that he decided to start playing video games again. A few weeks prior to this conversation I seriously encouraged Jo to stop playing video games for the sake of his soul; that it was a waste of time, and that he could spend that time praying instead of mindlessly staring at a screen. But this week, Jo's friends from school wanted to hang out and play video games and Jo came home to discuss the situation with his parents. He was torn because he wanted to be a holy Christian, but also liked video games and knew that spending time with his friends and doing things they liked would help him build a relationship with them so he could witness to them. He was coming down to their level in a fun and unimposing way. His dad encouraged him to play with his friends and not to reject or be afraid of video games because they aren't intrinsically holy themselves. This was an opportunity to meet his friends where they were at. His dad added that Jo liked playing the games and that wasn't a bad thing. He just had to make sure his other priorities came first.

When Jo explained this to me, I honestly thought, "The Regniers are not good Catholics, especially André. How could he give his son that advice? Doesn't he care about his soul?" Little did I know that André was speaking truth! But this realization came later.

The day my heart changed is one I will forever be grateful for. I regard it to be equally as important as my initial conversation in Grade 7 and I call it my 'missionary conversion.'

I was sitting at a table at a Church event in Grade 12 and who did I sit beside? André Regnier! He talked to me about the kind of Catholics who live their lives for themselves, caring only about their own spiritual growth and forgetting the many souls who also need to hear the Good News of Christ. He said those Catholics live within their own, self-made walls and how it was such a pity. I knew immediately that I was one of those Catholics and that I needed to let go of my selfishness and let the walls come down.

I went home and wrote in my journal, thinking and analyzing what André said. All I could think was, "Oh my gosh, I've been living for myself when there are so many people who don't know Jesus! The walls need to come down." I was convinced that this was true and was ashamed that I was living without any thought for my neighbour. And so I resolved to make a change.

Despite this new realization, it took a lot of time to actually change my way of thinking and doing things. I was used to thinking the world was bad and that what mattered most was my own spiritual growth, and now I needed to reacquaint myself with the world. In my heart I wanted to be missionary but barely knew how. I wanted to be in the world and not of the world, but had no experience. All I knew how to do was reject and fear the world, and that would get me nowhere when trying to relate to people who need to know Christ. Being relatable is key because inviting people to a relationship with Christ usually comes through having a relationship with them. Does anyone want to be friends with someone who is so unrelatable? No!

I know Christ and I love him. I have experienced deep fulfillment and joy in my relationship with God, and I know with certainty that this is why I was created. My hope is that every single person on this planet can know this same thing. But how can I be an attractive, relatable, effective bearer of this Good News if I reject the world and all the people in it? How can I share the love of Jesus with people if I look unapproachable or don't know how to have a conversation about things happening outside of a church environment?

Wheat Among The Weeds

In learning to live in the world but not of the world, it is important to search for the 'wheat among the weeds.' As Scripture tells us:

> *"The kingdom of heaven may be compared to someone who sowed good seed in his field; but while everybody was asleep, an enemy came and sowed weeds among the wheat, and then went away. So when the plants came up and bore grain, then the weeds appeared as well. And the slaves of the householder came and said to him, 'Master, did you not sow good seed in your field? Where, then, did these weeds come from?' He answered, 'An enemy has done this.' The slaves said to him, 'Then do you want us to go and gather them? But he replied: 'No; for in gathering the weeds you would uproot the wheat along with them. Let both of them grow together until the harvest; and at harvest time I will tell the reapers, collect the weeds first and bind them in bundles to be burned, but gather the wheat into my barn."* Matthew 13: 24-30

We need to sow and seek out wheat in our lives. But the reality of living in a fallen world is that the enemy sows weeds everywhere. Rather than freaking out and making the slaves fear or hate the weeds, the Master calmly tells them to let them grow and, when the time comes, he will take care of them. Similarly, we need not fear evil things that are of the world; we need to know they exist and calmly recognize that they are a danger, while seeking out and growing the good wheat.

Conclusion

Before we conclude, I think it's important to clarify that my siblings and I were not and are not super-evangelists. We do not have a long legacy as far as the eye can see of those who have come to the faith because of us. It is not our 'performance' that matters but fidelity to Christ's mission. The principles we discuss in this chapter were all ways that our *missionary identity* was claimed. We are not 'perfect' missionary disciples by any means, but what I think is important is that our faith was not limited to ourselves. Our great expectation and hope is that this chapter gave you principles and methods in raising your family as missionary disciples. Here are things to remember as you raise your children in the world but not of the world:

■ Balance surrounding your family with a good village and embracing opportunities for your children to be witnesses to their friends at school and in sports.

■ Introduce your children first and foremost to a relationship with Jesus. This should be more important than focusing on the rules of our faith. The rules serve the relationship, not the other way around!

■ Having a heart for the lost is having the heart of Christ. Be mindful of how you speak about the 'lost', since your children will catch your attitude towards them. This can either foster or discourage their missionary heart.

■ Be *in the world* as ambassadors for Christ, encouraging your children to represent Christ positively to their peers, in a relatable way.

■ Don't be *of the world*. Keep your eyes fixed on Christ, teaching your children to live differently, not being conformed to the world but being "transformed by the renewing of your minds" (Romans 12:2).

We cannot separate the term 'missionary disciple.' As disciples we grow in holiness and intimacy with Jesus, and as a missionary we strive to live the mission of proclaiming Jesus to all. Our families cannot merely be a monastery on a hill. They need to be a light in the world with an eternal impact. St. John Paul II acknowledges this: "As the family goes, so goes the nation and so goes the whole world in which we live."[22] Let us not miss out on what great things God can do in the world through our families.

Reflection / Action Points

1. How do you seek to strike the balance between protecting your children within your village, while also giving opportunities in the world where they can witness to their faith?

2. Are you passing on rules and devotions to your children, or are you passing on a personal relationship with Jesus? What is the message of 'first importance' you are passing on?

3. How can you support your children as they are exposed to the secular world? As they have conversations with their friends and classmates that test their faith, how can you coach them?

4. How do you speak about the lost? Are you modelling judgement or a missionary heart for the lost?

---

22. Pope John Paul II, *Homily of John Paul II in Perth (Australia)*, 30 November 1986.

5. How can you develop a heart for the lost for you and your family? Does your family have a missionary mindset, or do you need to ingrain new attitudes and methods to teach your children how to be in the world not of the world?

6. Are there ways that you can become a more attractive ambassador of Christ?

CHAPTER 3

Decision Making

Raising Children You Can Trust

MYLÈNE

As parents, we can do many things to try to form our children in the faith. We can surround them with a faith-filled community and have beautiful faith traditions, but more will be needed to prepare children to make the right choices in their life. My siblings and I have learned that there is so much more to being ready for the world than knowing about the faith: we needed to know how to choose to live out our faith in a world that mocks our choices. Forming a child's conscience involves good teaching and good practice at any age. Fundamentally, the choice they are facing is a temptation to disobey—that is, to sin. These days in our home, Max has to be trained to know not to sneak fruit snacks from the diaper bag because it's wrong. (They are needed for when we are out of the house and, frankly, it's a treat more than a healthy snack so I need to approve its consumption.) The preparation to make good decisions and not to do what is wrong and displeasing to God (and parents) will take Max far in his life and in his spiritual life. As discussed in the previous chapter, I have seen peers whose decision-making skills were poorly developed and spiralled from one wrong decision to another as their sin separated them from God. The truth is that sin does separate us from God, so we need to take it seriously.

In this chapter, we will discuss how our parents formed us to be able to make good decisions in our toddler years and beyond, and how we learned these lessons in the real world.

Approaches to Discipline

ANGÈLE – Our Method

Every chapter in this book began with a family gathering in the living room—a two to four hour discussion took place, in which we came up with the chapter content and delegated the writing points. The discussion on this particular chapter was very granular, looking at specific learning points from the toddler years to adulthood. Finally, someone pulled up from an ocean of specific scenarios and asked us, "Mom, how did you and Dad equip us to make good decisions in general terms? What were the guiding principles in all of these situations?"

My first response was that it was grace and an answer to prayer. That prayer was simple and it was said on my knees for each of my children. "Lord, I pray that this child would find joy in obedience." I was on my knees with a prayerful disposition even though I was in fact vomiting into a toilet. Yep, I had Hyperemesis Gravidarum with each of my kids, meaning that I was extremely sick throughout the pregnancies. Early on with Mylène I had an inspiration; to offer up my sickness for her, that she would 'find joy in obedience' (to the Lord's will, to her parents, etc.). I believe the Lord heard the cry of my heart and my wrenching stomach and that my children did grow up finding joy in obeying the Lord.

On the practical side though, there are things I can identify in our parenting that contributed to the formation of our children's consciences and decision making skills. The teacher in me would classify them as *three E's* to train children for good-decision making: example, explanation, and engagement.

1. Example:

The first E is 'Example' and I mean this in two ways. The first sense of the word I want to explain is the example of the parent. The child needs to see parents making right decisions. The example of our life aims to model doing the right thing (whether seen by our children or not). In other words, 'more is caught than taught' and 'practice what you preach' sum it up nicely. How can you expect a child to make the right decisions, or respond generously to God's will, when you are inconsistent and succumb to lesser choices? Now, to our shame, we did not set perfect examples. We totally did stupid things with our kids' full knowledge—like claiming a child was younger than they were to get kid-pricing at a restaurant or amusement park. Will our kids end up doing the same dishonest practice? Probably. Because we trained them well to lie about their age (something I have been doing ever since I turned 29, by the way). I'm speaking humourously but, like I said, I am not proud of it. This is not virtuous behaviour. But it does highlight the fact that example speaks volumes.

A second way we speak of example is with the consistency needed for standing your ground in discipline. How can a child's conscience be formed when you are constantly changing whether a behaviour is corrected or not? If sometimes your child is reprimanded for eating in the living room, and sometimes you turn a blind eye to such behaviour, how will they know what is right and wrong in your house? If you consistently model inconsistency, this will deeply affect the formation of your child's conscience. They will have trouble respecting the rules and authority and developing their virtue to do the right thing. What we wanted was for both our older and our younger kids to attest to having experienced the *same* family by-laws and principles held firmly by us as parents all the way through.

Part of the example that we set for our kids in decision-making is not to be too legalistic. Now, of course we want them to know right and wrong, and we want them to have a healthy 'fear of the Lord' and respect for the Ten Commandments and Church teachings. But some might be surprised at how moderate some of our choices are. In light of our missionary perspective, and desiring to be 'in the world, not of the world,' we recognize that not everything in the world is bad. We aren't afraid to take what is good and that which does not go against our faith and use it in a balanced way. For example, we could have chosen not to listen to any secular music, but our kids have had many dance parties with us listening to 70s and 80s music (with careful consideration of the lyrics, mind you).

This approach, however, means that we need to research and be informed on what is out there for kids. Sure, we aren't afraid of the world, but we don't exactly trust it either. We think about what we expose our kids to. We do our homework, we talk to other parents, we reflect, we pray, and we discuss it as a couple. Most often, the issues relate to TV programs, toys, and games that kid-culture pushes. I remember back in the day really trying to stop the kids from watching Arthur[23] for the sake of forming their consciences. It was a very popular cartoon when the older kids were in elementary school and they and their peers thought it was funny, but I didn't like it. I did not like the way Arthur's sister, DW, was always selfish, dishonest, and disrespectful to her family. My 'beef' with the show was kind of benign though, in the grand scheme of bad influences out there. So what I chose to do was let them watch Arthur, since it was such a big part of what their friends talked and laughed about. But I used it as a teaching tool to show them what was inappropriate about DW's behaviour, and what I would never tolerate. You can ask Mylène, Jo, and Caleb—they remember that I didn't like DW, and that I was right about her. This is a foretaste of the second point—explanation.

---

23. Arthur (TV series). Directed by Greg Bailey. Cookie Jar Group and WGBH-TV. 1996 – .

But before I write about the second 'E', I want to say that there were a number of decisions we made with great caution that we later relaxed on. For example, celebrating Halloween. I am very sensitive to spiritual realities and I did not want my family to promote the celebration of anything that gave glory to Satan rather than God. I did not want to pretend the devil, evil spirits, haunted houses, and witches weren't actual spiritual realities (albeit not like their fictional portrayals). And I really didn't like the idea of trying to frighten children, especially spiritually. So I advocated that we abandon the idea of celebrating Halloween in every way and instead celebrate All Saints Day with sweet little families at a parish hall.

Maybe five years had passed before I started thinking about the long game. I started thinking about my kids getting older and becoming bitter that they never got to dress up and go door to door to bring home a truckload of candy. Then I thought, "I don't want them to be angry teenagers who felt like they missed out on something really fun. This might be a seed for bitterness and rebellion that we will regret." So André and I talked and prayed about it, and decided to relax our approach and let the kids go trick-or-treating. However, there were some conditions we insisted on. We didn't decorate our house to look scary, our kids were not allowed to wear scary costumes, and on trick-or-treat escapades, they were to skip houses that were trying to scare kids.

2. Explanation

As mentioned earlier, when it comes to the variety of decisions to be made, we do our research to become informed. In the early years we did this by talking to other parents, especially the more established families we were modelling our parenting after. We also read up on issues and this became so much easier to do once the Internet was invented. (Yes, we parented before the Internet.) André and I discuss and, based on the data gained, we figure out how to approach the question before us. For example, would we allow our kids to read Harry Potter[24], collect Pokemon cards[25], or watch Lord of the Rings[26]? When we are at peace with our decision, we sit down to share our decision and explain our reasoning to the kids. And I think this is a big ingredient to our special sauce. I believe our kids respect the comprehensive answers we give when they are rooted in a fundamental understanding that we live out our own moral choices at a pretty high level (Point 1 – example). They know we consistently choose to

---

24. Rowling, J.K. Harry Potter (Book series). Bloomsbury Publishing (UK). 1997 – 2007.

25. Pokemon Trading Card Game. Creatures Inc.(Japan), Media Factory (Japan), The Pokemon Company (Japan), Creatures Inc. (United States), Wizards of the Coast (Hasbro) (United States), The Pokemon Company International (United States). 1996 – .

26. Lord of the Rings (Film series). Directed by Peter Jackson. New Line Cinema. 2001 – 2003.

do the right thing for the right reason. They realize from our example that we are not interested in being particularly legalistic either. But they also know that some decisions are rooted in the law of God—the Ten Commandments—and honouring all of God's law especially found in Church teachings. An example of this would come up in things like going against the grain of culture by not using the Lord's name in vain—even 'OMG'.

My 'go to' practical resource is commonsensemedia.org. We have gotten such helpful background as to the precise usage of bad language, sex, violence, etc. in media from this website. It gives helpful reviews from an adult perspective and suggests appropriate age levels. What we really appreciate are the objective facts that allow us to make our own decisions. There are other websites to help in this area, but I find this one the most helpful since it is more fact-based rather than opinion-based. This is probably sounding like a big infomercial for Common Sense Media. But wait, there's more! They not only review movies but also TV shows, books, apps, websites, and video games. This sort of information makes my explanation to the children much more reasonable than an abrupt, "No, you're not watching Zoolander[27]! Why? It's bad. You're not seeing it. End of discussion." What would you want to do as a 14-year-old if your parent barked like that at you? You would totally go see what you're missing out on because Mom's so unreasonable and mean. Right?

One of the most common phrases that came out of my mouth in my explanations were, "This isn't appropriate for a child of your age." For example, "It's not appropriate that a child your age is watching movies with that kind of language." Or, "It's not appropriate that a child your age wears make-up." Then it would be followed up with some reasons why it's not appropriate. Most often the reasoning in my own mind was, "If a child does such-and-such an activity at this age, what will they desire to do when they are older?" Here's an example of what I mean: there is a temptation to give kids an iPod/iPad with essentially unmonitored Internet access at age seven or younger. As we faced this situation and as our kids asked for this sort of gift, we asked ourselves:

- Is it really appropriate for a child of this age?

- If I give them this now, then what is going to satisfy their 'fun entertainment' desires when they are 12, 15, or 17?

- What will they have to turn to when they are older if they have experienced everything before Grade 3?

---

27. Zoolander. Directed by Ben Stiller. Paramount Pictures. 2001.

- What influences are they exposed to at a young age through the games/Internet?

- How can I protect their childhood with best practices for a wholesome, natural child development?

- How can I raise my child so he/she appreciates and values his/her own childhood days?

In our explanation, we often build off of the last question above, telling them what they should be doing as kids—that kids should be creative, should play, should be outside building forts, and should be coming up with games and skits. I find kids really understand that. Of course, that didn't mean our kids never got any of those fun, cool things, but we were very discerning in what we chose (i.e. if it was age-appropriate, fun, not harmful, and affordable). So with such an explanation, along with discussion and reflection, we have found that our kids could appreciate that they were actually having more fun 'acting like kids should' than having the latest big ticket item. (You will read my rant on toys in a later chapter.) I want to emphasise the word *discussion* in that sentence. The explanation is given in the context of a conversation, *not* a lecture. And that allowed the explanation to be well-received. I guess you could say we showed the children respect by laying out our parameters for decision-making in an atmosphere that was conversational, not confrontational. This leads us right into the third 'E'.

3. Engagement

We strive to engage our children in the process of making the right decision. Yes, it is richly rooted in a good explanation (as seen in point 2) but we feel it has to include engagement. André is very big on this aspect. He talks through a given situation very thoroughly with a child—the reasons why not to do such-and-such, the repercussions if they did make such a decision, and a spiritual consideration of the decision (namely WWJD—what would Jesus do?). Not always, but often, he would talk at length, covering all the angles and then eventually walk away after saying, "Well, you need to make a decision here. I know you will make the right decision."

I have to admit this got me concerned on many occasions. I'd be thinking, "André, you did not just walk away and leave the decision in their hands! They will totally choose the shiny temptation—not the right choice." But you know what—they almost always made the right choice. I honestly can't think of any time that they didn't choose well. If they did choose 'poorly', I think their enthusiasm was often short-lived with the guilt of their conscience convicting them of what they should have done, and what they should do to make up for the situation.

Now if a situation required us to force an unequivocal 'no,' we certainly would have done that without the option of a choice. We didn't feel handcuffed by our own method, but even a clear right/wrong decision involves explanation and a conversation of asking the child what they think they should do. The rare occasions when they didn't come to the right decision, we just trumped it—that's all.

This really works well when you start early. You can even build the conscience muscle of toddlers and train them to make the right decisions. Your children will make right decisions if they've consistently practiced making the right decisions. That means getting preschoolers to see that they need to choose to clean up the crayons they exploded across the table because it's the right thing to do. That means they share one of their cookies with their friend because it's the right thing to do. This kind of practice, that keeps happening as they are growing up, forms them and strengthens them so they can choose on their own not to dress immodestly, or swear, or cheat at school.

The real motivation for us in this school of conscience-building was to prepare our kids for their high school and university years. Our inspiration came from another missionary family we had known for years who work with Power to Change, an Evangelical ministry. They said that they put their children in public school so they could learn how to make right decisions in the midst of 'age-appropriate' peer pressure. I'll never forget what they told us, leaning in, looking deeply into our eyes, "Look, if our kids can't choose on their own to make right decisions when they are in Grade 2 with 'Grade 2 level peer pressure,' how will they be able to stand up for themselves and make right decisions when it really matters in Grade 11 with Grade 11 situations?" That made tons of sense to us. Although we wanted to protect our kids and hide them from all the evil lurking in the big, wide world, we knew that the best way to protect them was to train them to guard their own hearts and minds in Christ Jesus.

Like we discussed last chapter, this environment to grow conscience strength, along with the opportunity to be missionary, is what led us to choose to put our kids in the Catholic public school system. I can tell you that if any of our children were not able to cope with making the right decisions in their school environment, we would have discerned switching them to homeschooling or private school in a heartbeat. (Especially in the case of bullying or unbearable social pressures.) But our experience so far, is that this environment has provided many teachable moments to form our children's consciences and decision-making muscles in the context of their peers.

Throughout this chapter, you will see various age-specific situations and how we sought to form our children's consciences and help them make holy and good decisions. In each context, I believe that the principles of the three E's will be found: example, explanation, and engagement.

Marc and I have made a point to learn from my parents in strategizing how to discipline and form our own children. This has come with victories and failures alike. To offer a practical example of the three E's being used with small children, Marc will share his experience navigating the 'wonderful' world of toddler discipline.

MARC – Teaching Toddlers to Make Good Decisions

As a parent, I recognize that I can be very reactive. What I mean by this is that sometimes I anticipate a potential problem and, instead of quickly moving so that it doesn't happen, I can be lazy, which nine times out of ten prompts a negative reaction towards my children. For instance, I don't know if it's just my children or if everyone has experienced this, but they have the tendency to always, I mean ALWAYS, put cups on the edge of the table and it drives me crazy! Of course, on my watch, the contents of the cup inevitably spill. My reactive response would be to get angry and upset after the spill. My proactive response would be to teach my kids to not put their cup so close to the edge. This would require being attentive and stopping what I was doing to deal with it. There would be the added benefit of no mess and no temper tantrum from myself as well as from my children.

I have come to recognize that with my four-year-old Max, explanations matter. He wants to know why I am saying no. "Because I said so" is not a good enough answer. If I am proactive in my explanation and engage him in a decision, it sets him up for success in making a good choice. And even if he makes a bad choice, then it is still just as important to debrief using the 3 E's instead of just punishing him. For example, Max loves to snack. He enjoys a plethora of fruit, fishy crackers, and granola bars at Grandma's house. On one occasion, his grandmother, Angèle had just finished cutting up a pineapple and he was excited to have some. He grabbed a handful from the container and dropped a piece by accident, but quickly turned away to chase his Aunt Natalie. I called him back and said, "Maxy, you dropped a piece. Can you pick it up and throw it out please?" He responded, "No." I then explained why I would like him to pick it up and gave him another opportunity to respond promptly, knowing he wanted to get back to playing. He said, "No!" again, and louder this time. I said, "Max, please pick it up and throw it in the garbage or you'll have to sit down." He refused, so I picked him up and sat him down on the couch. Let's just say he was not a happy camper—tears streamed down his face, and he kicked and screamed. Once he calmed down, I used his wrong decision as a teaching moment. Instead of just waiting to receive an apology, I decided to debrief what happened, using examples and explanation, and engaging him on what the right decision should have been. In this scenario, Max learned through experience what a wrong decision felt like, and I believe this will prepare him to make the right decisions in the future. I know this is just a simple story that could have very easily ended with no confrontation if I had just grabbed the fallen fruit and thrown it out myself. However, as a parent, I have learned to see and seize opportunities to form my child's conscience, and these small teachable moments help form a strong foundation that will influence my children's future decision-making capacity.

Conscience-building in the young years lays a foundation for a finely-tuned conscience in the older years. Reflecting on our childhood, we kids have seen that the rules that my parents enforced were boundaries we fully understood and agreed with. We realized that making the right decision was something that we truly wanted to do, although we obviously weren't perfect. Alana describes seeing the tell-tale signs of how the Regnier kids were raised as she got closer to our family.

ALANA

Having worked for CCO in Ottawa, I became good friends with the Regniers. In their family, I saw a deep love for Jesus and a desire for mission woven into each and every one of their children. I remember sharing with Angèle how I wanted to raise a family like theirs. (Clearly all those people who asked the Regniers to write this book feel the same way I do.)

In dating Caleb, I felt I was given a backstage pass to their family life. It was clear that they didn't just become missionary disciples by happenstance; it was a series of virtuous decisions exemplified, explained, and engaged in the lives of each Regnier kid. I remember one day on campus, Jo shared with me that they never grew up watching *The Simpsons*[28]. I was shocked. I mean, you grew up in the 90s and weren't raised by *The Simpsons*? People often joke that TV or Netflix is a good 'babysitter' but think about it: We would never hire a babysitter who is going to set a bad example for our kids at home, and the same should apply for what we expose them to with screen time. As a missionary, I hear many university students express frustration with their parents about the things that they didn't let them watch or do. However, in Jo sharing this with me, his tone was not at all frustrated or jaded. His reasoning also wasn't just "because *The Simpsons* is bad—end of story." But, rather, it was formed from an example of life, and an explanation

---

28. The Simpsons (TV series). Created by Matt Groening. 20th Television. 1989 – .

that it does not align with the virtues that God calls us to. I could see from his conviction that it was a personal resolve to keep Christ at the centre—even with what he decided to watch on TV. This process of decision-making can make the difference between raising children with an 'eat my shorts' mentality about Catholic morals or raising children who are personally convicted and taking ownership in living out their moral decisions. (As I read this to Caleb, I'm having to explain that the 'eat my shorts' phrase isn't an Alana-ism but that credit goes to Bart Simpson himself!)

Valuable Lessons – Our Stories

The best way to grasp how my parents formed our consciences is to see the practical situations where we had to learn the hard way to do the right thing. Here are some stories that stand out for us kids as key learning experiences, where we were challenged to choose God's will in our lives.

JO – Trading Cards

When Caleb and I were still in early elementary school, a huge fad swept across the playground. It was a new card-trading game which had a lot of spiritual and magical elements and you could duel your friends. It was all the rage—everywhere you looked, kids were playing this card game. Caleb and I wanted to get our own cards so that we wouldn't be left out of the fun. Mom and Dad were uncomfortable with us getting into collecting cards with the costs it could incur and the risk of us getting too caught up in it. Caleb and I really pushed for it. We pleaded with Mom and Dad that it was just a fun card game.

Usually Mom and Dad research everything to the nines, but this time they chose to trust us and allowed us to buy the cards, with a catch. We had to use our own money. (They did this as a filter to see if we really wanted the cards badly enough to spend our own money.)

Even though I was only in Grade 3 and Caleb was in Grade 1, I can vividly remember the sequence of events that followed. We were ecstatic with the news and dumped out our piggy banks for the moola. Caleb and I each picked out a pack of cards at the local corner store, then ran home to excitedly see what we got.

As I sat in my room looking at the cards, I felt all the excitement quickly disappear. The names of the characters, and the words and images I saw on the cards were dark and heavy with spiritual themes of the demonic and evil kind. There were cards that had spells, incantations, and curses on them. I had never noticed that stuff before on my friends' cards. I felt this deep sense that this wasn't okay—that keeping these cards and playing with them was the wrong thing to do. It was like a supernatural moral sensing, a deep-set conviction that these cards went against God and were not good for me. I talked to Caleb and he felt the same way. With heavy hearts, we both approached Mom and Dad, showed them the cards, and told them that we didn't like what we saw on them. They asked us, "What do you think you should do about it?" We took some time to think about it a bit more, and then told our parents that wanted to destroy them. We chimed in that we wouldn't pass them along to our friends either. We were convinced that they were just bad for a kids' spirit. Wow! A seven-year-old and a five-year-old freely chose to say no to the latest fad because they knew, deep down, that it was wrong; even after having spent their own money on it! That was a big moment in our moral formation.

From that day forward, Caleb and I made sure we had nothing to do with that card game. On the playground we refused to play the game, or to sit and watch other kids play their cards. The thing is, we didn't do this because our parents told us we couldn't play it. We did it because we freely chose to follow our conscience. This would never have happened if Mom and Dad had not given us a choice, if they hadn't given us the opportunity to make a decision for ourselves.

This situation had a profound impact on me. It was the first time I made a significant decision on my own. This taught me an important lesson: I need seriously to consider and discern when I make decisions.

I feel that if I had not been engaged by my parents in making decisions—both big and small—while in the safe environment of my family, I would have had a hard time making right decisions as a teenager and beyond. I chose to live my life according to God's will because I desired it freely, not out of compulsion but out of love.

CALEB – Bullying

In elementary school, I had a short five-minute walk home after school. One of my neighbours, who was in my class, took the same path home as I did. We didn't really get along, so on our walk home from school, we would often bicker, call each other names, and, sometimes during the winter, throw snowballs back and forth at each other. I often initiated these little confrontations, and as I was doing it, I knew it was wrong. I might not have considered what I was doing to be bullying, because he would often reciprocate, but let's face it—I was actually bullying him.

One spring day, this boy (let's call him Tom) and I were teasing each other on the walk home. It ended with a couple of little shoves here and there until we split ways heading to our respective houses. At the time, I didn't think too much of what had happened. I had only been home for about 30 minutes when the doorbell rang. I opened the door to see a big, grizzly man towering over me. It was Tom's dad. He did not hold back from raising his voice at me. It was the scariest moment of my childhood. He angrily told me how my bullying had caused his son to cry whenever he came home. I felt sick to my stomach. I did not realize how upset Tom felt by my actions and words. And now I was finding out about it from his big, scary dad who was yelling at me. Before I could make any kind of a response, he slammed the door shut and stormed off. Mom heard it all from upstairs—I knew I was in deep trouble.

This was one of the first times when I truly felt my actions had real consequences. Mom was disappointed in me. When Dad found out, he was disappointed in me too. But even worse, I was disappointed in myself.

The way Dad helped me deal with this situation will stick with me forever. Dad explained to me that I would have to go over to Tom's house, ring the doorbell, look him and his dad in the eyes and say, "I'm sorry". How terrifying! How humiliating! But I knew I had a clear decision to make. I had to do this. Dad and I walked over together to the house, he brought me to the door, and I rang the doorbell. My hands were sweating, my heart was pounding, and I saw the silhouette of a big, grizzly man through the door's thin window pane. Tom's father opened the door, took one look at me, and, before I could say a word, he began to shut the door. Dad held the door open for a moment, asking him to allow me to apologize to Tom. Tom's dad wanted nothing to do with it and proceeded to slam the door in my face. Surprisingly, I felt at peace. I had not been forgiven by Tom for my actions but I knew that, with Dad's help, I had made the right decision—to humble myself and apologize. I walked away from that house feeling like a free man.

This experience taught me the importance of making decisions that are above reproach. Because of my lapse in judgement, I learned that I was responsible for showing exceptional virtue—in order to clean up the mess I had made, to try and repair any damage done. I know that Dad could have easily patted me on the head and told me that Tom's father had no right to come over to our house and yell at me, that 'it takes two to tango' and that Tom was just as responsible as I was for what happened. But I see now what that response would have formed in me; that it's okay to shift the blame to others when confronted and to have a victim mentality. Mom and Dad, I'm officially tipping my hat to you. Well played.

JO – Drinking

In Grade 9, I remember going away for the weekend to my friend's cottage. One night we snuck out of the house with a few cans of Coca-Cola, some red solo cups, and a bottle of rum. We went down to the dock by the lake. The entire time we were heading down to the lake, I was having an interior battle. On the one hand, I had my friends, who were promising that it was all harmless fun and going to be a good time. On the other hand, I thought about my Dad's rule: that my first drink was going to be with him.

We got down to the dock and my friends began pouring drinks. I refused immediately and I tried to put up a strong front. But my friends kept drinking and egging me on. Eventually I conceded and I took a sip. That sip became a gulp and soon enough I had my own drink in my hand. The whole time I couldn't shake the sick feeling in my stomach. Luckily, since we were still pretty young and my friends didn't want their fathers to know we took his alcohol, the drinks were not very strong. After an hour we made our way back to the cottage, jumped into our sleeping bags, and went to sleep. Well, not all of us.

I lay there, eyes wide open, my heart pounding, my stomach in knots, completely overwhelmed by guilt and shame. I knew deep down that I had made a major mistake. My dad's words kept playing through my mind on repeat: "Son, your first drink is going to be with me." I knew I had betrayed my father's trust; I had disobeyed him and God. I really felt what the prodigal son must have experienced when he said "I have sinned against heaven and before you; I am no longer worthy to be called your son" (Luke 15:18-19). I lay there for hours, wrestling with all this guilt. Finally, I got up and called home at 3 am. My dad picked up, obviously half asleep. I didn't have the courage to tell him what I had done. I just said that I didn't feel good and I couldn't sleep. He talked to me a for a bit, told me to grab some water and to try to sleep. As I got back in my sleeping bag, I made a vow: I was never going to do something like this again. I was going to have my first real drink with my dad.

A few years later all was restored. Dad and I went out for supper in Gatineau, Québec for my 18th birthday, my first time to be able to legally drink. It was a Sunday, and most of the bars were closed. So we ended up sitting in an East Side Mario's, surrounded by a bunch of old couples out for a lazy Sunday supper. Let's just say it wasn't the most glamourous environment, but it was in right order. We each had a beer and enjoyed them together; no guilt, no shame, just freedom.

Dating

This is a hard topic. I would argue it's the hardest topic to discuss. I admit this is the last thing I want to write about, but I feel that my story is important and needs to be shared. Also, the family determined that I caused the most grief with dating so that means I get the exciting task of sharing my story!

I grew up with a very strong conscience. I was always known as the good church girl who never did anything wrong. From a young age, my relationship with God was a close one and I really did have Jesus at the centre of my life. In Grade 11, I met a guy at a youth group retreat. A few months later, we developed interest for one another and so he asked my parents in a very formal and respectful way for permission for us to date. My parents said yes, outlining strict parameters such as a curfew and that we were not allowed to be alone with one another, opting to stay in public places. Although I was still attending youth group, my heart began growing farther and farther from God. While this boy was a practising Catholic, he had major wounds from his past and struggled with the faith as well as anger issues and drugs. In hindsight, it was not a joyful, healthy relationship. My personality and immaturity kept me from recognizing this and caused me to not have the courage to end this relationship. Sin entered my life as I allowed this relationship to take precedence and I fell into impurity, gossip, selfishness, and lies. This sin continued to separate me from God while, in my mind, my life was going great. I thought I was happy and that this was the way I wanted to continue to live. There was only one 'burden' in my life: my conscience.

It was a strongly formed one, so it was firing on all cylinders, nagging me and bugging me to no end. There was only one solution: to kick Jesus out of my life. So I did. I removed him from the centre of my life. It was easier that way. I pushed him away. I didn't pray, I went through the motions at Mass, and, through it all, kept my attention focused on myself and my boyfriend. Even so, during the midst of it, I remember confiding to one of my friends that I felt like I missed my best friend: Jesus. I stuffed those feelings deep into my heart and tried to ignore them as I kept living my life without him. After a long sequence of events, my parents had enough. They pulled me out of the eight-month relationship, said it was over, and I was left overcome by devastation and shame. I remember feeling empty; everything that I had replaced God with to bring me joy was gone. But I had already known God and, deep down, I knew he was where I had to turn. So I said to God, "Okay, I am going to give you one more shot." I opened my heart to him once more as I felt him asking me to give him every aspect of my life. After this full surrender and a good Confession, I felt fully alive and free. I was honestly in an emotional euphoria for weeks. I've never looked back.

I think my story shows that a well-formed conscience can never be fully thrown into the trash. Despite my decision to kick God out, I still had the resolve to save myself for marriage and reject other overt sins such as drinking and smoking. The work my parents did to instill in me an understanding of right from wrong was not all for naught, even in my rebellion. God doesn't hide from us. Even if we push him away, he is always knocking at the door of our hearts. I credit my relationship with God that I had when I was younger for my fast return to Jesus; it was automatic to run back to him when I came to my senses. I think that sometimes we feel as if a person falling away from their faith makes what anyone did to nurture their faith fruitless, but it doesn't. In fact, it is that work (all the strategies discussed in this book) that made sure that coming back to God was the first thing I would do.

What would we suggest to you as parents as you guide your children into the dating scene? Well, this is a tricky one. Why did my parents say "yes" to allowing me to date at age sixteen? They wanted me to have a healthy view of dating. They didn't want strict rules to breed rebellion. So they actually never set a dating age rule for me. Looking back, my whole family agrees that I was a little bit of a guinea pig for the family. My siblings never dated until after high school and my parents approached dating differently for them. I think they learned just as much from this experience as I did. As a high school student, I did not have the emotional maturity to recognize that this relationship wasn't good for me and to get out of it. My parents were trying to be loving and not overbearing by allowing me to make my own decisions, but they and I know that this backfired.

With the wisdom of hindsight, I have talked with my mom and dad about how that all played out. I was able to tell them, and they agreed, that I had needed them to guide me during that time of my life; that they had failed me actually. Of course, I might not have been able to verbalize that need at the time, but the older me knows it was true. Mom and Dad shared with me how heart-wrenching that time was for them. They didn't want to crush my self-esteem. They wanted to demonstrate their trust in me and were afraid to hurt me. Since I was a very easy-going person, I had never asked for much growing up. (Yes, I was pretty much perfect.) For the first time in my life, I really wanted something. I was so excited about dating this guy. Mom and Dad, seeing me so lit up, were afraid to crush my burgeoning spirits and enthusiasm. But what I actually needed in that moment was for them to parent and guide me, not to be afraid to hurt me. I needed them to be more concerned that I would hurt myself! I needed them to help me think clearly about starting a dating relationship as a teenager, whether this guy was 'worthy' of my affections. I can assure you that the bar my teenage heart had set for myself was simultaneously too low and too heavy for me to bear. Together, with the wisdom of age and experience, the three of us came to the conclusion that parents should own the right to approve or disapprove of any dating relationship, with a keen concern that this special someone passes the gates of being trustworthy, a solid Catholic, and of sufficient maturity. For sure, the guy I was dating was none of these things, and Mom and Dad failed to think it through with me. But we are all the wiser now!

When we discussed this topic as a whole family in our book preparations, we asked ourselves, "How are parents to ensure that their children date someone who brings life to them rather than suck the life out of them?" We came to the conclusion that the key is to raise your child with high ideals and standards for the person they want to be with. This should not simply be enforced through rules and a checklist that the person they date needs to meet. This would be a negative approach; the child would be more inclined to have a fearful, negative perspective of dating and rebellion is more likely. Instead, a positive approach involves painting the picture of what dating should be ideally. This must be done proactively with good conversations and with an outline of expectations when they are young so that, as they grow and dream about future relationships and marriage, they are able to dream with a higher, Christ-centred standard. I've overheard my dad having conversations with Natalie and Janna about this. It is wonderful to see the standards and dreams for relationships they have in their life. They have no interest in dating during high school and have a high standard for what they desire in the person they will marry—if they are called to marriage, of course. Along with these conversations with our dad, a major influence on them has been their older brothers in their respective relationships as well as my own relationship with Marc. They have been able to witness positive relationships on an intimate level and so their image of romance is vastly different than the world would have it shown.

NATALIE

My view on dating has been formed by looking at my parents and my siblings in their relationships. They all lead such good lives and that is what I want. They have healthy relationships where both people love the Lord.

When I think of a relationship, I think of two people who love each other and who want to get married to spend the rest of their lives together. They feel that God is calling them to be together and they know their relationship has a divine purpose.

This is why I want to wait to date until after I finish high school. I feel like you may like a person in high school but you're still just in the process of growing up. Being immature in a relationship can make it unhealthy and can lead people to do inappropriate things. That is why I want to wait until I'm more mature. Besides, so many people in high school only date because it makes them look cool, or because it's fun. But relationships are more than that! The kind of man I'm looking for is someone with whom I already have an existing friendship with—someone who is mature, loves God, has a sense of humour, and who connects well with my family. Family is so important to me that if he doesn't like my family, then I'll say goodbye to him real fast. When I think of marriage, I want to make a good man happy and put his needs before my own. God first, him second! I want my future husband to have the same outlook towards me. To me, dating is not about my selfish desires and pleasure but about loving the other person, making them happy, and following God together.

Technology in Teenage Years

Technology in the teenage years is an extremely important, pertinent, yet tricky topic. For many teens and young adults, technology and social media can get them into a lot of trouble. As the amount of teens with cell phones and other personal devices increase, so does the risk of being exposed to pornography, sexting, promiscuous behaviours, etc. This is a terrifying reality that no one is ignorant to. Many teenagers fall into the sin of promiscuous behaviour online. So how do you protect your children? Without a doubt, this is a new topic and a new reality that parents are going to have to face head-on.

CALEB

The first question is obvious: why not just forbid all use of unsupervised technology? Maybe that's the answer, and up to a certain age, we think that's a great idea. But when kids hit the teen years and they need/want a device to stay in contact with you and others while they're out, things get complicated. Forbidding these devices might not be the best option.

We couldn't come to a consensus on the specifics of this. Do you forbid personal devices until the age of 10? Or up to 16? We aren't exactly sure. But we think delaying your child from having a personal device for as long as necessary is a good approach. Having a family computer on the main floor, is a good option to hold them over until you do decide to give them a personal device. The specifics of ages and such are at your discretion.

Here lies the bigger question. How can you monitor the usage of these devices and protect your teens from being exposed to inappropriate content on the Internet or social media.

We can't say exactly what you need to do, but we can give you some principles.

Internet Usage:

It is a great idea to set up parental controls for safe browsing on your home Internet, or on their personal devices. *Covenant Eyes* (www.covenanteyes.com) is a solid option. It is foolish, in my opinion, to have no means set up to block 'unsafe' websites. Phones and other devices can even completely block Internet surfing in the devices settings; this is an aggressive approach but also a good approach. If they need to search something, kids can do it on a family computer. No matter how much you feel like your teen wouldn't go looking for trouble, don't leave it to chance. You can never be too safe. Err on the side of caution; trouble may be looking for them.

Social Media:

To be honest, this is actually the harder one, and, in my opinion, potentially more dangerous. Why? Because teens can have hidden and private online conversations with their friends and other strangers without you knowing. By 13 years of age (when you're allowed to set up an email and sign up for social media) your teen will be asking if they can make an account, or will be making it without you knowing. All of their friends will have *Facebook*, *Snapchat* and *Instagram* and they will want it too. When Natalie and Janna started asking these questions, Mom turned to me. I'm not sure why, but many people in the family look at me as the techy guy. Mom understood *Facebook*, but the others were new to her. Maybe you're in the same boat. Here's what I told Mom:

Big Brother Mode ... [ACTIVATED]

Facebook: For the most part, *Facebook* (www.facebook.com) is pretty safe. You can customize your privacy settings, even as far as to have it so that teens can send friend requests but no one can send them a friend request. This protects from strangers looking to add them.

Make sure that you are 'friends' with them on *Facebook*, so you can see what they're posting, sharing, and tagged in. I even think it's important to go as far as having them tell you their password—not because you'll check in on them for fun, or to needlessly snoop, but so they realize they should have nothing to hide. I remember Mom telling me that and I got mad at her, but when I thought about it, I realized that I should be okay with giving it to her because if not, it meant I was doing things that I didn't want her to see. Odds are that you have *Facebook* yourself, and have a pretty good understanding of what it would be like for your teen to be on it. I see the largest danger here is the private messages they can have through *Facebook Messenger*. This danger becomes worse when they have a personal device that they can use alone in their room behind closed doors.

Overall, I think *Facebook* is the safest out of the three big platforms I mention. I don't see it as being a huge risk that teens would get an account at 13, as long as they have tight enough privacy settings, you know their password, and they're not going to their room on a device to have secret conversations.

Instagram: If you're unfamiliar with *Instagram* (www.instagram.com), it is a photo/video-based social media. There is no article sharing or statuses—only pictures and videos. I see Instagram as a *larger* risk for your teen. There are far fewer parents on *Instagram*, which means that teens feel more freedom to post immodest or inappropriate pictures. This is a danger if your teen is the one posting but also if they are simply viewing this. Of course, it all depends on who your teen follows, but it is much harder to monitor what they are looking at.

The 'explore' page has a lot of adult content that you can't control. Your teen can view this if they search for it, or if their friends interact with these pages. I would *wait* to allow your teen to use *Instagram*, and when you do, I would suggest getting an account yourself, to make sure you know what they are posting and liking as well as ensuring that they have a private account so that people need permission to follow them.

Snapchat: *Snapchat* (www.snapchat.com) is a newer social media that is based on pictures and videos that disappear after a set amount of time. It is extremely popular amongst teenagers. I think this is mostly because their parents are not on it, and it is next to impossible to monitor. Anything you say or send will disappear. Even the premise of this lends itself perfectly to promiscuous behaviour. You could send an inappropriate picture or have one sent to you, and it would be gone five seconds later; no one would know. I would highly discourage allowing a teen to download *Snapchat* for these reasons.

To conclude, technology amongst teens is a scary topic parents need to face. Helping your kids to form their conscience in this area is extremely important. Have openness and dialogue with your child about what images and practices are morally prudent. A strongly formed conscience here will give your child strength to make the right choices.

The Fourth 'E': Evaluate

Now, I know my mom said that there were three E's in this chapter, but my dad ingeniously discovered a fourth E: Evaluate. This is what will be discussed in the following section. So let's just pretend there were four E's from the start, shall we? Dad's point is that parents need to evaluate where the child is at and what the child needs in order to grow their decision-making muscles. Approaching the daunting task of teaching our children to live a life of virtue and avoid sin, it is hard as parents to know how to protect and empower our children without being too overbearing.

For most Catholic parents, our instinct is to protect and shield our child from the evils of the world and sin. I know that I would love to have my kids spend the rest of their lives in a perfect, protected world where the worst thing their eyes will ever see is their mother pathetically screaming at the sight of a spider. This desire isn't necessarily wrong, but we must be careful not to allow a spirit of fear to overtake us. Fear is never of God. In parenting, our motivation to shield or not to shield should never come from fear but from wisdom and discernment. One scenario where evaluation warranted a courageous decision to shield us was in the sexual education program at our schools. Elizabeth's parents took the exact same approach with their children. Here is the reasoning behind it:

ELIZABETH – Sex Education

I am not sure what the sex education is like at your family's school, but both mine and Jo's parents took us out of the program in our elementary schools. Our parents saw that the content was too mature for us young children to handle and it wasn't the responsibility of our teachers to teach us such delicate, sensitive information. I remember being taken out of class during those periods and being as proud as a peacock because I knew that my parents were making this decision based on our faith (as they usually did) and because they cared about my good. They had explained that it wasn't appropriate for my age and I was okay with that. Plus, I was uncomfortable with talking about sexuality with my friends and teachers, so it gave me a way out of sitting there awkwardly.

This doesn't mean that I never learned about sexuality. Over time, my parents explained things to me when I was ready to hear it. They made it a standard that if I heard anything at school about sexuality or if I had any questions, that they were the ones I would ask about it. I remember a classmate in Grade 5 mentioning the word 'virgin' and so I came home and asked my mom what that meant. My mom sat with me in the living room and explained things to me and it wasn't awkward or weird because I was comfortable with my mother and I already knew that it was my parents who would educate me about these things. My parents approached sexuality with reverence and did not think it was something embarrassing to laugh about, like my friends at school did. I caught this attitude from my parents and also knew that sexuality was a beautiful thing, not something to be talked about all of the time in negative or degrading ways. I believe the way they taught me to approach sexuality formed my conscience in that area and also opened the door for me to feel comfortable talking to them about personal things as I grew older.

At the other end of this balancing act is the importance of actually empowering a child to make their own virtuous decisions and to trust them as they face the world themselves. This was a tough one for my parents and required much grace from God not to be held back by fear. Sometimes, my parents chose to let us experience the tough challenges so we could learn how to handle them independently.

CALEB – Pushed into the World

In my early years of high school, I had made my decision to be an intentional disciple, and I was convicted and ardent about living for Christ. It began to change the way I viewed my high school friends who began to experiment with alcohol and partying. The first time I was exposed to this was in Grade 9, when a couple of my buddies filled water bottles with vodka and were drinking it after school. (Looking back, I am sure it was only 20 percent vodka, 80 percent water.) I knew this was wrong. I saw it and it frustrated me because I knew that this behaviour was inconsistent with my desire to live for Christ, so there was no way that I would ever join them. On top of this, as Jo mentioned, I always knew that Dad had told me that my first drink would be with him. I felt no need or desire to have that drink with my friends; I wanted it to be with my dad. Obviously, I was an angel compared to Jo, since I never broke this rule.

Over the next two years, I really distanced myself from my high school friends. I would say that I almost segregated myself. I began to view them as bad because they drank. This was, of course, not true. My view of the world began to change: I started to view the world as inherently evil. My relationship with my friends became very shallow, and they rarely invited me to hang out with them anymore. It was not as if they had shunned me because I was practising my faith but, rather, because I had shunned *them*, thinking that they had turned to the 'dark side'. Looking back, I feel bad that I communicated to them what may have seemed like a 'you're not worthy to be with me' attitude. I even remember ripping on one of my best friends because I found out that he had drank at a party the Saturday before. I acted like I was his dad, and it caused a huge rift in our friendship that was never repaired.

It came as a surprise to me, then, that I was invited to a party one Friday night in high school. I knew there would be alcohol at this party, so there was no way that I would go. I told my dad that I had been invited to this party, explaining how stupid it was. To me, it felt like going to this party would be like stepping into the gates of hell. His response baffled me. He said, "Why wouldn't you go?" WHAT? Why would any father, in their right mind, ever, under any circumstance, suggest their 16-year-old son to go to a party with the guarantee of underage drinking? I was so confused. This went against everything I had been fighting for. Dad explained to me that going to a party doesn't mean I needed to drink; I could go and not drink.

This is such a difficult and grey area. It is so risky! Allowing teenagers to go to parties, hoping that you can trust them, could be a huge mistake and result in opening the doors to drunkeness and promiscuity. There is tremendous importance in evaluating. Dad evaluated me and knew that I would not drink. He trusted me, and I think he was able to sense a fear of the world in me. His evaluation led him to challenge me to have a healthy relationship with the world; to "not be conformed to this world" (Romans 12:2) but also to not live in fear of it, for "God has not given us a spirit of fear." (2 Timothy 1:8)

So I went to the party. I didn't drink and I had a good time with my friends, and it helped rebuild the many bridges I had burned. But, most importantly, it reversed my demonization of my friends which had taken place over the previous years. Compassion for them grew instead of indignation. I had a new desire to meet them where they were at and look for opportunities to build trust in the hopes of sharing my faith with them down the line.

ANDRÉ – Evaluating

What kind of dad am I to encourage my son, who chose to live his faith with great courage amidst his peers, to go to a party where there would be drinking and everything else that goes with it? I was an evaluating dad, that's the kind of dad I was.

I made a similar decision with my daughter Natalie when she was asked to go to a co-ed backyard sleepover party. Yes, with both boys and girls! The arrangement was that the boys wouldn't sleep in the same yard as the girls but rather, in the backyard just next door. You can see the conditions set up for possible bad and regrettable decisions here! I was confident in her ability to navigate right from wrong. At the same time, as a father, I am responsible to protect her and not let her go into a compromising situation.

The fact of the matter is that Natalie didn't want to go. I was proud of her that she was prepared to make a good and courageous choice, even when pressured by her friends to go. That could have been the end of the whole thing. But as I reflected on her situation, I wondered how I could use this context to form her character—to make good decisions without fear and judgment of the world, and from a missionary mindset.

I evaluated. I could tell she was not susceptible to being influenced by the behaviours of her friends. She had an informed conscience. She had a missionary outlook. She is an important person in the lives of her young friends, being an authentic and attractive witness of the faith. Was there a way to make this a win-win and for her to be 'in the world but not of the world'?

I talked to Natalie about all the things I had assessed about her and what she means to her friends, and I proposed a solution: I pick her up at 11 pm so she could hang out with her friends and have fun, and by leaving, she could still be a witness to her convictions about purity. She agreed with this approach rather than just outright rejecting her friends. I have to emphasize that my evaluation of Natalie's and Caleb's situations were significantly influenced by how they had *proven*, time and time again, that they were able to make *good* decisions. If I was *not* confident of their decision-making capacity, I would have acted differently.

When our children are out in the world, we aren't there to watch over them. They experience independence and autonomy. Such autonomy may give them a sense of secrecy, "Mom and Dad aren't here, they will never know." Faithful children are taught and are aware that they answer to someone much greater than their parents; they answer to God, who is ever present. With such a worldview, they know that nothing is done in secret. They are ultimately responsible for their decisions to God.

As Catholic parents, we are not alone in this task of evaluation and forming our children. We have the Holy Spirit always with us, infusing us with much needed wisdom, counsel, understanding, and the fruits of patience, goodness, hope, and love. We are never alone in our parenting and even if we get it wrong sometimes, that's okay! Thankfully, God knows we are weak and our acknowledgement of this weakness—that we need him in our parenting—will only strengthen us more. "I remind you to kindle afresh the gift of God which is in you through the laying on of my hands. For God has not given us a spirit of fear, but of power and love and discipline." (2 Timothy 1:7-8) So while it is a balancing act, the strategy parents choose is one that can and should be guided by the Spirit. We have no need to be fearful; instead, we should be confident that he is going to work here and he wants our children to live a life of virtue even more than we do!

A Relationship with Jesus is Key

As parents, we can do a wonderful job of teaching our child to make the right choices, but there is only so far they can grow. As I am sure you have already learned time and time again in your own lives, our efforts to do the right thing often fail miserably when we don't depend on Christ's grace. We are fully able to receive this grace in our lives when we give Christ full dominion and have a relationship with him. Your child can be wonderfully obedient, virtuous, and faithful, but it is only once they truly put Christ at the centre of their lives that parenting becomes so much easier.

NATALIE

Last summer, I went to a Steubenville conference in Toronto with our youth group. It was an amazing experience! During those two days, I personally experienced God. On the last night of Eucharistic Adoration, I was so filled with his love that I began to cry with joy. I experienced the fire of the Holy Spirit in my heart. Since then, I've been happier than ever! I've noticed that I am way less attracted to things that aren't good for my faith. My love for the Lord has really taken away the desire for things that would be wrong for me.

A lot of girls my age don't wear modest clothing (crop tops, short shorts, bikinis, etc.) but, it seems when I see these fashion choices, I have no desire to wear them. The reason I don't wish I could wear those kinds of clothes is because I know that dressing modestly is the right thing to do. Also, when I hear my friends swear, I don't even wonder if I should try swearing. People notice that I don't swear like everyone else or that I don't act like most girls.

For example, once when I was in school, one of my friends asked me if I had ever sworn. I responded honestly by saying that I don't swear. She then asked me to say a curse word but I said no. She wouldn't stop asking me, but I knew I wouldn't swear—even though she kept on pestering me and making fun of me. God was watching over me with love and I showed him that I loved him by doing the right thing. I've noticed the change in me since that personal decision I made to put God first in everything last year (2017). Because I practice my faith and have Christ in the centre of my life and because he matters to me and has filled me with his love, I don't want to hide my faith.

Conclusion

"Instead, put on the Lord Jesus Christ, and make no provision for the flesh, to gratify its desires." (Romans 13:14) Let us put on the Lord Jesus and encourage our children to do the same in all aspects of their lives! The decisions children make can be a source of great pride and joy or, contrarily, an area of deep hurt and regret. Through this chapter, we have shared stories of poor decision-making, and good decision-making. In all cases, it has been Mom and Dad's intentional effort to form our consciences which has resulted in our ability to make good, holy, and moral decisions. This I can say has remained with us in our adult years (for those of us who are adults, of course).

After reading this chapter, we hope that you remember:

- The Four E's:
  1. *Example* – model moral and just behaviour that isn't too legalistic
  2. *Explanation* – give the reasoning behind your decisions through conversation, not a lecture
  3. *Engagement* – involve the children in dialogue, inviting them to take personal ownership in the decision that is to be made
  4. *Evaluate* – assess where the children are at and whether they need to be shielded or empowered
- Give your children opportunities to make right and moral decisions according to their age so that as they grow older, they can independently make choices that reflect their maturity.
- A relationship with Jesus is key! Keep this at the back of your mind as you form your child's conscience, always looking to explain a decision through the lens of faith.

How does the ability to make good decisions prepare a child to be a missionary disciple? Why is decision-making such a great tool at your disposal in raising children as missionary disciples? If they are not strengthened to choose well early in life, how can they stay true as disciples and be missionaries to this world when they grow up? The world, the flesh, and the devil are always the enemy to serious followers of Christ and a missionary disciple must learn to say no to sin. Training a child to make good decisions roots a child in docility, to be ever ready to the promptings of the Holy Spirit in their conscience and say yes to God. Is this not an imitation of the greatest role model and disciple of them all, our Blessed Mother? When the mind and conscience is formed to make good decisions, the child will naturally grow in virtue and goodness, which will make them beautiful apostles to a world in need of authentic and compelling witnesses to Jesus Christ.

Reflection / Action Points

1. André and Angèle knew they couldn't fear the world but they also couldn't trust it. Are there areas you fear or trust in the secular world too much, where you should change your attitude for the sake of your children whose consciences need to be formed in freedom?

2. Do you find yourself reactive or proactive in the way you are parenting? Are you seeing and seizing opportunities to equip your children to make good decisions in the future?

3. Which of the Four E's are you strongest in, and which one do you need to work on the most? Choose an 'E' to focus on this week with your children.

4. Having Christ at the centre of your life as a parent makes a difference, but it's also a game-changer when your children have Christ at the centre of their own lives. Are there ways that you can be more Christ-centred in your parenting? Are there ways that you can encourage your children to consider placing Christ at the centre of their own lives? Could you send them to a retreat weekend, a conference, or a youth group event?

CHAPTER 4

A Culture of Respect

Respect at the Foundation of All Family Relationships

MYLÈNE

In doing our version of an 'environmental scan' of our home life for this book, we noticed that respect was a ribbon that flowed through almost everything in our family life. A deep respect is implicit in our interactions with each other and, specifically, in the area of discipline. A disposition of respect was furthermore expected in how we, as Regniers, acted towards others in the wider community. This culture of respect encompassed children respecting parents, parents respecting children, self-respect, respect for God and the Sacred, respect of authority, respect for life, respect of privacy, respect of property, and respect of the other.

Permit me to emphasize that respect in itself is an admirable virtue to foster in a child's human development but, in our family, we have seen how it has had a significant impact for forming our spiritual lives as well. Respect cultivates a desire to please, honour, and bring glory to God. Respect breeds fear of the Lord, docility, humility, kindness, selflessness, charity, obedience, generosity, and abandonment to God's will. These are all essential in forming children who will become missionary disciples of Christ in adulthood.

Respect is what we all desire to receive and what we are expected to give to others, yet it is not something that happens automatically. It needs to be built—but how? The definition of respect is "a feeling of deep admiration for someone or something elicited by their abilities, qualities, or achievements."[29] The Christian definition of respect brings us deeper than this, as it extends beyond simply seeing one's abilities and achievements to

---

29. The English Oxford Living Dictionaries.

having respect for a person's God-given dignity as a child of God. It's not so much what one does, but rather who they are that matters. Knowing this, the question remains: how do you build such respect within human relationships? Based on both definitions of respect, we would suggest that respect can be built in two ways: proactively seeking to see another person as a child of God who is inherently good no matter what they do, and also seeking to admire a person's abilities, qualities, and achievements (especially when they are different than your own).

We've noticed that respect isn't something you can just instruct and enforce. It comes largely through modelling in everyday interactions, especially in those teachable moments and the overall tone of your family environment. As a parent myself, I see that it requires consistency, effort, self-reflection, and diligence. Seeds are sown in mere moments but require time to grow.

Children Respecting Parents

As someone who is prone to be a 'people-pleasing, conflict-avoider' kind of person, discipline of my children has not come naturally. Luckily, my husband seems to be a natural and he has encouraged me in this regard. Often it feels like it would just be easier to let things slide, to pretend I didn't see something. But making the tough decision to stay firm in moments of difficulty with a child has rewarding results in the long run. The result is a disciplined child who has respect for their parents. I'm grateful for the wisdom in disciplining children that my parents have passed on to Marc and myself, which is rooted in a culture of respect in the home.

ANGÈLE – Discipline

God has entrusted five children to André and my care. We look at this responsibility with the same aspirations as St. Paul, "that we may present every man [and woman] mature in Christ." (Colossians 1:28) Just as spiritual disciplines perfect a disciple of Christ, so parental discipline trains a child to maturity. Our discipline of a child, therefore, is more than behaviour management; it facilitates the development of a missionary disciple in a school of respect.

I propose that any behaviour or attitude of a child which requires discipline is surely rooted in disrespect: disrespect towards rules, another's belongings, or someone's feelings. If disrespect is at the core of disobedience, then respect must be fundamental in training a child to be obedient. When we discipline a child, we are not simply dealing with behavioural issues—we are instilling respect. Respect goes both ways; we won't be able to nurture respect if we don't discipline our children in a respectful manner.

The keys to discipline that we have found in raising our own kids are being: 1. consistent; 2. timely; and 3. reasonable. Conversely, I might say that the pitfalls to discipline are: 1. being inconsistent; 2. not responding in a timely manner; and 3. unreasonable approaches.

Consistent means that you discipline in every opportunity that requires it and that your character is consistent with the behaviours desired.

Timely means that you deal with the issue immediately to capitalize on the teachable moment.

Reasonable means the way that you discipline needs to be controlled, not frenzied, and that the choice of the punishment must be a reasonable consequence appropriate to the behaviour and the child.

It is hard to speak of these keys to discipline isolated from each other. I see them in the form a Venn diagram of respectful parenting (see Figure 1). In a nutshell, the interdependency of our approach to discipline is: *be consistent with reasonable rules and repercussions in an absolute timely manner*—all at the same time. I will try to break down what I mean by each of these principles and offer some practical and real-life examples.

Figure 1:

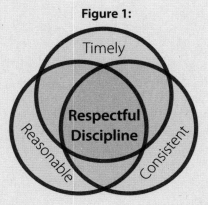

Key #1 – Consistent

If you can win at being consistent in your parental discipline moment by moment—at home, in the grocery store, at your mom's house, in the car, or while company is visiting—your child will be happier and you will save yourself a lot of heartache from disobedient behaviour.

I noticed that, when we were inconsistent, the kids were more likely to disobey. Lack of consistent discipline numbs children to rules and authority. If they can get away with not listening to their Grandma asking them to bring their plates into the kitchen as a toddler, then who and what will they not listen to when they are 8? Or 12? Or 15? Or 17? Consistency, however, gives safe parameters and, in a mysterious way, forms a child's character in respect. ("I was asked by my Grandma to clear the plates and she expects and deserves my respect to do so".)

Consistency also has another meaning—that your own habits, behaviour, and integrity model the behaviours you are trying to instill in your child (just as we outlined in the Decision Making chapter; forming consciences requires the 'example' of the parent). You practice what you preach. When you discipline your child about watching too much TV, you yourself model how much TV you watch. How can a child respect being grounded for having not cleaned their bedroom, when your own bedroom has an explosive night stand of books, cups, pens, and papers from work, as well as an open and overflowing suitcase in the middle of the floor from your last business trip?

I'm sure the principle of consistency seems pretty straightforward. I think it's the kind of statement about discipline that can get a quick nod and a yawn. "Of course, if you want to discipline, you have to be consistent." But it's hard work! You always have to be on. You have to make sure you discipline with the same approach in the same set of circumstances, and equally when the same infraction happens with another child. Oh, believe me—like elephants, kids remember. "Hey! When Jo didn't do his chores you only made him blah blah blah … how come I have to do xyz?" So for your own sanity and theirs, you need to think like an elephant too. You have to remember the rules you made up and then stay consistent.

Honestly, this is tricky to manage. I think if I could do it all over again, I would keep a little notebook of punishment by-laws. A policy manual for mom's reference. I am totally serious. Such a notebook would have been so helpful to keep things consistent, not only from one child to another, but also when the situation arose again. I wouldn't have had to determine the repercussions all over again. It is so helpful when you can be clear, concise, and confident in your response because you know what your usual discipline response is, and so does your child. Your darling elephant will likely remember, "Ya, that's what Mom usually does when I disobey that way." Or your older ones can chime in and say, "Yep. Mom did that to me too." Not only is this a calmer, more confident approach to discipline, but the child is calmer and more confident too. They know it's appropriate and aligned to the boundaries of this family. It is right and just.

The power of consistency is that it establishes security and safe parameters for kids. Children want to know their boundaries for safe play. Ever notice how kids are constantly testing the boundaries of what is allowed for them? "Hmmm, I wonder what happens if I try going here. What will Mommy say?" In my experience, children are happier with clear boundaries that are regulated and watched. They like to know where they belong and what they can and cannot do in their environment. Kids are unsettled in shifting environments and in a lack of routine, or with too many choices and options. So if your child does not get consistent messaging, parameters, and punishments from you, they will be confused and act out in that confusion.

Key #2 – Timely

Timeliness is the principle of dealing with the problem *immediately*, *swiftly* and *calmly*. A child—especially a young child—needs a quick response time in order to understand the problem. If the response time is too slow, the child can be confused as to what behaviour caused the punishment. As children get older, your responsiveness and time in which the punishment plays out also needs to be timely. I learned the hard way that deferred punishment does not correct behaviours. The best learning, or formation of behaviour, happens when discipline is as close to the misdemeanor as possible.

For example, we went to a waterpark as a family and six-year-old Natalie kept running off on her own, thinking she was one of the teenaged kids, I suppose. In a situation like this, it would not be very helpful if I had told her: "If you don't stop doing that, I'm going to ground you for two days when we get home" or, "If you don't stop running off like that, we are not going to watch a movie tonight." The threatened punishment might scare her into obedience but, if it doesn't stop her from running off, then what? I'll tell you what. Good luck dealing with the weeping, wailing, and gnashing of teeth that night or the next two days—not Natalie's wailing but mine while I struggle to keep her grounded or out of the TV room during family movie night. Believe me, I just ruined my own summer night, not hers.

Even if the punishment to be grounded or not watch a movie is a consistent punishment and a reasonable punishment, the problem is that it's not *timely*. *A child needs to feel the consequence as proximate to the misbehaviour as possible.* Six hours into the future or two days from now is too far away for a child to grasp. Their minds are too immature to really comprehend how much they will regret those repercussions. When they are actually serving the time, they won't even have the bandwidth to reflect on how they misbehaved because all they will be thinking about is how mean their parents are.

So let us go back to the crime scene: Natalie would not listen about running off on her own. She would not listen to the rules that had been clearly repeated to her. What kind of punishment would have been timely? It needed to be something that would stop this blonde cutie wearing a Walmart one-piece bathing suit and lime-green goggles from having fun in the sun, right then, right there.

"Natalie, if you run off again on your own without anyone in the family, you will have to sit here on the grass until they come down to line up for the next water slide. If you do not want to miss out on the fun, you need to stay with someone in the family." Ouch—that pinch was both felt and immediate. And it worked!

The enemy of timeliness (and consistency for that matter), is laziness. Laziness is the opposite of a timely response. I can have every intention, in principle, to be consistent but what often happens is laziness kicks in and I wimp out. *Laziness is the biggest attack on the greatest key to disciplinary success.* It's when I am too lazy to deal with a child and their behaviour that I shoot myself in the foot BIG TIME. When I let behaviours slip, once, twice … and then try to enforce the appropriate behaviour, I'm in for a battle. It takes way more energy to try to bring the kids back in line than if I had just taken the effort to pull myself off of that la-z-boy chair from the start.

The 'la-z-boy chair' is more than a little quip in that sentence. André and I often say to ourselves, "Get off the la-z-boy and respond! "We came up with the phrase watching other parents/families literally losing the parenting battle while in a la-z-boy. (I guess you could surmise that we were judging them, but I like to think that we were observing, gathering data, and drawing conclusions.)

What we witnessed was not so much that the kids were misbehaving—and believe me, they were driving everyone else crazy—*but more so that the parents weren't responding to the kids' disobedience.*

For example, I was once visiting at a neighbour's house when one of her darlings was dragging chairs across the kitchen, scrambling up on to the kitchen counters, and knocking things over in order to dig through cupboards to find a package of cookies. Although I cringed at what was happening and it wasn't my place to discipline, I was shocked that the mom did nothing, especially since she had just told this child that they didn't need any sweet snacks right now. Chaos was ensuing and she just kept chatting, oblivious to the kitchen shenanigans.

After some time, she yelled over her shoulder towards the kitchen. "Hey, get off that counter!" and "What do you think you're doing? You don't need cookies, you just ate!" Blah blah blah, yell yell yell, until the kid succeeded in the goal of attaining a fistful of cookies and fleeing the scene while leaving a catastrophe behind. Finally, our armchair parent was freed from the need to yell and was able to get on with our lazy afternoon visit. I was astonished when this imp wandered over several minutes later, cookies in hand, to casually sit on the arm of the la-z-boy next to her mom. Although I first pegged the behaviour as brazen cheekiness, I observed that this child was looking to see if her mom would do anything now that the crime scene in the kitchen had gone cold. "Will she be mad and react to my handful of cookies or not?"

I think that subconsciously, she was testing the boundaries. Maybe a little dialogue like this was going on in her precocious head:

> *"Did I really just get away with that cookie snatching? I wonder if I could get away with it again? She sounded really mad when she was yelling, but I don't know if she really was? I bet I can actually steal cookies whenever I want to, because mom didn't stop me. I don't think she really cares too much about it. I'm sitting here beside her and she's not even mad. Yay, I like these new rules. I wonder what else I can do. Hmmm, I wonder where she keeps the chocolate chips…."*

Through all of these observations, I realized that la-z-boy parenting seems like it's saving time and energy, when in reality, it creates more issues, more fights, and more time spent disciplining. Actually, the 'lazy' thing to do is to get up off the couch and discipline your children in a timely manner because in the long run, you are going to save yourself hours of heartache, anger, and frustration (freeing up a lot of time to sit back, relax and eat cookies!).

Timeliness also calls us to discipline in season and out of season. To win at timeliness, you have to be prepared to act—even if that means scooping up the child and leaving the grocery store or the park when the nonsense strikes. If your child starts misbehaving or perhaps having 'the gimmies,'[30] our approach is to be prepared to leave.

A specific example I remember was when I took the kids out to the playplace at *Burger King* one cold winter's day in Regina. Jo and Mylène, who were three and five years old, would not listen to me about some particular rule of the play place (either keeping their socks on, or blocking the tunnels, or something). They were outright ignoring what I was telling them to do. I warned them that, if they didn't abide by the rules, we would go home. Now, you have to understand that I wanted to get out of our townhouse desperately! It was February in Regina! Need I say more? I was going stir-crazy! I was so looking forward to enjoying a Coke, fries, and a burger and making some to-do lists while the kids played happily in the ball pit. I wanted to be there. I did not want to discipline. I did not want to pack them up in the cold after only 15 minutes of settling in. But when Jo and Mylène blatantly disregarded the rules and the warnings I had given them, I was faced with a choice: to turn a blind eye and act like I didn't see anything *or* to act with timeliness.

---

30. This is a reference to the MUST-HAVE classic book, *Berenstain Bears Get The Gimmies,* about kids having meltdowns in stores.

Now, let me unpack this scenario showing more than timeliness, but also reasonableness. The most reasonable consequence was to take them home. I could have tried implementing a 'time-out,' except that time-outs were always a disaster with Jo because he refused to sit. It just made things worse. I needed a real, timely consequence that made sense immediately, like: "We are leaving. Playtime is over."

I think I even gave them one more chance to comply (with a repeated warning) and then that was it. Upon the next infraction, I swiftly handed them their outerwear and announced we were leaving immediately. End of story. Well, not quite—I gave them a long speech the whole drive home about what went wrong, the necessity of respecting their parents, listening to the rules, the consequences of disobedience, and what behaviour I expected the next time we went out.

After that, all I had to say when heading out to the park, *Walmart*, or wherever, was a reminder of the respect I wanted to see and, if there was a problem, they would be given one warning before we left for home. They knew Mom was prepared to do it because I had done it before. I can honestly tell you that I *never* had problems with public freakouts after that day at *Burger King* (and the *Berenstain Bears'*[31] book was a huge reinforcement too).

By the way, it's my observation that sometimes kids have these meltdowns in stores not just because they aren't disciplined properly, but because the child is just done with shopping. This is not unlike how André is done with shopping after his '43-minute shopping capacity timer' goes off. You know he's 'done' when his eyes glaze over—his energy is zapped and he has shut down. Now imagine you are a three-year-old and you are done. You want a nap. You need food. You need to run, play, and get out of the uncomfortable metal basket of the store cart. I think we as parents can be so fixated on what we want to do, shop for, or look at, that we aren't prepared to stop doing what we want to do for the sake of the child. So we start bickering and snapping at the child because we are frustrated that he/she is ruining our shopping day. We need to put the needs of the child first—be it rest, nutrition, routine, or discipline. We have to be ready to walk away and do what is needed for the child's development. We need to show respect for the child.

---

31. Ibid.

Key #3 – Reasonable

Let's look more at reasonableness. The principle of being reasonable guides us to suit the punishment to the crime as well as our little criminal. The consequence shouldn't be too easy or too exaggerated. It should be appropriate to the child's age, the behaviour, and even the personality of the child. In light of reasonableness, I try as much as possible to go with consequences that fit the context. For example, you made the mess—you have to clean it up; you ate your brother's treat—you have to buy him a replacement with your own money. Finding reasonable punishment is a bit of an art and, when possible, I find that talking it through with your spouse is very helpful to finding a wise approach.

(See 'Bonus Features' for some examples of reasonable, context-appropriate consequences and discipline strategies)

Sometimes it's really hard to decide what is reasonable, especially when you are in the heat of the moment and want to blurt out, "You're grounded for life!" I found it helpful to say, "Look, you're in really big trouble right now and I'm really mad about this. I'm so mad that you do not want me to decide now what your punishment will be. I'm going to have to calm down a bit and think but, believe me, it's not going to be good. If you want any hope of the punishment being better than worse, then I strongly suggest that you be on your best, quiet behaviour until I get back to you." I wasn't saying all of this to build fearful suspense, because that would go against my principle of timeliness. The reason I was suspending the sentence was to ensure reasonableness. I knew myself, and I knew that in frantic frustration I would be likely to blow the situation out of proportion.

Reasonable discipline is done respectfully. For example, instead of shaming a child publicly or getting in a heated frenzy, get down to their level and speak firmly. I strive to discipline with my dignity intact, not as a stark raving mad mother. I want to model reasonableness, control, clarity, and confidence in my discipline rather than an emotional knee-jerk reaction of disgust, frustration, and bitterness.

Seriously though, how can a child respect an adult who is having their own XL-sized hissy fit? When I have to ask myself "Who's supposed to be the grown up here?", I know I'm slipping. I need to be the adult and discipline in a reasonable manner starting with how I talk to the kids. This exhibits respect for my own dignity and for the child's. So, in summary, be reasonable in your demeanor as well as in your choice of consequence.

The opposite end of the spectrum from this is being too lax or too soft in your approach—the la-z-boy parenting again. Permissive or lazy parenting diminishes the respect the child has for you as the parent. Although they may appear to be thrilled with the freedom of permissive parenting, they instinctively know your judgements are not reasonable or wise. Just like the little cookie monster snuggling up to her mom right after blatantly stealing Oreos.

Imagine if your kid stole your car for a joy ride to the next city with his high school friends. Would it be reasonable for you, as a parent, to turn a blind eye? No—lax, sloppy parenting is not kind or reasonable. And the effects of this parenting snowball into bad behaviour. Think about it. What would *you* do if your parents never really got mad that you went on a joyride? You would totally up the ante and go bigger next time. Why not steal money from mom's purse, take the car, and come back in the morning next time?

My take on it is that, consciously or subconsciously, a child is wondering, "Do you even care? Do you have any self-respect or control?" Disrespectful and sloppy, lax parenting means that children will lack safe boundaries and a moral compass. Children of all ages are innately looking to understand what is right and just and true.

As parents, whether we like it or not, we are icons of the Father's love, safety, and authority in their little worlds. We need to strive to reflect to them how our God—the righteous judge—makes good and true judgments, balancing both justice and mercy in his love for us. It has long been understood that a child's first perception of God is through their parents (especially through their father). They may see God as unengaged, passive, and permissive. Maybe they may see God as an angry policeman in the sky looking to nail them with a life sentence. But if we can balance justice and mercy in our disciplining we can help them have a healthy understanding of God too. And we won't just be raising mature well-adjusted children; we will be raising mature well-adjusted disciples.

Tying Them All Together

When we refer back to our Venn diagram approach, we can see the need for all three of these parenting principles, at all times.

If you are **consistent** and **reasonable**, yet don't discipline in a *timely* fashion, your child can miss the teachable moment and the connection between the behaviour and the consequence. The child may be unclear as to why they are being punished, and this could cause mistrust in the relationship. They just don't get why you're being mean and grumpy.

If you are *timely* and *reasonable* but not *consistent*, the child is likely to feel unsettled and unclear in the actual parameters and rules he needs to abide by. You can expect misbehaviours to keep happening because they are testing the rules.

If you are *timely* and *consistent* but not *reasonable*, you risk losing your child's respect. They will sense that you don't discipline well, either due to being lax or from overreacting. If your unreasonableness is demonstrated through laxity, your child might push more limits with more varied misbehaviours to see if you will actually discipline with stronger confidence. If your unreasonableness is shown in overreacting, you lose respect and you risk instilling fear and bitterness in the child's relationship with you.

So our advice, which will save you a lot of heartache in the long run, is to be consistent, timely, and reasonable.

JO – Respecting Parents

Growing up, one of the most awkward situations I was a part of was witnessing a friend fighting with his parents. I have a vivid memory of being out skiing with a friend, when he asked his dad if we could have a sleepover. His dad calmly said no. My friend began to fight with his dad, big time. I felt awkward in the back of the car while this back and forth exchange was going on. My friend eventually got so heated that he swore at his dad. "@$#& you, Dad."

Screeeeeeech! His dad had had enough and drove me right home. That drive home was so uncomfortable. The whole time I was asking myself: how could he speak that way to his dad?

One thing that Mom and Dad were very insistent on was that we kids did NOT get away with giving attitude or being smart towards them. Did I give attitude? You better believe it. Did I get away with it? Well, do prisoners escape Alcatraz? (Ok so some did, but I didn't.) Mom and Dad always insisted that we speak respectfully towards each other, and especially towards them. For me, as the resident 'fight-starter', this was something I dealt with on a regular basis. If I spoke rudely towards Mom or Dad, I was immediately reprimanded. I remember once getting mad at my mom and saying something disrespectful towards her. My dad sent me to my room and sternly told me, "You do NOT speak like that to your mother, and I will not allow you to speak like that to my wife." Looking back, that always stood out to me. I had no right to speak that way towards my mom and, had my dad allowed me to get away with it, I would have understood that it can be permissible to disrespect my parents through my words.

I remember other times being at a friend's house when they would start complaining or fighting with their parents because they wanted something. At first, his parents would say no, but my friend would continue to push. Eventually, his parents would give in. I never understood this. If I did that at home, especially in front of friends or company, I would be punished and my friends would be sent home. There was no way I would come out a winner. Mom and Dad were the boss, and I knew that, as much as I wished I could be in charge. They demanded respect. This did not just apply to outright disrespect, but also to smart comments or sarcasm. The way we speak towards people, especially towards our parents, forms the way we think and act towards them. As my dad always says, "If you say something enough times, eventually you will believe it." This is so true, and is actually confirmed in Scripture. "The good person out of the good treasure of the heart produces good, and the evil person out of evil treasure produces evil; for it is out of the abundance of the heart that the mouth speaks." (Luke 6:45)

Parents Respecting Children

Parents' respect for their child will manifest in very different ways than a child's respect for their parents. However, they are equally and mutually important. To respect a child is to love them in all the uniqueness of who they are, treat them with the care and dignity they deserve as children of God, and assure them they belong and are loved. This is something that my grandparents did extremely well, as my dad will explain.

ANDRÉ – Respecting a Child's Dignity

The Christian idea of respect surpasses what a person does, but appreciates who a person is through their God-given dignity. In this environment of respect, we are more free to be ourselves in our strengths and our weaknesses. As a child and even as a young person, the place where I felt the most safe and secure was my home. I did not need to showcase abilities and achievements to gain respect. Rather, admiration was founded on me being who I was: a member of the family.

My mother always had an immensely respectful response to us as her children, despite our weaknesses, and we had many. I remember being in a French school play as a young boy. I was not very good at French, I was not good at remembering lines, and I had a short attention span which made it difficult to be on stage. My teacher knew me well, so she chose the appropriate part for me in the play. I was to play the part of the family dog, where my only role was to come in for one scene and bark. The big night arrived; the set was up, the lights were down, and the auditorium was full of proud parents. My big moment arrived and I came in for three whole seconds to bark as loudly as I could: "Woof woof!" (that is, "Ouaf ouaf!" en français). While leaving the stage, I could see my mom in front beaming, her eyes saying to me with great pride, "That's my son!" In that moment, I felt like a million bucks. I knew that in my mom's eyes, I deserved a Tony Award.

My parents also showed us kids great respect in how they dealt with the dreaded parent-teacher interviews. It is true that my siblings and I were not the best students, which was reflected in our report cards. We all feared our parents going directly to our teachers and talking about our bad performance. To our surprise, my parents would come home and, rather than reprimand us for low grades, they'd tell us that our teachers liked us and considered us good people. However poor we were as students, we never disrespected our teachers and they knew we were good kids. And that's because we were always respected at home and taught to be respectful; it was modelled to us and expected of us.

Disrespecting a child and their dignity is far too easy to do. Respecting them is the decision not to view them as 'just a kid' and disregard what they say and do. I remember one time when my son was two, he began to explain something to some friends that sounded ridiculous to the adult ear; everyone was giggling at his silly talk. However, he kept insisting. Luckily, I had spent a modest amount of time with this kid over the past two years (i.e. every waking moment). I had learned that he rarely spoke nonsense. He was always communicating something that was real to him in his little world. While everyone else was ignoring him, I got down to his level and did some digging, and I discovered what he wanted to communicate—that the colour of the balloons were the same colour as his shirt.

In parenting this toddler, I had to learn how to listen. I mean *really listen* to what he was trying to say and use my detective skills to decipher his language. I noticed that his attempts at communication were always rooted in something real and legitimate, rarely just babble to hear the sound of his own voice. Imagine how frustrating that would be to a child who is genuinely trying to communicate something to his parents, only to see them laugh it off and disregard what he is saying. All he is asking for is a little r.e.s.p.e.c.t.

Another thing I've noticed is how parents show disrespect in how they speak about their children, even when they are present. When friends get together for a playdate, kids run around and play while the moms get a chance to chat about motherhood. And it can be all too easy to start talking negatively about the kids, while they are in earshot. Moms start to complain about their experiences disciplining their toddler, they might tell bed-wetting stories, or embarrassing things the kids have said. It seems harmless but think about the perspective of the child overhearing this. Imagine how it can hurt their little hearts.

I remember chatting with a mom I had met at the park one spring day. She began to share how difficult her three-year-old was and how he was not as smart as his younger sister. She continued to tell me stories about him and his behaviour as he was quietly playing with a truck right at her feet. While he was not looking at her, I knew that his little mind had absorbed these words and I quickly changed the subject. Surely this mom loved her son and she was simply venting, but my heart was breaking for this little guy. The gaping hole evident to me in this situation was *respect* for the dignity of this child.

What I *try* to do when I'm talking about my kids with them in the room, is to invite my child into the conversation. For example, if I am sharing about how my son is very particular, I will simply engage him and say, "Max, you like having your books all lined up neatly don't you?" This way, I am acknowledging his presence in the room as I speak about him. This is the same way that I would quickly engage another adult friend if I was telling a story about them while they were in the room. It shows our respect for the individual present, and makes us more cognizant of how we are speaking.

One thing that all parents soon discover is that kids get emotional and fluctuate between being difficult to handle or easier to handle. Just as I feel that I've reached my breaking point (or, more honestly, after I smashed through it and I am halfway to the point of insanity), they turn into obedient, delightful children. I have noticed this pattern often and I have tried to make sense of it. I think one reason is that they are testing the limits. They are subconsciously seeing what they can get away with through misbehaving. If we, as parents, keep strong and hold our ground when it comes to enforcing rules and correcting behaviour, these values eventually settle in and the child starts behaving well naturally.

Other moms have suggested to me that children tend to act out when they are going through changes in their environment or growth. When a child feels unsettled because they feel their little world is not operating the way they are used to, they express this discontent through being emotional or troublesome. Small children are unable to process difficulties in the same way as adults. Their response is to lash out emotionally in all areas.

During Christmas time, our routine is obviously thrown out the window—days are spent with extended family, we are traveling long hours, and we're sleeping in different beds. Our kids usually have a noticeable change in behaviour. Specifically, they are more whiny, disobedient, clingy, and temperamental. I think this behaviour is a response to the fact that they are missing the comfort and familiarity of their home routines and environment. They respond to this environmental instability with emotional instability.

So where does respect come in here? Well, as parents, Marc and I need to respect the way that our children are feeling, that they are not their normal selves and can't really control how they express their stress. Instead of responding to their behaviour with anger, annoyance, or bitterness, we need to respect that they can't navigate out of the funk that they are in. We can *lead* them through it by responding with firm, compassionate, yet calm direction. We can accompany them, show them sympathy, and try to help them handle their emotions. So when I know some big changes are coming our way, I try to anticipate how the children will process it. I try to respect that their idea of normal is important to them. I try not to change our routines any more than I have to and, when I do, I am prepared to guide them and hold their hand through it so that they will come to learn how to handle these changes maturely.

MARC – Patience

Life with a toddler can be a constant test in patience; it means learning how to dial back on your reactions as a parent so that you can guide your child appropriately, as well as acknowledging and respecting that your child is just that: a child. I remember when Max was two-and-a-half, I laid him on the change table naked and went to find him pyjamas. Soon, I heard wailing and, when I looked over my shoulder, I saw a fountain of pee erupting skyward before landing directly on his face! It was already past his bedtime and now I had to give him a bath. As I frantically washed him, I was furious and, somehow in my head, I thought he was disrespecting me and procrastinating his bedtime. After I finally struggled to get his arms and legs into those button-down pyjamas, I held him tightly in the dark. Normally at that point of the bedtime routine I would sing, but that night was different. I was not in a singing mood. But as I swayed with Max in my arms, he surprised me by breaking the silence with a little song: "JESUS, JEEEESUS, Jeeeesus!" I guess he was trying to be cute and funny to break the tension. But I wasn't in the mood for cute and funny. I was so done with this bedtime gong show. I wanted to scream "Stop it! Stop invoking the name of Jesus!" But instead, I let out a big sigh, bit my tongue and placed him in his crib.

Looking back on it, Max's actions were not out of disrespect towards me; he was just being a two-year-old. He missed the song that was a normal part of our routine; he wasn't trying to spite me. I realize now that my reactions do have repercussions in parenting. I could have responded to him with bitterness and anger, reflecting outwardly the annoyance that I was feeling inside. Instead, I kept my emotions in check and dealt with him calmly (or as calmly as I was capable of at the time). The law of magnetism is of utmost importance in parenting. The way I talk, carry myself, and react to things can all be projected in how my child reacts to things. For instance, if I am angry or frustrated easily, Max picks up on it and imitates my behaviour when he finds himself in a similar scenario.

Ultimately, if I want Max to be respectful, I have to show him respect. I have to teach him his dignity and worth as a son of God, and as he takes his identity in his sonship he will naturally learn respect for himself and others. I know that, as a father, I have to model what respect looks like so that he, in turn, can learn to respect himself, others, and, most importantly, God.

As children get older, their emotions and opinions should still be respected. My parents often brought us into the conversation for big family decisions. Ultimately, the decision was theirs as the heads of the home, but they allowed our voices to be heard as we discussed the options before us.

I remember when Natalie was two years old, my parents had a conversation with us about whether or not they should try to have another baby. This is a curious question to propose to children, but since my mom had Hyperemesis Gravidarum for all of her pregnancies, having another baby meant that the entire family would have to work hard to help Mom around the house, including us making simple meals and having increased responsibilities. My parents acknowledged this was going to have to be a family effort and respected what our opinions would be. All of us were eager to have another baby in the family, so we were more than willing to do the extra work involved. This is not to say that every family decision or new baby must be preceded by consent from all of the children. I share this story to illustrate just one example of how my parents sought to bring us older kids into the decisions they were contemplating. They regularly showed us that our opinions and feelings about these things mattered. If we disagreed with whatever they were planning to do, then my parents discussed the situation with us so that we came to a place of understanding. In all of this, they were respecting our dignity as members of the family, even if the decision was ultimately theirs to make.

As a family, we realized that along with respecting emotions, personalities must be respected too. Temperaments, strengths, and weaknesses make up who your child is and how they engage with the world and people around them. I believe the beauty of family is that it is made up of individuals who all grew up in the same circumstances, yet each one turns out a unique wonder. However, this uniqueness inevitably brings conflict. It's difficult to live with someone who doesn't do things the same way you'd like them to be done. It's even more difficult to raise someone whose personality clashes with your own (whether due to similarities or differences). I believe that it's very important to develop an awareness of your spouse's and children's temperaments, so you can learn to respect them in their unique personalities. Being aware and conscious of these differences has helped us to avoid a lot of conflict. For example, I will not get offended when Natalie isolates herself in her room for the evening because I know she needs her alone time. I also do not get frustrated when Jo talks my ear off about his latest culinary masterpiece for the third time that day, as I know Jo loves to share everything he is excited about. But if Jo were to hide up in his room for the evening, I would immediately know something was off.

This is something our parents were always attuned to. We enjoyed talking about our personalities growing up, and each of us was respected in our uniqueness.

CALEB – Respecting Temperaments

As a teenager and young adult, I had the opportunity to attend many amazing retreats, conferences, and prayer nights. At these various events, I had many powerful and intimate encounters with the Lord, and my parents were always eager and excited to hear what God had spoken to me over the weekend. They knew that the time would have been filled with moments of personal prayer, Mass, Confession, Eucharistic Adoration, small groups, and talks—so how could I not have grown in my relationship with Jesus? And, of course, they were right. It was these opportunities that helped me to know Jesus intimately. So when I came home with my sleeping bag in my left hand and a Bible in my right, I could have sat down with Mom and Dad and told them for hours how excited I was about how I had encountered Jesus. I could have told them how I encountered God's infinite mercy in the Sacrament of Reconciliation. I could have proclaimed how I heard God's voice through reading his word in Scripture. I could have even announced how I had grown in fellowship with young men who had experienced the same thing. Instead, I was silent. With great excitement, Dad would drill me with questions, "How was your weekend?" or "What did the Lord speak to you?" and even "How was Adoration? Did anything stand out to you?" My response: shoulder shrug, shoulder shrug, and maybe an unenthusiastically mumbled, "It was good." I appreciate how infuriating and saddening that was for my parents (especially Dad), but for some reason I couldn't bring myself to talk. I needed time to process, I needed space and, most importantly, I needed them to respect that I never resented them for asking me the questions. In fact, I think it would have communicated disinterest or a lack of concern for me if they didn't. But I really appreciated that they backed off and gave me space, recognizing that it was hard for me to be open because of my personality.

Jo, on the other hand, would often come home from the same retreat with a Bible in his right hand and a megaphone in his left. Jo would go on and on about every single moment of the weekend. He would spare no detail of his spiritual growth from the retreat. A very stark difference to my secrecy.

When my parents would give me space, it showed me how much they respected my personality and even my weaknesses. I always knew the door would be open when and if I was ready to talk (followed by a barrage of questions of course). Is this not the way Jesus knocks at the door of our hearts? He is "standing at the door, knocking." (Revelations 3:20) He never forces the door open. My parents helped me to understand this reality in their sincere care for who I am and how I am.

Respect for Others

Our parents put a lot of work into ensuring that we respected them and that we knew we were respected by them. But in order to raise us with a missionary mindset, they also taught us to respect those around us. Our culture today tends towards being self-focused. We see people fighting to get respect regardless of how that affects or impacts others. I've even seen this play out with parents.

One thing I have witnessed amongst this generation of parents is a refusal to accept any input from others. I see this most often with my secular friends, but it remains something we should be aware of. Parents want respect from others on their parenting decisions and they are extremely defensive towards anyone making comments or suggestions in regards to their children or rules. I suspect this is rooted in pride. The way we parent and the decisions our children make is obviously a sensitive topic; if anyone were to correct or criticize me in any way, I would be really hurt. This attitude of self-protection says, "These are my kids and I am the only one who has any say over them—back off!" This is dangerous. This self-righteousness and disrespect of others will bleed into the children who are absorbing all that their parents do. If our children see us disregarding what their grandparents just told them, they will absorb this attitude and treat their grandparents with the same disrespect. This goes for all adults and authority figures. I see it as important to treat adults with full respect when our children are present so that our children don't feel entitled to treat adults poorly. If we disagree, we can approach them later, in a respectful manner, without the repercussion of our children learning to be bratty.

My parents were always careful to guard their words about other adults in front of us kids. This was especially relevant when it came to teachers. We had good teachers, not-so-good teachers, solid Catholic teachers, and teachers who taught their own brand of "spirituality". We would come home complaining and, while my parents took the situation seriously, offering us advice on how to respond to our teachers, or by confronting the teacher themselves, they never fell into speaking poorly of them in front of us. They would say "Yeah, your teacher said that Jesus wasn't God; they obviously don't know the truth and we will have to tell them what the Church teaches." We weren't allowed to mock our teachers or disrespect them in any way. Our teachers were authority figures and, no matter how flawed they were, we had to treat them with the dignity that their position of authority afforded them. This approach worked, as we all treated our teachers with respect, and they often came up to our parents to comment on how well-behaved we were. As an example, one of my religion teachers, who constantly taught things that were far from Catholic teaching, and with whom I had many peaceful confrontations, really liked and respected me even though I was regularly trying to show how he was wrong. I got a 99 percent in that class.

In the spirit of honesty, I must admit that we don't have a perfect record. When we were four and six, Jo and I had an ongoing feud with our bus driver. It was quite the drama. We even threatened him saying that our dad was a wrestler and could beat him up. Needless to say, we were disciplined appropriately when the bus driver brought Mom and Dad up to speed on the situation.

JO – Respect for Other Adults

Mom and Dad always insisted that, as children, we refer to all adults as "Mr. or Mrs. [insert last name]". Growing up, every one of my parents' friends were always addressed as Mr. or Mrs. by us kids. They insisted we do this as a sign of respect. We were kids and they were adults. Adults make the decisions, they are the big bosses, and were are not yet their equals. It is sort of like how teachers are never referred to by their students as "Steve" or "Susan" but are called Mr. or Mrs. as a sign of their position of authority. Imagine what would happen in a class where students started to call their teacher casually by their first name. I think, very quickly, the teacher would lose authority over the class because, now, they are on the same playing field as their students.

I remember some adults would say to me, "You can just call me by my first name." I felt like a deer in headlights. I did not know what I should do or say. I asked my mom and she told me I should continue to call her Mrs. [insert last name]. She said, "Even though she said to call her by her first name, believe me, she's actually going to find you very charming by using Mrs."

If my parents' friends told us to do something or to stop doing something, we obeyed because they were adults and we were kids. In establishing this rule, Mom and Dad were laying a foundation for us: we had an innate respect for authority. As we grew up and developed in our faith, we had a built-in trust and understanding in the authority of God and his Church. You could call this fear of the Lord, which means I recognize that he is God and I am not; that he is greater than I am and deserves my obedience. Because of the way I was raised, I was prepared to understand that, in the spiritual realities, I do not get to make up the rules or choose which rule I am going to listen to or ignore. It was natural for me to get that God is the boss and I am not. Growing up, I never struggled with the rules of the Church, because I knew that, if the Church told me something, the right thing to do was to listen.

I remember one Sunday at church, we were early for Mass (for once) and sitting in the pew as a family. Our pastor came up and asked me if I could altar serve since one of the servers could not make it. To my mom's dismay, I said, "No, I don't really want to." The priest went on his way, looking for someone else to step up. As soon as he was out of earshot, Mom turned to me and said "Jo, if a priest ever asks you to altar serve again, you say 'yes' immediately." In that moment, I was embarrassed, realizing I had committed a major faux pas. Yes, priests and parents are human and they make mistakes. But at the same time, they have a God-given authority that I need to respect and honour. These formative experiences set the stage for my eventual desire to be obedient and docile to God's will for my life. "Speak Lord, your servant is listening," (1 Samuel 3:9) is a response of faith which captures this disposition of docility and respect for authority. Imagine how the tone would change if Samuel had replied to the voice of God with, "Speak, buddy, I am listening" or worse, "No I don't really want to."

Do not underestimate the power of training children to address people, especially adults, with respect. It prepared my siblings and I to respond in docility and obedience to the living God. One more thing: now that I'm a married adult, I would prefer if you all addressed me as Mr. Regnier from here on in.

ELIZABETH – Respecting Siblings

When I was younger, I knew that it was not appropriate or loving to speak negatively about my brothers and sisters in the presence of my friends. I think it is both something that was taught and an attitude that was caught. I know my parents stressed that it is not loving to gossip, especially about our family, but we also had a natural knowledge based on the respect that was displayed and enforced within our family. We loved each other very much and we knew to respect each other. We obviously fought as children just as other siblings do but we were taught always to say sorry and forgive each other. My brothers and sisters were my best friends. So when I was at school or with other young people my age, I remember being horrified when they would talk about their family members with anger. I would often hear "I hate my brother/sister," and I never knew how to respond because, even though I fought with my family, I could never speak that way, especially in front of my friends. I remember mentioning this to one of my sisters and she was shocked because she felt the same way.

One day in elementary school, my friend said that his brother was a stubborn kid. I responded saying, "Yeah, well my sister is SO stubborn." I immediately felt bad for not respecting her in front of someone else. When I got home from school and saw her face, I almost cried and so I decided to be particularly nice to her that evening to make sure that she knew that I loved her, even though she had no idea what I had said about her.

Respecting our siblings was an important part of my family life, and it extended beyond speaking nicely about my brothers and sisters in public. As children, we were not allowed to take things from each other's rooms and, if the door was shut, we had to knock before entering. If my brother or sister had a friend over, I could only join them if invited. When we shared secrets with each other, we were not allowed to tell anyone else—not even Mom and Dad (unless it was dangerous, of course)! We learned to respect the differences in each other as well, particularly differences in temperaments and the little quirky tendencies we all had.

One other thing that my parents enforced between us kids was forgiveness. Whenever we fought, we had to take time to think about the situation and then resolve the conflict verbally. If I hurt my brother or sister, I had to apologize. If they apologized to me, I was expected to come to a place where I could say, "I forgive you." Our readiness to forgive each other regularly and repeatedly came from our undying respect for each member of the family. And the humble process of apologizing and forgiving only increased our respect for one another.

Respect of Spouse

We have emphasised that the way we talk about other adults reflects on the way that our children treat them. This principle is equally relevant in the ways we treat and speak of our spouse. Our children see this and pick up on it. How can I expect my kids to treat Marc and I with respect when we ourselves are not treating each other with respect? Practically, this is often applicable in the way we approach rules and decisions as parents. When I reflect on the way my parents worked as a team to raise us, I am struck by how well they kept a consistently unified front. I have little memory of them ever disagreeing on a rule or decision (in front of us). If Dad told us that we were not allowed to watch TV, Mom would uphold the exact same rule. You know the classic move a kid pulls, of going after the other parent if one parent says no? Yeah, that never worked in our family. In fact, I remember Mom calling my bluff once asking, "Didn't you just ask your dad about this and now you're coming to me?" Busted.

Our parents rarely contradicted each other. If they did disagree on something, they would discuss it away from us. The respect they showed one another fostered a culture of respect in us children towards both parents.

ANDRÉ – Respecting Spouse and Family In Public

If we want our kids to respect the people around them, respect has to be taught and practiced first in the home. Our kids saw the respect Angèle and I afforded each other. There is so much that can be said in this regard but I want to focus particularly on how and why it is important to show respect of the family in a public setting.

Although respect is part of the DNA of the family unit, it still has to be earned, fostered, and protected. Such respect comes with the knowledge that we all have strengths and weaknesses. How do we respect someone in their weaknesses? You and that individual know that he/she is weak in certain areas and, out of deference to their honour, you do not expose their problems to others and publicize their vices. You want the world to see the best of this family member, not laugh at their worst. That doesn't mean some teasing cannot happen but it crosses the line when it becomes 'laughing at' and not 'laughing with.' I further recommend that you seek to affirm their strengths even more than you joke about their weaknesses.

I would like to begin with an experience I had with a friend. He and I were part of a small group of men who gathered regularly for years to encourage and challenge each other in our faith. This group was a great place for us to have an open and honest discussion of what was going on in our lives. Often, this gentleman would begin to share with us the difficulties he was having with his wife and her weaknesses. It is important to understand that he loved her and was committed to her in good times and in bad. I understood he needed to talk about his struggles, but I felt uncomfortable and saddened by how he was dishonouring his wife in front of us all. This caused our perception of his wife to become increasingly negative.

One day we went for lunch and he started venting about his wife again. It was as if he wanted me to validate how bad his wife was. It was at this point that I confronted him about how he was speaking about her. I said, "Sure, she has weaknesses like all of us, but it is your job, as her husband, to protect her reputation and in doing so you will be protecting the reputation of your family and even yourself. When you speak about your wife in this way it reflects badly on your care and protection of your family."

This situation reminded me of this Scripture verse:

> "In this same way, husbands ought to love their wives as their own bodies. He who loves his wife loves himself. After all, no one ever hated their own body, but they feed and care for their body, just as Christ does the church."
> Ephesians 5:28-30

If I speak to people about the weaknesses or failures of my family, I am actually disrespecting and dishonouring the person I am speaking about, the listener, and myself. There may be a place to talk to trusted friends in order to receive advice for moving forward, but this type of conversation should not be the norm.

How powerful it is for our children's self-image when they hear their parents tell others how much of a blessing they are and what a joy they bring to the home. How wholesome it is for your children to hear you only speak well about your spouse. This does not mean we should be bragging to others about our kids and spouse all the time. But it does mean that if we are going to talk about them to others, it should be positively and not negatively.

A Family United in Respect

Not only does a healthy dose of respect benefit our relationships with others and with God, but it also contributes to strengthening the well-being of the family as a whole. A family that respects one another is able to have deep trust, grow closer together, and move forward as a united front.

CALEB – Winning as a Team

I would argue that only a family that has high respect for each other can act as team. But what do I mean by a team? A team is a collective group acting towards the same objective. We see this in sports: a hockey team is a collective group of men or women who act towards the same goal of scoring goals and winning games. If even just one player is acting outside of that objective, the team suffers. Of course, when I say that families should act as teams, I'm not referring to sports. (Mom would undoubtedly not be characterized as a power forward). If a family's team goal is not to win games or score goals, what can a family's common objective be? I see that my family strives to be a family who brings greater glory to God, builds up his Kingdom, and personifies the joy of the Gospel (i.e. having fun!) in the process.

Every member of my family, even the youngest, knows that we are on this Earth for more than ourselves; that life has a greater purpose. God has more in store for our lives than for us simply to live. It is because of this that we are writing this book. Is it not out of a desire to have a family of missionary disciples that you yourself are reading this right now?

Earlier this year, Natalie led her very first night at youth group, just as Joel, Mylène, and I had done dozens of times earlier in our teenage years. She did a great job. A parishioner who has been heavily involved with youth ministry at our parish for close to two decades said to my dad, "Your family keeps pumping out leader after leader! It's like a family business you have going." Is this not what a parent would desire for their family? That their children be protagonists in building the kingdom of God? But what I found most interesting about this man's statement was how he referred to us as a business. I thought it was an interesting way to view family. It reminded me of a discussion I had with Alana about Patrick Lencioni's The Five Dysfunctions of a Team. I'll let her tell you about it.

ALANA – Lessons From Lencioni

Patrick Lencioni is a notable consultant and speaker who proposes in one of his books the five key dysfunctions of teams. When these dysfunctions are avoided, the result is team health and success. The more we discussed it, Caleb and I saw how these leadership principles apply to building strong families too. I want to focus on the first two dysfunctions in particular and how they play a very important role within the theme of respect.

The first dysfunction is 'Lack of Trust'. While it is well known that trust is the foundation of all good relationships, Lencioni specifies that great teams utilize a special form of trust:

> *"The kind of trust that is necessary to build a great team is what I call vulnerability-based trust. This is what happens when members get to a point where they are completely comfortable being transparent, honest, and naked with one another, where they say and genuinely mean things like "I screwed up," "I need help," "Your idea is better than mine," "I wish I could learn to do that as well as you do," and even, "I'm sorry".*
>
> *When everyone on a team knows that everyone else is vulnerable enough to say and mean those things, and that no one is going to hide his or her weaknesses or mistakes, they develop a deep and uncommon sense of trust. They speak more freely and fearlessly with one another."* [32]

Many families struggle to form this intimate kind of trust. It can be difficult to discuss our downfalls and mistakes; it can be hard to admit that we messed up to our siblings and parents; it can be especially hard to apologize when we know we have hurt each other. When a family is unable to be weak and exposed in front of each other, this kind of trust will never be formed. This is very closely related to what we are saying in this chapter. To foster this trust, you need to be open and honest with your children.

Something that Caleb and I did before our engagement was talk about some key principles to define our relationship. One was open and honest communication. This actually happened the same day we had this discussion about the five dysfunctions—go figure! We were inspired. One thing I admire in Caleb is his ability to ask good questions. I believe he learned this from both André and Angèle because I've experienced the same kind of 'digging' questions from both of them. This was not something I was totally used to, and I'm still growing in this

---

32. Patrick Lencioni, *The Advantage: Why Organizational Health Trumps Everything Else In Business*, (San Francisco: Jossey-Bass A Wiley Imprint, 2012, p. 27.

skill of asking questions (because I have seen it is an effective skill and tool of a missionary disciple). I mean, being asked, "Why are you feeling this way?" or "What is God saying to you in this?" or the classic André question, "What do you mean by that?" communicates that I care about you, I respect what you have to say, you can trust me, and in this house, we value openness and honesty.

I started to see the value of facilitating deeper sharing, instead of keeping conversations at a surface level; relationships don't go very far in terms of trust or respect when we keep it in superficial gear. Go deeper; ask more thought-provoking questions. This kind of vulnerability leads to a family that can talk freely amongst each other. If we are unable to talk freely amongst each other, the second dysfunction arises: a 'Fear of Conflict.'

Conflict may seem to be an indicator of a lack of health within the family team, but Lencioni is referring to a specific kind of conflict:

> *"Contrary to popular wisdom and behavior, conflict is not bad for a team. In fact, the fear of conflict is almost always a problem.*
>
> *Of course, the kind of conflict I'm referring to here is not the nasty kind that centers around people or personalities. Rather, it is what I call productive ideological conflict, the willingness to disagree, even passionately when necessary, around important issues and decisions that must be made. But this can only happen when there is trust.*
>
> *When team members trust one another, when they know that everyone on the team is capable of admitting when they don't have the right answer, and when they're willing to acknowledge when someone else's idea is better than theirs, the fear of conflict and the discomfort it entails is greatly diminished. When there is trust, conflict becomes nothing but the pursuit of truth, an attempt to find the best possible answer. It is not only okay but desirable."[33]*

Healthy conflict within the home is, in fact, a great indicator of high trust and high respect. I see this often in the Regnier house, even in the writing of this book. Caleb was notorious for derailing the train, saying, "I'm not sure if we really need to talk about this," or "Is this chapter really necessary?" These questions always led to some conflict and groaning, but it also led to more unity and buy-in as everyone felt free to share their ideas and come to an agreed-upon decision together. They were able to do this because of the foundation of trust, respect, and open and honest communication. It can be hard to bring up our

---

33. Ibid. p, 38.

disagreements when trust is low because we are not sure if conflict will hurt the relationship, or we are unsure that we have the right kind of relationship to tell them we are upset or to correct them. We see this in the relationships we have that are more shallow. I would not tell some of my friends if I was upset by something they did or said, because the relationship is less formed. But with a close friend, I can actually bring up behaviours that upset me, because I know that our relationship will not be damaged.

To wrap things all up and put a bow on it, if there is a strong culture of respect, the family can act as a team with a common objective—in our case, raising missionary disciples. Lencioni teaches us that by building trust and allowing healthy conflict, the health of the team (family) will thrive, and this is rooted in respect for the other.

Conclusion

Respect truly is foundational to a healthy family unit. Creating a home that operates with respect will help a family experience more peace, love, and true freedom. Almost more importantly, we have written this chapter because we believe that the principles and methods discussed on respect will help you to raise your family as missionary disciples. Here is a reminder of some key points:

- The foundation for all respect is recognizing the God-given dignity of each person. Building on this, we seek to admire a person's abilities, qualities, and achievements.
- Discipline is fundamentally about instilling respect. We suggest disciplining with:
  - *Consistency* – in every opportunity that requires it, with consistency in punishments used
  - *Timeliness* – as quickly as possible
  - *Reasonableness* – remaining under control and suiting the behaviour of the child
- Parents need to respect their children by loving and affirming them directly and in how they speak about them to others. This also includes treating them as more than 'just a kid' and respecting their temperaments, strengths, and weaknesses. When children feel respected by their parents they will be more inclined to respect others.

■ Children need to be taught to respect other adults, especially those in authority. How parents speak about and treat other adults affects the opinion of the child towards those adults. The same goes for spouses; a child will maintain respect for their mother and father as long as the mother and father show respect to each other.

It was God's design and desire that children respect their parents. We believe this is a reflection of the relationship of God the Father with us. Parents have a unique opportunity to reflect the Father to their children and to teach their children how to honour, obey, trust and love God. Thanks to how we were raised, it was easy for us kids to see God the Father as good, to *respect* and want to honour his authority through a holy fear of the Lord. This attitude was formed in us since birth. "Happy are those who fear the Lord, who greatly delight in his commandments. Their descendants will be mighty in the land; the generation of the upright will be blessed." (Psalm 112: 1-2).

Reflection / Action Points

1. Children Respecting Parents: Would you discipline your children in a consistent, timely, and reasonable manner? Which one of these three principles are you the best at, and which one would you like to improve? Do your children know you are the boss, not them?

2. Parents Respecting Children: Do you respect your children in how you speak about them, especially to others? Do you see them as more than 'just a kid?' Do you find ways to relate to and respect the different temperaments in your children, especially if they are different from your own?

3. Respect for Others: How do you model respect for other adults to your children? How do you teach your children to respect each other, as well as their possessions and secrets, etc.?

4. Respecting Spouses: Do you honour or dishonour your spouse and family when speaking about them publicly?

5. Remember that your family is a team and you need to work hard to build respect and trust in order to work well together. Do you see any of the discussed 'dysfunctions' in your family (absence of trust, fear of conflict)? How can you work on making those areas functional?

CHAPTER 5

Home Life

Creating a Place for Your Family to Gather and Thrive

MYLÈNE

Stepping into someone's home for the first time is always a lovely experience for me. I am fascinated just looking at the layout of the living room, dining room, and kitchen, and I love to witness the way they decorated and placed the furniture. Walking through a home is a unique way to experience the family that lives there. The pictures on the fridge, the pieces on display, and even the shoes piled near the front door are all exhibits in this family home, a living museum of sorts. It is so interesting to discover the place where everyone seems to converge, whether it be crowding around the kitchen as the hosts prepare dinner, sitting around the dining room table with drinks and snacks in the centre, or perched on couches in the living room engaged in casual conversation. Time might be spent playing cards, participating in a loud game, having a large group chat, or enjoying small conversations spread throughout the home. Every home has a different culture, a different way that time is spent and community is fostered. It reflects the personalities, history, and style of the family who lives there and the way in which they feel 'at home.'

The Regnier Home

Home is our favourite place to be. Period. The Regnier home is one that often involves wrestling matches, pool parties, loud music, laughing, embarrassing stories, and food, lots of food. It is a place that we, as children, always want to go back to. As a family, our relationships aren't simply familial; we see each other as some of our best friends. Isn't this something all parents want? When my kids grow older, I hope that home will be a place they will always want and look forward to come back to, not a place where they feel like they are forced to be on special occasions.

Our family dynamic has obviously had its ups and downs. We definitely went through those socially awkward teenage years where I am sure my parents struggled to make the home atmosphere fun. Now, we are in a pretty good season, with Janna and Natalie old enough to engage with us adults yet young enough to have fun playing with my children as well. Jo and Caleb have fully developed their comedic abilities. (They went through some awkward years. Didn't we all?) So laughing is an almost constant reality when we are together; we are rarely bored. This chapter will seek to address how our family came to this place in our time together, how my parents created a home life that nurtured our relationships together, and most importantly, how a positive home life is a key factor in raising missionary disciples.

The feeling of being 'at home' is something I personally treasure. I have always loved having a pleasant home to spend quality time in with those around me. When Marc and I bought our first house, it was gratifying to create my family's space. I designed my furniture layout and decor in a way that reflected the cozy feeling that I wanted my family to experience. My priority was having the living room as the central place in the home with comfy couches and pictures on display; an ideal spot for family time with the kids.

This is largely based on my experience of family life growing up. The place where we most often converged was the living room. From low-key family chats to gatherings with company, community was fostered in the Regnier living room. I realized that this same pattern has naturally become central in my own home. Company comes in the door, and I automatically walk them to our couches where we engage in conversation. When supper is over and the kitchen is tidied, Marc and I gather the kids in the living room and spend our time there until bedtime. That's just what we do when we are together and it's what the Regniers have done for generations.

ANDRÉ – A True Living Room

Despite being separated by distance and busy raising our own families, my siblings and I are still close and continue to enjoy being together.

What is interesting to observe is that what we do when we are all together now is similar to the way we interacted when we were all in the same home 40 years ago. Like any other family growing up, especially in our teenage years, we had a lot of distractions that could easily take us away from family time. The way that my parents dealt with the competing priorities of their kids was to create a family dynamic that would be captivating. What I can remember growing up was being in the living room or, more accurately, our three-ring circus in the middle of the house, doing handstands, somersaults, or pyramids, always ending up with my dad asking us to hit him in the stomach as hard as we could. Yes, it was possible that someone could get seriously hurt. I guess that was a chance my parents were willing to take in order to create a environment where their kids could play together and have a good time. Dad was usually instigating the activities and Mom was a sideline encourager.

Angèle and I have intentionally worked at creating a similar three-ring circus in our own home. Our two sons have often remarked how incredible it is that their mom never gets uptight about roughhousing (even though at times, things were knocked over).

What is your family's way of bonding and spending time together? Is it playing board games with the kids? Make sure you have lots of games and a nice table with comfy chairs to sit in while you play. Do you enjoy going outside and being active together? Have a garage stocked with all the outdoor fun necessities and a backyard that is a haven for you to spend time together! Our family loves to swim, so my parents made sure to get a house with a pool in the backyard. And let me tell you, that sucker gets a ridiculous amount of use out of it. Find what nourishes your family life and prepare your home to cater to this. Not only should a home be a comfortable place to sleep, eat, and relax but it should also be a place that sets the stage for family life to be enjoyed and strengthened.

ELIZABETH – The Doucette Family and Music

My family likes to play music. Growing up, we would often gather together in the living room and play praise and worship music. As younger children, we would dance along. We also had a piano on the main floor next to the main entrance, where we would stop while walking through the house to play a few songs. No matter where you were in the house, you could hear the piano playing and people singing. That was important for our family and my mother acknowledges that she intentionally kept the piano in a central location to encourage the family to spend time together through music.

Our family experienced what St. Augustine meant when he said, "He who sings, prays twice."[34] Music brought us closer as a family, but it also brought us closer to God. As people started getting married and moving out of the house, we transitioned to singing and playing music together when we gathered for holidays.

When Jo first met my family, he was amazed at how music was such a big part of our family culture. The Regniers are many things but musical is not one of them. It was cool for him to experience a different family culture and see how we came together.

Back to the Regnier living room. I should mention that the way the Regnier living room is used now—talking and laughing together—was not always the case. The majority of us are adults or teenagers now, and with age, our tastes have become more refined, consisting of lively conversation while sipping some strongly brewed coffee. Okay, 'refined' may not be the right word, to my mother's dismay. Regardless, it is important to note that our tastes have changed, just as every family is constantly evolving as the children grow. As kids, we would have had little patience for sitting around the room talking like we do now. Instead, much of our living room time was spent playing. My parents always insisted that our family room be fully carpeted because wrestling, playing, and circus tricks in the middle of the living room floor were an ever-constant reality and we needed a soft landing. It seems that our family's priority was to have fun over 'class.' On the plus side, Dad became very close with the local carpet cleaners.

---

34. St Augustine. Cited in *Catechism of the Catholic Church*, 1156.

ALANA – 'Journey'

As André mentioned, his parents created a captivating family dynamic so that the kids did not want to miss out on all the laughs going on at home. I have experienced this first-hand in the Regnier's home life; I mean, who would want to miss being there when something spontaneous like 'Journey' could make an appearance any minute? And I'm not talking about the band.

Journey (noun), is a Regnier original game that involves jumping into sleeping bags HEAD FIRST, and—wait for it—racing down the stairs from the top floor of the house to the basement, not to mention with a main floor obstacle course.

You can't see anything, unless you're sneaky and try to use the faint daylight peeking through the seams. It's dark and hot, and the intensity rises with the sound of other family members cheering and guiding you through the course. Things get heated as others on the 'Journey' bump into you or slide past. The stakes are high and, to get to the basement first, it is not uncommon to see a doggy pile of sleeping-bag-covered crazies sliding down the stairs. Needless to say, it is a rush, and always results in all of us gathering in the living room and humourously replaying the 'highlight reel', while nursing some bruised knees.

But more than feeling like I would be missing out on these fun times if I was away for a weekend, I am captivated by, and gravitate towards, the deep and significant conversations that happen in their home. I've seen the practice of having guests over—CCO staff or students, clergy, or other family friends—which facilitate an environment for these conversations. I know the family isn't shy to jump into topics like relativism, the end times, or what it means to have Jesus at the centre of your life. Needless to say, these conversations contribute to the excitement of home life.

Freedom in the Home

Our home was always *our* home, not just my parents'. They created a space that served the purposes of our family. While Dad made things fun, Mom did a masterful job of creating a living space that was beautiful, yet could be played in. Her priority was not creating a magazine-worthy space but, rather, a family space.

ELIZABETH – Order in the Home

One of the first things that I noticed when I came into the Regnier home was that there was not a big emphasis on having a perfectly pristine house. I noticed that, although their house wasn't dirty, it wasn't always tidy either. They seemed to often allow fun to trump order and, although I was uncomfortable with it at first, I grew to respect it.

Knowing Angèle well enough to know that she is a detailed person, I was curious how she felt about the 'lived-in look' of her house. She sighed. Yes, she was aware that shoes were out of order in the entrance and the floor wasn't swept during clean up after dinner and that drove her crazy. But what mattered was that the family was taking time to be together and she wanted to encourage their bonding. I understood that tolerating some of the mess was an intentional choice on her part to die to her preferences. She told me that nagging the family to have them keep the house spotless wasn't the battle she wanted to pick. She compromised a certain level of clean and tidy that she could live with in order to keep the tone of the home softer. Angèle emphasised, however, that it is important for the kids, especially preschoolers, to have order in the home. A tidy home is a safe and calming environment for children and they play more peacefully, as opposed to getting stressed from the chaos.

As I start building my own home environment, I want to be mindful to have a home that caters to what my kids need. I want home to be where my kids have fun first, but where they also feel at peace amidst the order. It's not about *what I prefer* or *how I prefer it*, but *what my kids need* and *how they need it*. By focusing on what my kids need over my preferences, I will create a family culture that is rooted is selflessness, love, peace, joy, respect, and freedom.

I appreciate that I grew up in a home where I truly felt it was my home. Now, I love watching my kids play with their toys or run around the house with full comfort and freedom. This is *their* place and they are aware of this from as early as infancy. It is so heartwarming to know that this space, that I put thought into forming, is central to their little worlds. As parents, let's create a comforting home that our children are free to live in.

NATALIE – Feeling Comfortable at Home

At home, I always feel safe and that I can be myself without feeling judged. At times, I am very loud like my siblings (it's the atmosphere I grew up in) yet my parents only allow me to be loud when it's time to have fun. Obviously, this doesn't mean that there is constant screaming and roughhousing but, once or twice a week, when we are in the mood to play, we feel free to do so. But I don't think this is the case for everyone. Sometimes, when I'm at my friends' houses, I see my friends being more cautious with their actions. They seem not as free as they would be elsewhere, which makes them want to leave. It's obviously very important to respect your parents, but to feel comfortable in your house is a completely different thing. Sometimes when I am at a friend's house, we feel like we can't laugh or sing loudly or else their parents will get upset, which I think strains their relationship with their parents. I wish it wasn't the case for my friends, but it is one of the reasons why I enjoy inviting my friends to spend time at my house.

I think a key reason we always felt freedom in the home was due to the way in which our family consistently sought to take ourselves lightly. We weren't always perfect in this regard, but there was a culture in our home that had more of an air of laughter than seriousness. It was a comfortable atmosphere, one in which we were free to fail and where we could feel comfortable to laugh at our mishaps without judgement. Mistakes and mishaps don't have a strong hold on us because we just laugh them off afterwards.

CALEB – Taking Ourselves Lightly

Home needs to be a place where joy and laughter abounds. Fights will happen, mistakes will be made, but what better place to be stretched and corrected? The home can act as a microcosm for the outside world. We can make our mistakes and learn from them in a place where the consequences are small and mercy is always available.

Jo and I didn't always get along, but we were eventually able to recognize how we were not the best brothers to one another. Mistakes were made. But through choosing to take ourselves lightly, Jo and I were able to bring joy into our relationship. We can now laugh at the many jerkish things Jo did and roll our eyes at my many annoying antics. Even today, the first thing I do when I apologize to Jo is laugh at my mistake in front of him.

Each member of the family has learned to be able to laugh at themselves, whether it be following a dramatic outburst, a fight, an embarrassing moment, or a selfish action. This is so healing and it's rooted in *holy goofiness*, which Alana spoke about in a previous chapter: we take God and the mission seriously, but not ourselves!

I believe this is a powerful and easily transferable principle that Mom and Dad taught us. It is this ability to laugh at one's weaknesses and mistakes that makes home a place of safety, a place where you are free to mess up.

Home Entertainment

The culture in the home is greatly influenced by the things we have in it to entertain us. It is important to be intentional about the forms of entertainment in our homes.

ANGÈLE – Toys and Boredom

I'm a toy minimalist. My theory is that kids only really like toys that are other kids' toys. Think about it. What does practically every kid do when they go to another kids' house? They pull out every stinking single toy into the light of day. They have some kind of need to see everything this new toy bin has to offer. But I guarantee that if you were to own all those toys, they would be lonely and ignored, taking up tons of space in your playroom.

Why am I a toy minimalist? I have a number of reasons.

I believe kids get overwhelmed with too many choices, so I keep the playroom and the options less busy. I would purposefully hide half of their toys in bins and rotate them out every four months or so. It made everything new and interesting again. Of course, if some toys were favourites, I noted that and kept them available at all times.

Space matters a lot for play: meaning you need to give kids space. Maybe it's the prairie girl in me looking for wide open spaces, but too many toys overwhelms the room, so kids can't spread out with the games they are most enjoying. When play was done with a particular toy and one of the kids wanted to do something else, I was on top of getting them to clean up what they were just doing to make space for the next game. Even when the kids were just babies, I would always clean up after them. Yes, I don't like mess, but mostly because I believe too much mess for kids makes them stressed and unhappy. They can't enjoy a new toy or game because there's too much 'noise' in their space. By cleaning it up, they can appreciate the new toy they are looking at.

I believe kids also need space to engage their imagination. I prefer toys that make the kids think of imaginary games. Blocks, dress up clothes, stuffed animals, forts, barns, and castles are the kinds of toys that allow kids to create a story and an adventure. I find there are too many toys that entertain a child or do something for a child, when it should be the child doing something with the toy. Honestly, our most 'techy' toys got the least amount of play after the first few experiences with it. These toys leave no room for imagination. Imaginative play is incredibly important for a child's mental development.

I believe giving children too many toys, or the latest toys, is not good for a child's moral development either. I think it plants a seed of materialism—that they need things, many things, the latest things, the shiny things, to fulfill them and make them happy. Frankly, too many flashy toys spoil our children. It is not good for a child to get everything he or she wants. It is not a lesson in real life. As I've noted previously, if a child gets everything they could ever want when he/she is two, four, seven or 10 years old, then what are you going to do when this child wants the things they think a modern 13, 15, or 17-year-old is entitled to?

Not only am I a toy minimalist, but I am also pro-boredom. Being bored is good and healthy for your child. Let them have some thinking time. Let them think of what they could do to have fun. Boredom is a school for creativity, thinking, and mindfulness. You might have to help your child use boredom to think of activities to do, but try not to propose too often. Boredom teaches us that happiness doesn't come from being entertained. Let your child discover what they like doing and what they like thinking about. As they say, "Only boring people can be bored."

Any parent knows that expensive or varied toys don't actually create the best, satisfying play environment for kids. But lots of cardboard or blankets do, not to mention sticks, rocks, water, and dirt. These rudimentary (and free) items allow for great times of play, creativity, and imagination. Memories are guaranteed. One summer in Prince Edward Island, we spent a rainy afternoon of fun racing twigs down a tiny little stream to the ocean. The boredom of the cool weather that day forced us to think of things to do other than swimming and tanning. I came up with the idea (yes, I'm taking all the credit for this one), but the kids quickly caught on and embraced it. In only a matter of minutes, I was the picture-taker and race official for what became one of the most memorable days of the trip.

Even though I made up the twig race game, I actually don't think kids need to have parents play with them constantly. They do need their parents nearby, accessible, and within earshot to help and delight in their creative ideas, though. I strongly believe that constantly making up games for your kids and playing with them robs them of developing their own imagination and thoughts. There's nothing wrong with a few suggestions to get them started on a game, but I recommend leaving them to play the game as much as possible. For example, hand them a bunch of kitchen utensils and an apron and tell them to pretend they are a restaurant, then walk away. Let them fill in the screenplay. When I was studying for my Bachelor of Education degree, I remember learning how, as teachers, we shouldn't give the kids cookie-cutter art and crafts where the students deliver identical, highly pleasing wall art for the adult eye. Instead, we were encouraged to give them the mediums, methods, and inspirations to let them create. The product is not the win. The creative process is.

Having said that, André totally plays with our kids all the time! So what am I saying then? The way he plays with the kids is very physical, fun, and spontaneous, which models creativity and imagination to them. It's like he enters into their world and lifts the lid of their imaginations to see how creative they can be.

I have to admit that his play with them gets competitive at times. I'm thinking about those games of hide and seek. There's a hilarious story of a time when André went hiding and told the three older kids, who were in Grades 5, 3, and 1, to come and look for him after counting to 80 or something. They got distracted having to count for so long and, while waiting for Dad to hide, ended up in a game upstairs with their stuffed animals. Meanwhile André was hiding in the basement. His initial excitement over his primo hiding spot was transforming into impatient frustration. He started yelling, "Come find me!" and "Hey, I'm over here!" The only person that heard him was me in the kitchen. I could hear the kids happily playing in one of the bedrooms upstairs. I yelled up to the kids that Dad was waiting for them and even I had a hard time getting their attention. The next thing I heard was André stomping upstairs, declaring, "I'm not playing anymore." I will always remember Mylène coming down to the kitchen and saying to me, "I think Dad's mad." It was so funny.

As my mom mentioned, kids are drawn to simplicity. We, as adults, are the ones who believe that our kids need things to be happy. This is true in my own home. I get pressured by Instagram posts of babies wearing adorable outfits sitting in their nursery adorned with gorgeous toys and decor. I feel like I am missing out, that my child is missing out, that they just need that one toy to make their lives so much better. But guess what? If I buy that item, my kid plays with it a couple times, or maybe more because I keep desperately handing it to them so that they love it. After that, I keep seeing more Instagram posts that make me feel like my playroom is continuously insufficient. When I stop looking at social media and start observing my children, my minimalism sensibilities return. A child's imagination transforms the most futile of items into an endless font of entertainment. For a long time, the most popular 'toys' in my home were two industrial grade, brightly coloured fly swatters that became, in my son's eyes, everything from a vacuum cleaner to a sword, and have helped him become a scorpion with a stinger and a toy-pushing digger. I can barely remember the endless amount of uses he has made out of those things. All the while, the epic, interactive, robotic toy Marshall from *Paw Patrol*[35] sits on the toy shelf, untouched. My children's imaginations regularly amaze me, and watching them unfold is one of my favourite parts of parenting.

Technology

Let's talk about something else that harms imagination: technology. TV is a normal reality in the life of toddlers and kids. Their little minds are being fed with songs and images and a constant flow of entertainment. Why make the effort to get children to imagine, play, or explore when, with the touch of our fingers on a screen, exciting adventures will be projected before their eyes?

In my little family, I have had to move through the struggle that technology is to us all. This is something that is equally as relevant for parents as well as for children. As a new mom, with little to no interaction with the outside world, except through a small mobile device, I have definitely struggled with technology addiction. As I am writing this, it is Lent and I have given up social media, so I am at a stronger place than usual. To my surprise, I have not had a fear of missing out, like I thought I would. Social media and technology, while not bad in themselves, can be harmful. It is far too easy to waste time scrolling and searching and watching. Recently, I realized that I was not allowing myself to sit still and let my mind wander. In moments where I had nothing to do, I would look at my phone. When I was rocking my baby to sleep, I would *need* my phone with me so I had something to do. How many opportunities to think and feel and reflect have I missed? How many moments of silence have been stolen where God would have spoken to me or nudged me to do something that would have furthered his glory?

Our kids are also seeing us. While we as parents can do all we can to try and limit screen time for our kids, are we living out an example for them? How many times have I told my kids, "No, you cannot watch a show right now," and then turned to my phone to check out my latest notifications? If I don't want their lives centred around watching a screen, my life must reflect the same. We do not want to raise a generation of kids

---

35. Paw Patrol (TV series). Directed by Jamie Whitney, Charles E. Bastien. Guru Studio and Spin Master Entertainment. 2013 – .

who are dealing with the emotional repercussions of having parents more concerned about *Facebook* than their child's life right in front of them.

Handing a child an iPad and putting on a show or game to play is far too easy a solution for our child being grumpy, bored, or loud. While I would not hail our methods as the ideal, Marc and I have tried to limit how much our kids watch shows by selecting a certain time in the day when TV time usually happens and with a limited amount of time to watch it. For a season, this was only ever in the mornings while Marc and I prayed. Currently, TV time only ever happens after lunch during baby's naptime. That way, the question: "Can I watch a show?" rarely arises at any other point in the day.

We also purposely don't download games onto our phones for our kids to play with. In a technological age, I would prefer not to introduce *one more thing* into my childrens' lives that I have to fight to limit. I know many people are able to manage the game usage in a fun, healthy way. For us, it's easier just to not have it as an option at this point in our parenthood. Recently, we went to a social event with a group of kids present. All of the children received devices so that they were distracted while the adults ate. It saddened me that the background noise of giggles and laughter as kids play was absent from the room. Instead, they were all seated at their tables, staring at a screen. Max was offered a device that had games for little kids. As a child who had never played video games, he sat there for half an hour, determined to 'play' as he aimlessly pressed the screen at different points—completely unaware of what was going on in the game. I had to snicker.

MARC − Television and Home Life

My home was a place where I was loved, taken care of, and could just be lazy!

As much as I loved it at home, one drawback was that the TV was the centre point of the household. With no exageration, the TV was always on from the moment we woke up to the moment we went to sleep. Even if we weren't watching it, the TV was a constant background noise. So much screen time meant there was little time spent in conversation or quality time together. Because of this, my home became a place of boredom to me where I felt like nothing really ever happened. We were so immersed in the next thing on TV or with our other screens, that I became a constant consumer, never really being satisfied. We absorbed more and more content, to the point where it seemed to me that nearly everything we talked about revolved around something we saw on-screen. How true is this in society today, when it's easier to sit and scroll on our phones than it is to carry on a conversation with a loved one?

I remember the first time Mylène came to visit my childhood home, she was stunned by the constant hum of the TV. Being used to only having the TV on when they intended to watch it, she did not understand the concept of not keeping her eyes fixed on a screen that was on. I started to think about whether this was part of the reason I looked outside the home so much to have fun—I wasn't having the kind of social interactions I craved simply by crowding around the TV to watch the latest shows. Having family time centred around a screen didn't leave much to be missed if I wasn't there.

This isn't to say that all of my family life was wrapped up in watching shows. My family loved each other very much and enjoyed time with each other. My experience in this area, I think, is similar to that of many families who are living today in this technological age! However, let us not allow our families to be drawn too much into that allure of technology-driven entertainment to the detriment of furthering our familial relationships. The memories that I hold most dear growing up were the times where we spent quality, face-to-face time together. These are the moments I want to fight for in my children's lives. The atmosphere I want to cultivate is one where my kids feel that they are missing out by not being at home. I want our family life to nourish them and be a place for them to live life to the fullest.

Sibling Relationships

While the setup of the house, the choice of toys, and the culture in the home are all important components in creating a strong family life, the most invaluable underlying foundation to family life is the individuals within it. While every person is important, I will argue that there is a subunit of individuals in our family who actually bring the most life, joy, and virtue to our home: babies and small children.

Our case is unique in that we had a large gap between the youngest two and the oldest three. This gives us a unique perspective to clearly see the difference that a baby makes in a family. While I wouldn't say that our family was dull and dreary before Natalie was born, I will say that a whole new level of life (literally and figuratively) was brought into the family. My brothers and I were headed into the awkward years of no longer being little kids anymore and bickering was our bread and butter. As soon as babies came into the picture, though, an immense light shone within our family.

I cannot describe to you how much joy, it was for me as a girl to have my baby sisters brought into my life when I was in Grade 6 and Grade 8. I was just the right age to be able to take care of them responsibly, yet have fun playing with them. Their presence was so life-altering. They were the reason

I eagerly ran home from school everyday. It was so fun to watch them learn and grow. Everything we did as a family was so much more engaging because we were watching our little sisters experience it for the first time. It was perfect timing when my son Max was born, as Janna had just passed the cute little kid stage, so we had a new little life to dote on!

Not only do small children bring with them laughs and giggles, but they also call everyone to virtue. Babies make people more generous. When the girls arrived, everyone in our family became softer with one another. Fighting became less common. As older kids, we were naturally challenged to come out of ourselves and care for someone smaller than us.

Babies and small children have this knack for kicking up the selfless notch in those who take care of them. As siblings, we had to accept that we were needed to help out with the girls. I remember that once I hit babysitting age, I had multiple nights where I was unable to go out with my friends because I had to stay home and babysit. I could have complained or resisted this responsibility, but I understood it as just that: a responsibility. It was a part of being in a family.

My Dad always said that the greatest gift a parent can give their child is another sibling, and we definitely felt this to be true. Once Natalie and Janna had gotten out of their toddler years, my parents announced that they had a major surprise for us. My brothers and I were bubbling with anticipation, as we were pretty sure what my parents were going to announce. We burst out what we were all thinking: "Are we having another baby!?" My parents, shocked, said "No … we are going to Disney World!" They were met with a mood-killing response: disappointment. Disney was a second-class announcement compared to a new sibling. It wasn't until the next day that we we started getting excited but it took us a few hours to get past the initial letdown.

JANNA

I have never had younger siblings before so having nieces and nephews in the family is awesome. I love hanging out with little kids; they keep me happy. Usually kids my age go on their phones a lot but little kids are fun to be with because they are constantly playing and are enjoyable to be with. They are the best cure for boredom for me. I love carrying them and running, doing tricks, or singing with them. I love having a niece and nephew because they love me a lot and I love them. I also enjoy taking care of them. It's hard work, but I like having the cuddles with them. Whenever I am taking care of them, they are never bored, and I like that they are happy to be with me and play with me.

When children are small, they are cute and cuddly, but as they get older, the sibling dynamic becomes tougher to live out. Growing up, I had many frustrations with my brothers. They had horrible taste in TV shows. They always interrupted games with my friends. And Jo especially knew just how to find my weak spots and push me to my breaking point. Even with this, I always knew that once we passed the gates of high school being over, we would no longer bicker. Luckily my intuition was correct. Now my brothers make me laugh instead of yell, a notable improvement.

CALEB – Sibling Bonding

When Jo and I were younger, we would bicker quite a bit. Jo was notorious for the 'x100' method. Meaning, if I were to hit or kick him, he would hit back 100 times harder. This is very typical for young siblings, but it did make me very sad. Jo always found me annoying and whiny (Not sure why he thought this; I have always been an absolute angel!), and I always found him to be mean and unreasonable. I'm sure Jo could easily share some stories about how annoying I was, but, since I am writing this section, I get to tell my side of the story.

I remember video games with Jo, usually with me beside him watching him play. The stress levels would rise as he would get to a difficult level that he was unable to beat. After failing on multiple attempts, Jo would stand up and throw me out of the room, exclaiming "You're bad luck!". Outside of the room, I would quietly stick my ear to the door to listen, trying to imagine what might be happening in the game. After a few minutes I would quietly crack open the door and crawl back into the room, trying to be as unnoticeable as possible, lest he hear me and kick me out once more.

We joke about this often today, but as a boy, in my mind, Jo was not my friend, and I was not his. In the midst of the bickering and wrestling, Mom always said two things. The first was: "Jo, one day Caleb is going to be bigger than you, and he will beat you up. Be careful." (Well, LOOK AT ME NOW! Revenge is so so sweet. I've got about 20 pounds and 15.5 centimeters on the guy, but who's counting?) The second thing she'd say was: "You don't know it yet, but he's going to be your best friend someday." And she was right. Today Jo is my best friend. When things are tough, or when things are exciting, Jo is the first to know. We enjoy ourselves when we are together and I laugh most when I am with him. This occurred through natural maturing, but also through our home being a place of fun and tradition, a place where relationships could grow.

Family Priorities

We need to be choosy about certain aspects of our family life. Just 'going with the flow' will ultimately result in us drowning in what life throws at us, but if we maintain family priorities, these things will become a strong rock foundation for our families. Our family is a strong advocate for mealtimes being enjoyed together as a household. The vice of gluttony may be a factor here, but let's try to ignore that, shall we?

JO – Family Supper

Regniers love food. We love to eat Chinese, Thai, Vietnamese, Polish, German, French, Italian, Canadian, American, heck we would even eat British food … okay, that went too far. There is nothing we enjoy more than sitting down as a whole family for an amazing meal with good red wine. This may not come as a surprise since everyone eats food. I respond to that by saying, yes, everyone eats, but not everyone *eats*.

It can be easy to frequently eat supper sitting in front of the TV, or have family members simply eat when they feel like it rather than wait for the whole family to gather. I think this can become unhealthy, and it's something I am passionate about reversing. Our family takes meals very seriously, and Mom and Dad worked really hard to ensure that the importance of the supper table was preserved in our daily life. *Every night*, we would sit down as a whole family for supper, and it was deeply unifying.

For example when Elizabeth got back from her mission trip to Mexico City, we had a Mexican night. I opened a can of refried beans and poured them over some stale chips … just kidding. We all got dressed up, I was wearing my luchador mask, we had mariachi music blasting, and we began to make our own homemade mexican food. Elizabeth shared with us about her mission trip, and we rejoiced with her about all that God had done. We continued the fun late into the night. Obviously, this isn't an everyday occurrence, but it happens often enough that it has become a running joke. We make so many extravagant family meals, that we come up with reasons to celebrate in order to justify it. Why did we make fresh gnocchi, roasted red pepper alfredo sauce, and homemade caesar salad dressing? Well, to celebrate Caleb doing his chores two days in a row … not exactly the best reason, but we'll take what we can get.

When I lived at home, our everyday meals were a simplified version of this. Mom prepared a meal with help, the supper table was set, and we all sat down together to eat. We talked, laughed, shared about our days, told stories, and discussed our plans for the next day. Sometimes we had meals where there was hardly any talking, usually on nights where the food was SO good that no one bothered to look up from their plates. We didn't rush our daily suppers, but sat back and enjoyed them and each other; it was our daily touch point.

I am sure some are reading this and thinking, "That sounds nice, but my family's life is WAY too busy for that!" I completely understand that. Life is busy. But at the end of the day, we make time for what we love. Our family's supper time is a priority because we choose to make it a priority. With Mom and Dad heading up a nationwide university student movement, and all of us kids in school, involved with CCO, sports, clubs, and youth group, not to mention jobs and social lives, suffice it to say our lives are pretty busy. Despite this, growing up, we were able to get together practically every day as a whole family to share a meal. Even if supper was on the table and I texted saying my bus was going to be 20 minutes late, I knew the family would wait until I got home before eating. Mom and Dad set the tone, and we understood that family meal time was a priority.

The reason we were willing to go to those lengths was that eating supper as a family was practically sacred to us. Food is a gift from God, and he gave us a desire to eat—not just as a utilitarian function but as a means of communing with others and enjoying his creation. But even more than this, think about what happens during Mass on Sunday. We gather together around a table, to share a meal. On the altar is the Bread of Life that we come to eat, through which we enter into communion with God and our family of faith. Not attending this meal is a serious sin—Sunday Mass attendance is not considered an optional part of our faith life. Without it, our relationship with God and our communion with each other falls apart. If the family is the domestic Church, then perhaps family meals matter. Gathering around a table to share a meal is integral to the communion of the family. Without this, the family can easily begin to fall apart.

Jo brought up the conflict that many families face in trying to cultivate their home life: how busy we all are. Being busy and trying to balance all the demands that life throws at us is a major life-sucker to parents and children alike. Parenthood can feel like a juggling act. My mom will discuss how she managed to 'balance it all' and the reasonings behind the things she prioritized in order to set the stage for a flourishing home life. Everyone's juggle will look different, but it's important that we are selective about what we are choosing to bring into our family.

ANGÈLE – Balance

In our contact with young parents, we are unfailingly asked about how to find balance in family life. The question is loaded and complex. It is asking how to deal with the constant demands of parenting and have time for self-fulfillment: recreation, relationships, achievements, hobbies, and interests. Certainly the 24-7, 365 days/year reality of parenting is a huge adjustment for young parents. There is a longing to have time to do the things that brought enjoyment, satisfaction, and fulfillment in those memorable kid-free days.

This question comes to me often from working moms who are certainly pulled with work, the home, children, husband, and personal well-being—not to mention: extended family, friends, neighbours, parish, and recreational needs of the whole family. The pressure can be overwhelming to fulfill all your duties, care for the people in your world, and take care of yourself.

Finding a way to strike a balance can seem overwhelming with all of the moving parts. I want to break it down in two sections of immediate ways to integrate balance and then share from my personal experience how I intentionally sought some balance in our homelife through staying home with the kids.

Balancing Extracurricular Activities

A challenge to finding balance in our home life is managing extracurricular involvements. We have been very choosy about the clubs that kids got involved in, considering the toll that they take on our family, in particular our family supper time. Now I'm a bit opinionated about extra-curricular activities, because I think they can easily become disordered. I see a temptation in treating our kids and their activities like a trophy case to show off to the world. Everything our kid does or succeeds at becomes like a collection of boy scout badges (for the parents). I personally don't share the propensity to build up a child's 'activity resumé' so intently. Is your child *really* going to make it to the Olympics or perform on Broadway? What is the cost to your family life and the development of the child in the pursuit of competitive dance, gymnastics, or soccer? (And what is the financial cost?)

I believe busyness drains family time and raises the child in a culture that says you *need* to be busy, you need to experience many things, you can't be bored—you need to be entertained. Busyness risks the child taking their identity in the things he/she is doing or succeeding at. These kinds of activities and all the chauffeuring that goes with it particularly affect the family meal time.

So my biggest practical advice for balance is to be ruthless in pruning everyone's extracurricular activities. I challenge you: do a purge for three or four months and see how your family balance is doing. A friend of mine, after moving their family of eight kids to a new city, said that having no sports or dance or music classes was so refreshing. She said it was like pushing the 'restart button' for their family.

Extracurricular activity and balance even applies to Mom and Dad's involvement in ministry, which I'd like to briefly touch on here even though it comes up elsewhere in the book. Even though I'm an absolute advocate of being a wholehearted, generous disciple in the mission of the Church, balance, prudence and wisdom are needed here too. Sometimes we can get ourselves overcommitted and too busy serving the Kingdom. Sometimes we enter seasons in our personal health (mental, emotional, or physical), our children's needs or other family life concerns when we need just to pull back, take a slower pace, have a narrower mission outlet, or even withdraw for a time—in order to have the energy to deal with immediate concerns while pressing deeper into the Father's heart. That might mean pulling back for a few months, it might mean a year or more depending on your situation. (The fear I think we all wrestle with, is the fear that if we dial back from ministry, our zeal will wain and apathy will permanently take over.) A more proximate fear might be, "How will I be judged by people in my church or community for pulling back from ministry?". What I think is important here is proper discernment: *know in your heart of hearts* that you are being invited by the Lord to slow down, go deeper and invest in your home life *for a season*. A spiritual director can confirm for you when this is important for a period of your life and that the Lord is inviting it. There is an opportunity, even here, to offer up your ache to be (more) engaged in the mission for the salvation of souls.

Balancing Personal Time and Couple Time

Then there is the question of balance when it comes to 'me time' or couple time. My first comment, at the risk of being a bit blunt, is that there is just much less of this kind of time in family life, and that's okay. Self-gift is implicit in the marriage vocation. In marriage and family, we imitate Christ and give of ourselves out of love, ideally without counting the cost. Again, I'm just being a bit opinionated here, but I think that we believe we need 'me time' because 'the world' tells us that we need it. Our culture is very individualistic and hedonistic, really; it promotes self-gratification and *not* self-gift. I encourage you to find enjoyment in small pleasures—like monthly or weekly outings for a date night, or an hour to take off when the kids are in bed to go to Eucharistic Adoration, to get a coffee, to go to the bookstore, or to go shopping. André and I each had our own men's and women's small group that met almost weekly and was a great outlet for our personal and social lives. The men met for early breakfasts, which was awesome because it was generally quiet around the family when he was gone. I would get together with my friends Tuesday evenings. André would put the kids to bed that night and so that was a double bonus for me. It was self-gift, not selfishness, that motivated making time for our sharing groups, or an occasional retreat for that matter. André and I covered for each other so we could share our lives with friends and care for our spiritual well-being, which in turn benefited our marriage and children. In short, it was a wise investment.

Making time for your relationship with God through a daily conversational prayer life and time for self-reflection is huge for experiencing balance and peace. I recommend doing an examination of conscience and trying to get 30 minutes of quiet for prayer. (I talk more about this in the last chapter.)

Balance also involves understanding each other's needs for outlets of fun or self-care and giving each other freedom to do the things we needed to do. For André, that was the need to go for runs daily, and play hockey with the guys once a week. What I needed to feel like 'a grown adult woman' in a kid's world was to take time to try and look nice: visits to the hair salon, pedicures, make-up, and dressing in style when going out of the house were important to me to feel good about myself. There was a time when I didn't take care of myself at all, wearing the same Value Village sweats every day for comfort and warmth, and then, after some comments from friends, I realized I had let myself go in my self-deprecating motherhood. On the flip side, a few years later I went to volunteer at Caleb's Grade 2 classroom, and I dressed nicely—fashionable jeans, belt, crisp white shirt, and nice heels. Caleb came home from school and was excited to tell me, "Mom, my friends think you are nice." I was confused, "But Caleb, I didn't help those boys at all. I just helped you and Michael." He repeated, "Yeah, but they really thought you were nice." I hadn't even spoken to them! And then I realized, "Ah, they thought I *looked nice*." I learned that day that it's not just important for me to feel good about my appearance, but that it obviously means something to my kids too.

As far as couple time went, we would always talk in the evenings when the kids were in bed, or over a cup of coffee on Saturday mornings when the kids were watching cartoons, or hire a babysitter for a date night once a month. Opportunities for weekends away happened sometimes, with the help of free babysitting from our moms. All of it requires some creativity and flexibility according the needs of your kids and your season of life. With time for talk, special fun, and closeness, I think the biggest win all around is that it fosters unity as husband and wife—and this is the foundation of your marriage and whole family environment. It makes me think of the parable from Matthew 6:46-49 that speaks of the wise man who builds his house on rock instead of sand in order to withstand the storms of life. This was the Gospel reading at our wedding and our theme was "Built on Christ". Thirty some years ago, we concluded that, if we were established in Christ as individuals and in unity as a couple, we would be able to withstand all that life would bring.

Ultimately, the guideposts that helped me maintain a healthy life balance were: 1) a consistent daily prayer time, 2) the fellowship of sisters in the faith with whom I could share my heart and struggles, 3) unity with Andrè on decisions and 4) making the environment of the home a priority in decision making. This means, that I weighed opportunities and decisions based on the impact it could have on the peace, joy and stability of our children's lives and our home life.

Balancing Work and Home

I will now address the question of the working moms about how I have found balance, from my own perspective. Please understand, I do not claim to have the definitive answer to this, and each family needs to find their own way. I do not want to come across as saying my way is the best way. What I will be expressing is my experience of and discernment of *my* decisions that I made as a mother. I know every family's decisions will look different.

When I am asked by moms about balance, they seem to think I'm some kind of super mom who is a full-time executive, spiritually strong, and has raised a good family. I think they see in me a role model of someone who has been winning at the balance game for decades. What they don't know is that what they see in me has only been my lived reality since 2014, when, out of submission to a request from CCO's president, I took a full-time position to work as one of the Vice Presidents in our organization. It was a huge adjustment for me in managing our family (meals, groceries, laundry, extra-curricular involvements). I had never worked away from the home before!

Not working outside of the home was an intentional decision. When women ask me about balance and career, I refrain from giving them my thoughts and avoid the subject. But in writing this book, I can't really dodge answering the question. You may have some great reasons to disagree with me in certain areas, and that's okay, but I'm going to answer the question in all honesty for those who can benefit from my personal experience and insights.

As I've heard more and more young moms talk about this issue, I am seeing a trend of being the 'I-can-do-it-all-wonder-woman' modern woman. I feel the need to offer that an alternative voice may be needed to add some balance to the discussion. My caution is that the current trend could hurt and burn out children, families, marriages, and women. Some young wives I've talked to feel it would be selfish and lazy for them to raise their kids as a stay-at-home mom. They've whispered to me, "Angèle, what do you think? I really want to be home with my children, but I don't feel like I have the freedom to choose it. What will people think of me not keeping a career?".

It was important to André and me that I raise the kids. I guess this may sound kind of old-fashioned, but it had always been the desire of my heart. This was a counter-cultural decision to make in the 90s; hardly anyone stayed home with their kids. All my peers pursued full-time careers while raising their children. My perspective on it was that I wanted to be the one to influence how my children behaved, how they thought and spoke. I wanted to be able to see all their firsts: first steps, first sounds, and first adventures. Knowing that children are a gift from God, I wanted to give myself entirely to care for these treasures. When Bishop Scott McCaig visits our home, he almost always brings up the fact that the enemy of our souls has made the family his latest and greatest target. Christian families may want to consider a more radical approach to counter worldly trends in light of the spiritual realities at play.

Now just because I stayed home to raise our children doesn't mean I just read them storybooks and baked cookies all day. Inside joke on that comment. When Jo was in Grade 4, he begged me to homeschool him. I told him I was too busy to start homeschooling. (Truth be told, I had tried homeschooling for two years and found I was always fighting with the kids and, in a flash, I could see my frazzled future trying to homeschool this stubborn kid. So yeah, I wasn't going there.) Jo's angry reply to my rejection was, "You're not busy! You just stay home and eat cookies all day!"

But what *if* I just stayed home reading storybooks and baking cookies with the kids all day? What's wrong with that? It's beautiful, actually! How wonderful to be a mom that gives herself in such attentive, tender ways to her children day in and day out. But I noticed that when I was raising my toddlers, I was looked down upon for being a stay-at-home mom, while neighbours who ran childcare out of their home were considered respected professionals. What is the difference in what she did, or what a nanny did, and what I did? Nothing—just the paycheque. I might sound a bit defensive, but I am just being honest.

Raising children, keeping a clean home, planning and preparing healthy meals, and staying on top of household and family responsibilities is a lot of work! Stay-at-home moms are always active and, if the needs of the children should slow down, they will naturally migrate into other projects. In my day, and in my mother and grandmother's day, stay-at-home moms were industrious women and community leaders. They were the ones initiating and leading committees, events, and various service projects. They would volunteer and be active in the parish, school, and extra-curricular interests of their children. Stay-at-home moms always end up serving or leading in these domains out of their giftedness and desire to make a better life for their children and community. My mom, grandmothers, and great-grandmothers managed massive gardens to provide food for the family throughout the year. They sewed the children's clothes to save money. Some of them actually made income for the family through providing services out of the home: selling cream, eggs or perogies, hairdressing, sewing alterations, making silk-flower arrangements, or even as a sales representative for gravestones (yes, seriously). Today, some women choose to earn money by working from home in a variety of ways. All of these money-making initiatives barely took a mom out of the home, and I think that is the point.

Balancing Volunteering

For my part, my working as a young mother was volunteering with CCO. I have been a part of our leadership team for decades (since I am a co-founder), and I have been brought into many strategic meetings to lend my strengths and gifts. When Caleb was in full-time school and before we had Natalie, I started working part-time hours a couple days a week from home as an internship trainer, while the kids were at school. When Natalie and Janna were babies, I planned my work to happen only during nap time (1-3pm) or I would hire a CCO student to come in for one day a week when I would sequester myself in the basement to do non-stop conference calls. In 2009, when Janna no longer napped and wasn't yet in kindergarten, I took a leave from CCO because I knew I would have a hard time balancing my growing work expectations and her little needs (as the only child in the home with no siblings for playmates). When Janna joined her older siblings in full-time school, I worked pretty much full-time, from home. So as you can see, I applied my gifts but kept the children and home life as my main focus.

A wise parenting mentor told me that kids don't need *quality time* as much as they need quantity time. And furthermore, she told me, kids need a parent at home even more when they are at school, because it is precisely when they come home at the end of their day that they are bursting to talk about what happened to them. Think about it, what is the first impulse of a child when they walk through the door after school? "MOM?!" You reply, give them a fistful of those cookies you've obviously been baking all day, and listen to their stories while prepping veggies for supper. My take on it is that kids need to know I'm around. I need to be accessible but I don't need to be solely occupied with them. Quantity time is powerful for kids because your constant presence equals safety and security, and this is a huge need for a child's psyche.

This might seem like I am not addressing the question of balance, but I found that the way I was most able to balance it all was by either being a homemaker full time or working from home. This made raising my children and maintaining a functional home life much more doable. While financially it did mean living off of less, we found that if we were honest with ourselves, we would spend what we had. For a long time we lived off of a very low salary, and I was amazed by how we were able to sustain our family with so 'little' by living simply. We were discerning about all our spending choices, and we knew why we were choosing to live that way. It was for the sake of our children as well as for our own sanity.

I will admit that, since I've been working out of the home full-time, it has been a huge stressor, and I would much rather be able to work from home. I have had to make major adjustments and found it hard to have brain space and energy for my kids. I've had to focus on strategic meal-planning so as to have meals table-ready in under 30 minutes. I have invested in an Amazon Prime membership so I can order things I need for the family from anywhere I happen to be as it pops in my head. (This has been a lifesaver to have gifts for birthday parties, Christmas, etc.) My most recent inspiration has been to hire a house cleaner. It's seriously the best for my peace of mind. These are just some of the ways I am trying to bring balance for me, so I'm not a stress-case at home.

Hiddenness: An Additional Note for Stay-at-Home Moms

I'd like to say a few words to address those moms who are choosing to stay home with their littles. (Some of these words may apply similarly to stay-at-home dads.) Although the conviction and love to stay at home with our children can be strong, there is often a real death to self and loneliness in living out that decision. There is a feeling of being left behind. There can be a feeling of losing your identity and value. These emotions, this near grieving of your 'other life' will affect the tone of the home life. Let's talk about that for a bit and how to navigate it.

Here was my situation. I was in the isolation of my home—in a new city—3,500 kms away from extended family—in winter—in Canada—with three kids under the age of five. I was making so many acts of the will to dig deep and lovingly care for my family. No one was there to see or applaud. I was also keenly aware of my failings; being impatient, abrupt, and that was gnawing at my conscience. Meanwhile there was the temptation to feel sorry for myself because I was missing out. My colleagues in CCO were out there in the great adventure of our mission, reaching souls for Christ and 'changing the world'.

Me? All I was changing was diapers (mind you those puppies were handmade cloth diapers thank you very much). It felt like my own identity and value was at stake. Here I was, co-founder of CCO, I was the key developer of our strategy and materials, but I felt like no one remembered any of that. I was perceived as the dedicated wife and mom in the background. I was hidden. As I heard another young mom express it, "I feel so little in a world of littles."

If I could go back in time to give myself some advice during those early parenting years, I think I would say, "Angèle…."

■ You *are* doing a good, important thing here.

■ You are a part of the mission by making it possible for André to go out and do the work you both are so committed to. That means; don't make him feel guilty for going. Know how important his work is and give him the emotional freedom to go. Make a soft environment for him to leave from and come home to. Avoid guilt trips, emotional manipulations, pouting, or angry silence.

- Remember your husband's success is your success. When he wins, you win. You are a team.

- You *are* contributing to the mission. Your faithfulness to your family vocation is a powerful form of intercession and graces for God's mission in the world.

- This hidden time, which also exposes your own weaknesses in how you respond to your children, is a great time for personal purification and growth in virtue and holiness. This is a school of holiness for you in self-gift and self-denial. It is a school of love. And since kids are more merciful than adults, they are a safe place to grow and practice overcoming vices in daily life.

- If the hidden life of the Holy Family was part of God's Plan for the world's salvation and the revelation of Jesus Christ, then maybe you should believe it's a model for you and you family too and not be afraid of the implicit hiddenness. It's a co-operation with God's saving plan. There are many saints to turn to for intercessory help who can relate to the hidden world of mothers and domestic life: Our Lady, St. Gianna, St. Marguerite d'Youville, St. Monica, St. Elizabeth, St. Helena, St. Zelie etc.

- Know that your dignity and value is going to be under attack. Don't believe the lies. You are more than a job title, what you do, your accomplishments or recognitions. This time in your life pulls all that away and can leave you feeling vulnerable, but really it is an opportunity to find out how the Lord sees, loves and values you. The truth is you are first and foremost wildly loved by the Father, you belong to him and he will love you eternally—just because you are his. Let him love you.

- You will not be in diapers and toys forever, but so much good can come in these years for you, your husband, your children, your children's children, and the kingdom of God.

- The home and the environment you are creating is forming godly children who will multiply this investment into the world faster and more effectively than you can.

- The enemy of our souls despises your femininity, your motherhood and your children. You remind him of Mary, the woman whose offspring crushed his head. Part of what you are experiencing is rooted in his attack on the family. Be confident. Your motherhood and your Christian home is a spiritual powerhouse from a spiritual perspective.

How can I speak confidently like this? Because, my dear young moms, I am on the other side now. As a grandma, I can clearly see the fruit of the *investment* we made in creating a home life which fostered the growth of joy-filled, life-long missionary disciples.

You've got this.

Conclusion

Creating an environment that is free, fun, orderly and comfortable will make home a safe place where your children can be free to learn, grow; and yes, even be weak and fail. Here are some highlights from this chapter on making your home a place where your children can love to thrive:

■ Every home has a culture unique to the family. Find your family's common interests and intentionally take time to do those things.

■ Order is important in the home, but so is fun. Children need to know that they can be free at home, so find a way to balance cleanliness and rowdiness, while assuring each family member that they are free to take themselves lightly when they mess up.

■ Be intentional with how you handle home entertainment, whether with toys or technology. Encourage imaginative play!

■ New life encourages responsibility, generosity and self-gift. That is why babies can be such a gift to parents and older siblings, contributing to home life in a unique way.

■ Every parent questions how they should balance work and family life, extracurricular activities, time together as a couple, and time alone. Make these decisions based on the needs of your family and stability of your home life, as well as on your relationship with Christ and what he is calling you to!

Our 'place' was home; home is where the heart is. When home is a place where *life* happens, children feel less of a need to experience life, joy, and fulfillment outside of the home. Often, young people turn to the wrong crowd or a morally questionable atmosphere because they are searching for a place of belonging. We never had to do this because we knew where we belonged. We didn't have to go searching for counterfeit love, we were experiencing the real stuff. We were experiencing a reflection of Christ's love in the family and thus discovering God for ourselves was an easy and natural transition. I truly believe home life is designed to be a microcosm of the joy found in a life in Christ. And in closing, I will let Jesus have the last say: "The thief comes only to steal and kill and destroy. I came that they may have life, and have it abundantly." John 10:10

Reflection / Action Points

1. What does your family like to do (music, art, board games, cook and eat food, tell stories, etc.)? Whatever your common interests are, find ways to incorporate them into your family time this week.

2. Would you say that you take yourself lightly? Do your children have freedom to fail and do they know how to take themselves lightly? How can you encourage your children or spouse to laugh at themselves when they mess up?

3. Is your home a comfortable place where your family feels safe, peaceful, and free? Does it cater to what your children need and how they need it?

4. Angèle shared suggestions of how she and André found balance in their family life. What do you think about what she said? More importantly, what does your family need to be happy and stable? Bring it to the Lord and ask him these questions too.

CHAPTER 6

Traditions

Why Have Traditions?

MYLÈNE

Traditions are an extension of the experience and spiritual significance of a good home life. Due to the weight we place on traditions in our family life, onlookers might say we are obsessed with how we observe Christmas, Easter, birthdays, and even Labour Day weekend! But in our family book-planning discussions, we quickly and unanimously identified them as a huge part of our family's special sauce, and so we could not avoid reflecting on and reminiscing about them, giving them their own chapter to illustrate how necessary they were in creating the home life that formed us children as missionary disciples.

JANNA

I like having the same traditions every year because I feel like our family never changes and that we are together and not separated from each other. I know what's going to happen and I get excited about doing the fun things again and again. I also don't like changes very much, so I look forward to doing the same things. It matters to me that the whole family can be together for these kinds of special celebrations.

Janna expresses the experience all of us kids had. Our family traditions were deeply meaningful to each of us. As we discussed this, we asked ourselves, why were traditions so powerful for us? How did we benefit? What role did they play in forming us to become missionary disciples?

Our first observation was that traditions harness the power of repetition. Children love repetition. Ask anyone who has swung a child up in the air. Did the child not respond, "Again, again!"? Growing up, the *anticipation* of our family traditions, with the knowledge of what was coming next, was almost as exciting as the events themselves. We eagerly anticipated the fun that we knew always happened when we were together as a family. Routine is invaluable to a child's development. Countless experts have emphasized that children need routine in their normal everyday lives so they feel that they have some sort of control over their surroundings, and to help them feel confident and independent. Children thrive in this kind of an atmosphere, and we realized, so does our family. The consistent repetition of our times together as a family helped us to feel secure in our sense of home. We could be confident in the consistency and with this, we felt secure in our family relationships. We knew family was always going to be a part of our lives and because of this, we never questioned our love for each other.

In light of how we celebrated traditions, we kids knew that home was where the really important stuff happened. We felt treasured because our big life milestones were celebrated and valued by our family as a whole. Tradition made us feel part of something bigger than ourselves. And when it came to tradition, we were never lacking. I never understood in the movies when the main character spent Thanksgiving or Christmas with their friends, or their new boyfriend or girlfriend, opting not to go home. Often, spending time with family for these big occasions is portrayed as a burden to be avoided. I can say with certainty that this is not the way that God would have intended familial relationships. The concept and experience of 'going home' with the awareness that home is where one belongs during these special occasions was central to our family experience. Even if I am in another city, or spending time with my in-laws, it is such a security to my heart to know that the family is at home (wishing I was there with them), doing the same things we have done every year. The holidays should not be a season of loneliness or frustration; it is meant to be a time of community and celebration of Christ, with the deep knowledge that you are *seen* and *wanted*. Traditions are the context for a culture of family togetherness rather than loneliness. We feel our emphasis on tradition was a large reason why we kids didn't turn to harmful, worldly places growing up.

In all the fun that traditions provide, family members forge a trust with one another that strengthens the bonds of their relationships. On campus, CCO missionaries see every day that developing trust and building relationships is foundational in the work of evangelization. We believe the principle holds true for having a platform to witness and evangelize our children's hearts, too.

We were impacted by each and every tradition incorporated into our family life, from the greatest to the smallest. They fostered emotional security, created strong bonds that set the stage for spiritual mentorship from our parents in the future, and followed the firm example that the Church has given us. Traditions are the parents' opportunity to create the culture that their children will be formed in. We believe this culture can be a significant factor in whether children continue in their faith or not.

In the rest of this chapter, we are excited to share with you all the juicy details of how we celebrate as a family.

Regnier Traditions

While everyone's family traditions are unique and different in their own beautiful ways, we will give you an idea of our family traditions and our memories surrounding them. We'll share why they are important to us, how they nurtured our spiritual lives, and how they built a bridge of trust that was essential in all of our choices to follow Jesus and become missionary disciples.

CALEB – Advent & Christmas

When it comes to Regnier traditions, there is no time more regulated and policed than Christmas. Virtually every week and day is carefully planned and concretely placed within the Regnier Christmas cycle. The duty has been assigned to me to accurately describe this premium time, where family tradition is at an all-time high.

Let's start with Advent. I believe that the traditions practiced in this season of preparation made even more of an impact on us than the traditions of Christmas Day itself. Advent is all about waiting and preparing for the birth of our Lord, preparing the manger of our hearts for the joy of the Incarnation.

In our family, each week of Advent marks a new stage in the preparation of our hearts and home for Christmas. Two things that are consistent throughout all of Advent are: Christmas music played virtually 24/7 and 'Kris Kringle' or 'KK' for every new week. Every Sunday, the Advent candle is lit and everyone picks a name of someone in the family, for whom they become 'KK'. The 'KK' does secret acts of kindness, such as little affirmations hidden in lunch boxes, praying for them, or cleaning their room while they aren't home.

Another way we prepare during Advent is through decorating the home slowly, adding more decorations as the weeks progress. This process reflects the journey of waiting that is taking place. As a child, I was always looking forward to what would change in the next week of Advent. I think this is why I never felt the need to peek in at my presents; I wasn't impatient for Christmas because Advent was already so exciting.

One of my favourite Advent traditions is one that most actively prepares our hearts for Christmas. We go to St. Patrick's Basilica in downtown Ottawa for the Sacrament of Reconciliation. As a young boy, the idea of going to Confession was not very attractive; it would be very easy to complain or be annoyed. Mom and Dad were smart and found ways to make this experience magical and accessible to a young boy like me. After Confession, we would go out for supper and then drive around to look at Christmas lights. By doing it this way, Mom and Dad weren't dragging us kids to Confession; rather, we were excited and prepared for the full experience (even if sometimes I was just looking forward to getting chicken nuggets at the restaurant). This tradition has been essential towards preparing my heart for Christmas and recentring my focus on Christ.

Now on to Christmas. For me, the beauty of Christmas doesn't come from a special gift or an extravagant surprise, but from the power of tradition. If I could describe Christmas in one word, it would be 'magical.' It may seem like the concept of a magical Christmas contradicts the spiritual nature of the season. Can the 'magical' and the 'holy' be reconciled? I think that as long as the spiritual aspects of Christmas are woven into tradition, there can and should be an understanding that Christmas is magical *because it is holy*.

Christmas Eve is super special, with the summit being midnight Mass. The whole family gets dressed up and enjoys the celebration of Jesus being born. After Mass, we head home for a *Reveillon*, the French tradition where there is a post-midnight-Mass feast. We stay up late into the night eating and laughing, but Mom and Dad stay up the latest to put the gifts under the tree.

Christmas morning is marked by the excitement of coming downstairs to see baby Jesus in the manger, accompanied by a sight that is gloriously seared into each of our memories: the glow. The 'glow' is the light which shines from each corner of the living room, emanating from the lights on the tree reflecting off the shiny Christmas wrapping paper. As exciting as this sight is, before any presents are opened, we gather around and draw our attention to the fact that baby Jesus is now in the manger and we pray together.

We spend the rest of the day together, enjoy Christmas dinner as a family, and then socialize late into the night to finish off the day. It sounds cheesy and cliché, but Christmas for me is not about the gifts; it's about anticipation and love that is shared as a family—fostered through building and claiming strong, unmovable, and unique Christmas traditions.

JO – Lent & Easter

Don't tell Caleb, but Lent and Easter are a bigger deal around here than Christmas. Even as a kid, I always looked forward to Lent—it was an exciting time. Lent? Exciting? I realize this probably comes as a shock and you're probably thinking that Mom and Dad paid me to say this ($100 sounds about right). But it's true! We looked forward to Lent because we knew it was a time to grow spiritually, through prayer, almsgiving, and fasting—as a family.

Although we each had individual things that we gave up, here are some things we tried to do every year together:

■ Fast from watching TV with an exception to movies with 'redeeming qualities'. This essentially means that, although it may be a secular movie, there is a spiritual dimension to it that has heroic themes of forgiveness and redemption (reminding us of Christ). Some examples include:

◆ The Count of Monte Cristo (2002)
◆ Ben-Hur (1959)
◆ The Scarlet and the Black (1983)
◆ Les Miserables (1998 version)
◆ Cinderella (2015 version)
◆ The Robe (1953)
◆ The Mission (1986)
◆ Silence (2016)
◆ The Ten Commandments (1956)
◆ Jesus of Nazareth (1977)
◆ The Passion of the Christ (2004)
◆ The Prince of Egypt (1998)

■ Fast from junk food and desserts
■ A weekly Rosary
■ Commit to daily prayer
■ Fast from video games

Mom and Dad really emphasised that this was a time of spiritual growth, where we could draw closer to the Lord. When we were in high school, during Lent, they tried to help us grow our morning prayer lives, which were otherwise non-existent. I remember one year Mom and Dad brought a smoothie and a bagel to our rooms ten minutes before we normally woke up. This was to encourage us to get up and take time to pray before our day began. Isn't that an amazing idea? Well, after a week, all of our bedrooms started to take on a new aroma. This was because of a certain rapid growth that was taking place, mould-style. You see, we weren't waking up; we were just putting the smoothies under our night stands and going back to sleep. Mom and Dad's plan to help us pray didn't really work at the time, but we understood what they were communicating: that relationship with Jesus is key. Lent was a time to focus in on that. It's not even about the fasting. We kids could have fasted all we (or Mom and Dad) wanted, but without a relationship with Jesus rooted in prayer, our parents knew that fasting would not have borne much fruit. And, like our smoothies, eventually our spiritual lives would have started to stink.

Lent was a time of sacrifice and we wanted to embrace it with a joyful anticipation of things yet to come. I can confidently say that the Triduum and Easter are some of the most highly anticipated days of the whole year for our family. We take our fasting and prayer to a whole other level over these holy days. These days are quiet, reflective, penitential, and deeply spiritual. For the whole weekend, we don't go shopping or see any friends; it is spent closed-in at home, with the exception of going to Mass. We come together, pray, talk, eat simply, and meditate. These days are also filled with joy and excitement, bursting at the seams, but we have to keep that joy veiled as we prepare for the Resurrection.

To give you an idea of what those days look like, here are essential elements of our Triduum Traditions:

- Holy Thursday
  - As younger kids, instead of going to Mass, Mom would stay home and re-enact the scene from Holy Thursday. We'd read it from the Bible, eat pita bread and drink grape juice, and wash each other's feet.
  - As we got older, we went together to Holy Thursday Mass followed by a Holy Hour of Eucharistic Adoration (sometimes less than an hour).
  - We use art and decor to enter into the holy days. We use window writers to draw a symbol or picture for each major day of the Triduum, with a Scripture passage under each picture that sums up the events of the day. We also have a shelf that Mom decorates every morning before we get up. On Holy Thursday, there is a cup with bread and a statue of Jesus beside it.
  - Fasting through simple meals of soup, bread, cheese, and fruits.
  - At the end of the evening, we watch 'The Passion of the Christ' together, with whoever is old enough.

■ Good Friday

- ◆ For decoration: new window art and the shelf is covered in red fabric and a crucifix is on display.
- ◆ Prayer time in the morning both individually and as a family, usually sharing about what we reflected on the night before in holy hour.
- ◆ More fasting through simple meals.
- ◆ Quiet family time together, no exciting activities, no playing outside. Really trying to enter into the sombre day.
- ◆ Good Friday service at Church.
- ◆ Often we watch 'Jesus of Nazareth' together.

■ Holy Saturday

- ◆ For decoration: new window art and the cross on the shelf is covered in a purple sash.
- ◆ We take our individual prayer times.
- ◆ Family discussion where we talk about what the Lord has been speaking in our personal prayer. (This of course grew deeper as we grew older.)
- ◆ Dad reads to us an ancient homily that depicts Jesus' descent into hell to save Adam and Eve and all the faithful who died before him. This is found in the Office of Readings, always on Holy Saturday.
- ◆ We decorate Easter Eggs, with food dyes and crayons, making both silly and spiritual eggs.
- ◆ More simple meals, and a sombre atmosphere throughout the day since Jesus is in the tomb.
- ◆ The long awaited Easter Vigil Mass!! It's the highlight. We always have a big spread of decadent food ready and waiting to eat after the Vigil, even though it's so late at night.

■ Easter Sunday

- ◆ For decoration: new window art and the shelf is filled with flowers.
- ◆ Our wake-up tradition, which Natalie will explain.
- ◆ We pray together, thanking Jesus for his death and Resurrection.
- ◆ We have an Easter Egg hunt in the living room (the eggs are hidden the night before by Caleb, the resident Easter Bunny).
- ◆ We open our Easter baskets. The reason Mom gives presents is that she wanted us as little kids not to see Christmas as better or more important than Easter.

- Easter morning breakfast: Mom's homemade gooey cinnamon buns, maple-glazed ham, hash browns, and the eggs we painted on Saturday.

- Before eating the eggs we have our egg fight where we smash the eggs 'pointy end' to 'pointy end' and then 'butt to butt.' Whichever egg doesn't crack, wins.

- We spend the rest of the day together playing games and preparing food and desserts for Easter dinner. (Desserts of note: chocolate bunny-shaped cake, lemon tarts and cross-shaped sugar cookies.)

As a testimony to how special these days are, even for the younger ones in the family, here is what Janna and Natalie love about the Triduum.

JANNA – Holy Thursday

I always enjoy the Triduum, especially Holy Thursday. Since I've gotten older, I like staying after the Mass in Eucharistic Adoration to pray with Jesus. Dad taught me how to pray quietly during this time, and it's very special to be able to stay with Jesus for one hour in the Garden of Gethsemane—during the time he would have been praying to his Father. I find that Jesus really speaks to my heart during this time every year, especially through reading the Psalms. I remember one time, I was feeling fearful of some things while praying. But that night, Jesus made me feel safe through what I read in the Bible. Psalm 128 is my favourite and I feel God has given me promises that he will take care of me. I feel a little bit like Mary as Elizabeth said to her "Blessed is she who believed that the Lord would fulfill his promises to her." (Luke 1:45)

NATALIE – Our Easter Morning Wake-Up Tradition

Easter morning is just the best! Janna and I have always been in a race to be the first to wake up so we can wake the other up in order to wake up everyone else—including the neighbourhood. Here's what I do: if I'm the first to wake up, I quietly run downstairs to see all the Easter decorations, flowers, Easter baskets, and presents. I try very hard not to notice any of the Easter eggs which are hidden all over the main floor (cheating isn't cool). Everything looks so awesome and joyful. I get super excited and run back upstairs to wake up Janna. Our tradition is to go downstairs together, run outside and scream out, "JESUS HAS RISEN!" super loud. I wouldn't be surprised if we wake up the neighbours.

All in all, it is a very busy few days, that are jam-packed with symbolism, liturgy, prayer, fasting, sharing, art, and celebrating, and these things come together to form OUR tradition.

We don't just do all these things for the sake of doing them, or because it's fun. The reason we practice our traditions so religiously is because they are meaningful to us. We look forward to each and every aspect of our Lent and Easter traditions; each part has a story and significance in our lives. These traditions bring our family together in a special and powerful way. These traditions (even the silly ones) all help us enter more fully into the mysteries of Christ's death and Resurrection. How does *your* family like entering into Lent and Easter?

Pilgrimage

Tradition, of course, isn't limited to just Christmas and Easter. Many Catholic families have developed beautiful traditions to celebrate Saint feast days, baptismal days, and other milestones. Going on pilgrimage as a family is not only a traditional Catholic practice but one of our traditions as well.

ANGÈLE – Pilgrimage to Montréal

L'oratoire St. Joseph de Montréal (St. Joseph's Oratory in Montréal) has had a huge impact on my life and in my coming to the Catholic Church. I first encountered this impressive Church in 1980, on a trip to Montréal with my grandparents, having never left the prairie provinces before. As a small-town farm girl raised a Lutheran, I never knew churches like this existed! St. Joseph's Oratory was built under the inspiration of St. Brother André Bessette and is the largest shrine dedicated to St. Joseph in the world. It captured my imagination with its grandeur and massive presence. The piety of the people moved me, especially those who mount the stairs to the Oratory on their knees in prayer. It was so amazing to see! I knew I was on holy ground and I was absolutely smitten.

When we moved to Ottawa in 1997, I was excited to be in striking distance of the Oratory and to bring André and the kids to experience it. It quickly became a part of our family's annual rhythm to make pilgrimage there on the long weekend in September. There are always a few changes in how we do it, but the most consistent parts of the pilgrimage involve stopping at Real Bagel on Chemin Queen Mary for wood-fired Montréal sesame bagels (so good!) and eating them 'tailgate party style' in the highest parking lot of the Oratory. We then enjoy a sauntering visit around the Oratory and often take in our Sunday

Mass, Confession, or the outdoor Stations of the Cross. The highlight is always lighting a candle and praying in the votive room. Here, you find a dimly-lit room filled with pilgrims, thousands of flickering candles, and hundreds of crutches and canes hung on the walls in memory of healings from the prayers of St. Brother André during his days—and of course through the intercession of St. Joseph. The kids each get money for their own candle and can choose to light it themselves. This is very exciting, especially since you can mount several stairs to light a candle as close as possible to the statue of St. Joseph. Each of us is encouraged to pray for our own intentions at a variety of kneelers dedicated to different spiritual roles of St. Joseph (patron of workers, families, the dying, etc.). The whole visit to the Oratory, especially the candles, is very experiential for children and moves their little hearts of faith in this expression of public piety. Our girls really love the massive statues of Christ's passion in the Stations of the Cross on the side of the mountain. They would pose in the scene and make themselves part of the story—a childlike and concrete application of Ignatian meditation.

Sometimes the pilgrimage includes a visit to St. Kateri's tomb in nearby Kahnawake. Sometimes we go downtown to visit one of my favourite churches of all time, Notre Dame Basilica-Cathedral in Old Montréal. (In my humble opinion, if you could artistically portray the 'temple of the Holy Spirit,' which is in the heart of Our Lady, it would look like this church!) Sometimes we just walk around Old Montréal and enjoy the buskers, the vieux port, and the poutine. We always end our pilgrimage with a picnic at Parc Mont Royal. And, once the sun begins to fall, we walk ten minutes further up a path to get to the Kondiaronk Lookout to look at downtown Montréal and the St. Lawrence River at night.

As delightful and charming as such a day in Montréal is, for us it quickly became much more than a treasured tradition—it was a necessity, a life-saver. We *needed* to go. The kids thought we were just going to do our typical thing in Montréal, but André and I were often going in exhaustion and desperation.

Maybe it's just because it was the end of summer and we had just had everyone home for two months. Maybe it was because of the distress of school starting again. But the reality for us in our parenting was that, by Labour Day weekend, we were at our wits' end. One child was his own special flavour of August angst.

Of course you've already read how Jo has been nicknamed: 'Fight-Starter'. I don't need to go into the antics and challenge that Jo was for us, but honestly, we felt really exasperated and didn't know what we could do to discipline and parent him into appropriate attitudes and actions. I felt lost and exhausted. I didn't know what to do about him. He was often angry and we knew that he was fundamentally angry at himself for getting so angry—so often, so quickly.

In my desperation for supernatural intervention, I too, prayed in the votive room with St. Joseph. I laid out the pain and chaos I was feeling. I had no idea how to deal with Jo's outbursts, and I needed divine intervention. I asked St. Joseph for his powerful help and protection for my family life. I knelt there and begged the Lord for freedom from any influence of the enemy in my life, my family's life, my son's life. Tears would well up in my eyes, I would wipe them, and then it was time to carry on with our pilgrimage.

Without fail—WITHOUT FAIL—within 48 hours of our pilgrimage to the Oratory, there was a 180 degree improvement in Jo's behaviours. He was pleasant, peaceful, calm, agreeable, and happy. André and I would look at each other and our eyes were communicating, "Who is this kid?" I know that encouraging the kids to go to Confession in the Crypt chapel was also a big part of their experience and certainly instrumental in Jo's healing.

One particular year we decided to picnic first, then do the Oratory in the evening so we could be there at night. The Oratory is even more spectacular lit up at night than it is during the day. Unfortunately, our plans imploded. Our afternoon picnic at Mount Royal was an absolute disaster. Mr. Fight-Starter was on the move. He was angry about everything and blaming everyone about it. He was mad about the drinks, the snacks, the location of our picnic table, the lack of good toys, the other people in the park, the song Mylène was humming, the way Caleb looked at him, the cloud blocking the sun … you name it, he was annoyed by it. No matter what we did—whether we used the kind approach or responded in firmness—it didn't make a dent in his crankiness. I remember André and I being so frustrated that we announced, "Pack up kids—we're going home right now. This trip is done." Huffing and puffing, we started packing up the cooler and tablecloths at which point Jo asked, in a screaming voice, "You mean we're not going to the Oratory?"

"Nope, we're going home right now," André replied sternly.

"Well what was the point if we don't go to the Oratory anyways?" Jo yelled back.

Silence.

I can't speak for André, but I was incensed. "After all these behaviours, and you think I want to take you to the Oratory?"

It took every meagre ounce of humility I had to give in and agree to go to the Oratory—but we would leave the very minute we were done. I'm sure I stomped and fumed throughout that holy building. I couldn't believe it. I don't like losing arguments and I had just given into my misbehaving kid's wishes. (I know, I know, he wanted to go to church—I was blind with anger).

So we did the thing. We stomped around the Oratory, hastily lit the candles, each offered short, terse prayers to St. Joseph. Mine went something like this, "Lord, I don't know how to handle this. St. Joseph, I don't even want to be here right now and I honestly don't know if you can even help us this time. It's pretty bad. *sigh* Amen."

We certainly did it at a brisker, more efficient pace than usual, but we did the usual things and then we got into the car in silence and drove home with McDonald's drive thru fare for supper. I felt pretty raw and wrecked when we got home. I couldn't wait to get to bed.

The next day, as happened all the other years, there was a different Joel Regnier in our home; a pleasant, funny, and fun-loving child. St. Joseph had come through on his intercession for grace for us despite how terribly we visited his house. What a gratuitous and unmerited grace it was that particular year. I will never forget it.

When people ask me for the ten-second answer of the secret sauce to our parenting, I always say two things: the wonderful influence of CCO role models in my kids' life (a previous chapter), and St. Joseph. Consistently, when we had nothing left in us as parents, St. Joseph's intercession turned the tide *without fail*. We are forever grateful and try always to make it there each Sunday of the September Labour Day weekend.

St. Joseph, pray for us.

St. Brother André Bessette, pray for us.

JO – Reflection on the Oratory Pilgrimage

I have always loved our family pilgrimage to the Oratory. I love the story of Saint Brother André because, unlike other Saints, I felt a closeness to him, physically and temporally. I could see what he saw and touch what he touched. In this, I also grew to love St. Joseph. Mom and Dad used to buy me little statues of St. Joseph to have in my room; in fact, I have one they bought me beside my bed even now in my own home. I also loved our pilgrimage because it was a time for our family to be together. When Mom and Dad told me the stories of my meltdowns prior to and during our trips, I was shocked because all I remember was the joy and fun! I do remember being a bit of a 'freak-out kid' growing up and so I grudgingly accept the title of Fight-Starter. But when I heard just how drastically St. Joseph acted in my life, I was so amazed. I felt an even greater closeness with the earthly dad of Jesus!

I remember a letter my Mom wrote me years ago when I was on a retreat. In this letter, Mom explained to me the role St. Joseph played in my development. She said Mary and Joseph were just as much my parents as Mom and Dad are. I remember tears filling my eyes and feeling so blessed to have two sets of such amazing parents; parents who put up with all my antics and prayed unceasingly for me. I would not be the man I am today if not for all the prayers offered at the Oratory.

The Everyday Traditions

MARC

In joining the Regnier family, I have noticed that in addition to these large annual traditions, there are normal, everyday traditions that should not be left out. These traditions are less flashy and exciting, but they are invaluable. Developing and nurturing these family relationships in everyday life will make it so that your family *wants* to be together. The key is consistency. Mylène has explained to me that before youth group came in the picture and their Friday nights were free, they eagerly anticipated Fun Fridays, which consisted of a fun supper and running to *Blockbuster* to choose a movie (this was, of course, back when *Blockbuster* still existed—the collapse of video stores has ruined the fun of movie nights forever). Although Fun Fridays were before my time, we have moved this weekly time together to Sunday brunch. Because some of us have moved out of the house, this has become the time for us to come together regularly as a family, no matter how crazy the week has been. While Mylene and I are now in a different city, it is something we eagerly look forward to whenever we are in town visiting.

We could go on explaining all our traditions but, for your sake, we won't. I think St. John put it best: "But there are also many other things which Jesus did; were every one of them to be written, I suppose that the world itself could not contain the books that would be written." (John 21:25)

Forming Traditions

As you can see, our family has a strong attachment to traditions; even the suggestion of changing a tradition is known to wreak havoc. Recently, Mom suggested moving the Christmas tree to a corner in the living room instead of in front of the window and, with the backlash she received, she may as well have initiated World War III. Battle lines were drawn and protests were thrown at her from every direction. Needless to say, the tree will be remaining in front of the window next (i.e. every) year.

Our traditions weren't always practiced so sternly. In fact, they changed often as our family got older and circumstances and interests changed (we kids hit a point where making a shamrock craft just wasn't fun anymore). I remember when our family moved to Ottawa from Saskatchewan when I was five years old. For the first few years, we would always try to drive or fly back to see family for Christmas, but eventually it hit a point where it was just too expensive to go back. As a kid, it was very hard for me to let go of the many Christmas traditions with cousins, aunts, uncles, and grandparents that I was used to. It felt so boring to stay in Ottawa with 'just' our family. It didn't feel like Christmas to me. My parents worked hard to make Christmas special even though we weren't in Saskatchewan. After a couple of years, traditions were established and I no longer felt like Christmas in Ottawa wasn't Christmas. The traditions and fun that my parents worked to put into place worked, and no longer was it boring just to be with my family—it became magical.

ANDRÉ – How Traditions Are Made

Where do our traditions come from? How can we develop them in our home? As I see it, there are four means by which tradition can be established. The first is that it follows you into your new family; it's what your parents and their parents before them did. The second is the Church's liturgical calendar and civil society which both, throughout the year, provide plenty of rich moments and opportunities to build tradition around. Third, the natural life events that invite yearly remembrance and celebration. Last but not least, I think most family tradition comes about organically.

Let me explain the traditions that are passed on from generation to generation. Take a moment and think of what things your family is doing that you did as a kid growing up. I know for me growing up, my family always went home after midnight Mass on Christmas Eve and had a *Reveillon*. Happily, my family today continues to keep this party going—although I must admit that as I get older, the late nights become harder and harder. If you want to keep tradition strong in the family, sometimes you have to pay the price and make the sacrifice.

Angèle grew up on a farm in Saskatchewan. She remembers harvest time in early October when she and her mom would cook an old German family recipe for plum dumplings (yummy!). She has continued this tradition to this day and makes her awesome plum dumplings in the Fall. Yes, tradition that is passed on does not have to be food-based, but it sure brings a smile to your face and your tummy!

The Turkey Stuffing Method

As our older kids left our home to get married and start their own families, we encouraged them to take with them some of the tradition from our family as well as from the family of the in-laws. The counsel that was given by God to our first parents, " ... *a man must leave his mother and father and cling to his wife ...* " (Genesis 2:24) is a really important principle for stability in the home. The last thing us men should ever do is compare our wife's cooking to what we were used to (i.e. "That is not the way my mom made stuffing!").

Turkey stuffing is, in fact, one of those classic dishes that is passed on from one generation to the next. Since Angèle and I got married in October, Thanksgiving was the first time we got to celebrate as a couple. This gave rise to a marriage principle we call the 'Turkey Stuffing Method'. This is the way we approached forming *our* own traditions. It involves taking the best from both of our backgrounds and combining them into something new! It isn't an 'either/or' situation but, rather, a 'both/and. 'We didn't do things her parent's way or my parent's way; we did it our way. Angèle's family always had raisins in their stuffing, while my family liked ground beef in ours. So we incorporated both of these into our very own Regnier-Hoffman family stuffing—and it's even better! The 'Turkey Stuffing Method' of bringing the best of both worlds will help you develop a new tradition that both your mothers will be proud of. This is important. To do this, you have to be open to talking about what is important to your family. Then you have to be creative in how to integrate the two traditions.

ELIZABETH – Living the 'Turkey Stuffing Method'

Coming into the Regnier family around holidays was both fun and intimidating. My large Catholic family has our own traditions which are very different from the Regniers.

I remember one Easter when Jo and I were first starting to be friends. I invited him to come to one of our public Easter celebrations and I completely expected him to say yes. He awkwardly avoided giving me a response and went home with his family. I later understood that he said no because he didn't want to leave his family and their fun traditions that he was accustomed to. A few years later when we started dating, similar situations would happen on both ends. I would invite Jo to visit my family and he would say no, and when he would invite me to join in his family traditions, I would also refuse. Within the first six months of dating, I remember thinking, will this relationship work? We can't seem to let go of our own family and traditions to experience the other's, so how will we ever marry? That's when we had to have the compromise talk.

That talk happened multiple times over the next few years, stretching both Jo and I to let go when it was hard and be open when it was necessary. As an engaged couple, we had to discuss compromise regularly, particularly when planning for our future home and family. When bringing traditions into a family, compromise is important! The two become one in marriage, tying their families, experiences, and traditions together. Both people come from families with traditions or ways of doing things that should be honoured and replicated in their own families, if desired.

André and Angèle encouraged us during this time to learn to make sacrifices and compromise. This was something they struggled with themselves, particularly André who was from a family with a very strong focus on traditions (sound familiar?). Thus, we adopted their 'turkey stuffing method' of compromise.

While planning our wedding registry, Jo and I decided that we would ask for Christmas ornaments and so we had to make a decision about what theme we wanted for our Christmas decorations. This question was a vital one. It could make or break the new relationship we were entering. Seriously. Knowing that we both loved how our own mothers decorated for this special season, the question was: how could we compromise to make our own decorations perfect for our new family, without feeling like the other family's ways were preferred?

We sat down and discussed exactly what things we liked and didn't like about our childhood Christmas decorations. My family's colour theme is red and gold. Our Christmas tree is packed with ornaments that range in age from my great-grandmother's heirlooms, to ornaments handmade by us children. Amidst these are pops of gold and red in the form of poinsettia and golden icicles, and a gold and white angel finishes the touch at the top of the tree. Our Christmas tree lights are multi-coloured and they flash to the beat of the music box attached to them.

Jo's family decorates in gold, silver, and white to match their living room. Their tree has white lights – many white lights that create a soft, warm glow in the room. At the top of their tree sits an ornate golden star.

Both of our families have beautiful Christmas decorations, so how could we possibly decide? Well, as we sat and spoke about it, we decided that we wanted the white lights and star from the Regnier's traditional decoration, with the red and gold theme of the Doucette's traditional decoration. It was exciting to come to a conclusion that was ours, but had influence from both of our families! We believe that this way is the right way to do the Christmas decorations, since it is the Jo and Lizzy way.

ANDRÉ - How Traditions are Kept

While many traditions are passed on by family, by the Church or civil society, there are some traditions that simply develop organically. Here are a few tips on how to decide what is a good organic tradition to keep.

The first tip is obvious: go with what captures the attention of the family. One year, when we were decorating the tree, Caleb came down the stairs looking like he just walked out of a classic Christmas movie with a turtleneck sweater, a scarf swooped around his neck, and a Santa hat on his head—blasting Bing Crosby Christmas classics. Jo scrambled through our toques (that's Canadian for a knitted winter hat) to join the scene, which made for more laughs. The next year they both remembered how funny they were the year before, and so they did it again, but even better. Every year since then, our family looks forward to seeing what the boys will come up with for their 'cheesy classic Christmas look'. Establishing a tradition does not need to have any real or serious significance other than that it brings the family together in laughter and joy.

Second tip. Encourage the tradition to be developed. Anticipate it and prepare for it to be repeated again. For example, Angèle dug out the Santa hats, and the classic scarves and put them on the counter, knowing it would spark the boys to do their thing.

Third tip. Let it grow and let it fade as needed. We never hesitated to one-up our traditions year after year. We took satisfaction in upgrading and improving our favourite ideas. On the other hand, never be afraid to let a tradition go away as quickly as it came in, when the right time comes. How do you know it is time to let go? In most cases, the age of your kids will determine that. The way you celebrate needs to be purposely adjusted to the ages of your children. And should you drop (or upgrade) a tradition and they make a big stink about missing it, then you know they really love it and you can bring it back next time. The principle is to develop and change the way you do things, but at least continue to do something.

Traditions or celebrations do not have to be the most creative or elaborate, just meaningful for the family. And it is not about finding new things to do every month; then kids get bored! Our traditions and memories together were rarely expensive or elaborate. They were simple, but we knew our parents sincerely enjoyed creating an atmosphere where special fun happened in our home. We didn't need to go out and do something exciting in order to enjoy ourselves—home was where it was at! Simplicity in family life allows families to have more valuable quality time and decreases a sense of entitlement amongst children. This fosters a culture of contentment and gratitude that will influence the way they approach their lives and their faith.

Traditions need a balance of continuity and being open to new and improved ways of doing things that suit family life at the time. We do add to our traditions often, trying out different recipes or activities, and sometimes these ideas stick with us as if we had been doing it since the dawn of time but other times they are discarded and mocked for years to come. Now, your family may not become this analytical about your traditions, and that's okay. What we want to emphasize, though, is that traditions and the way that families celebrate together *is* important.

Traditions in the Church

ALANA

If we look to the Church, we see that she is the ultimate example of following traditions in family life. After all, the family is the **domestic** Church. Following the rhythms and cycles of the year along with the Church is a wonderful way to live out our calling as families to be the domestic Church. While it may be shocking, *the Church is even more devoted to tradition than the Regnier family is!* Every year, the Church feasts, fasts, and worships in the most predictable way possible! This repetitive life of tradition makes Catholics feel at home and a part of something. The yearly liturgical season brings us through a process of encountering Christ. As families, this is a perfect opportunity to follow the Church's lead and to fully embrace and engage with these occasions. Spending an Easter at the Regniers, you would quickly sense that the death and Resurrection of Christ was undeniably important. You can see the family answered the Church's call to engage fully in the season of Lent and Holy Week. I saw the fruit of living out the traditions of the Church deeply and how it gave the family the opportunity and context to talk about spiritual things at every age. It is as if the Church is providing a yearly roadmap for people to walk through their spiritual life with their families. If the Church so faithfully follows tradition, it must be something that we should pay attention to and follow in our own lives.

The familial security that traditions can bring about reflects the security that is perfected in a relationship with God. The sense of togetherness and belonging that family traditions create can foster the same sense towards the Church and its traditions. While on a mission trip to Poland with the Regniers in 2016, we had the opportunity to go to Mass in another culture and a completely different language. Even though we did not understand what was being said, we knew what was happening and we still felt connected and engaged in the Mass. That is the power of tradition. It creates a deep connection that surpasses time, language, and situation. The family of faith is brought together in Christ through traditions. Sacraments, feast days, and liturgical seasons all serve to mark milestones, rights of passage, and commemorations of important events. Tradition is integral to our faith and family life, and is essential to our lived relationship with Jesus Christ.

Conclusion

The togetherness tradition engenders, allows for trust and relationships to grow in the family, which has a positive effect on the overall atmosphere of the home life. This in turn fosters spiritual openness.

Christian parents everywhere desperately try to reach their children, to get them to live out the faith. While it is not always the case, many times there may have been a poorly established 'accompaniment relationship.' By that I mean the process of intentionally accompanying children on their walk with and towards Jesus. Remember that you are walking along the road to Emmaus with your children, gently and intentionally modelling a life of faith and helping them to grow at their level. You are co-operating with the Holy Spirit as your children move towards embracing Christ fully. I say 'move' intentionally—move versus being brought, or dragged. This creates the circumstances for the children to choose to follow Jesus. This modelling of parenting is heard in the words of St. Paul, "Be imitators of me, as I am of Christ." (1 Corinthians 11:1)

In our experience, family relationships are nurtured and strengthened through traditions. Traditions not only create positive associations with members of the family but, since many traditions are connected with the faith, it also creates positive associations with Christ and his Church. Here are some things to remember as we close this chapter:

- Traditions grow the kind of trust in a relationship where a child will want to follow your guidance because they feel comfortable, safe, and secure. This trust and receptivity is foundational for you to evangelize your children.

- When forming traditions, look to (1) what your family did when you were young, (2) the liturgical and civic calendars, (3) natural events that come up in family life that deserve regular celebration, and (4) whatever comes up organically.

- Remember the 'Turkey Stuffing Method' and compromise when needed. Besides, it makes for a good story every year as you're celebrating your tradition!

- When keeping traditions year after year, choose ones that capture the whole family and know that they do not have to be super elaborate to be a good tradition.

Our parents poured creativity and energy into our family traditions as children, and that built strong bonds of love and trust. This fostered a freedom in our young hearts to receive how they were forming and leading us—which was to become a disciple of Christ.

Reflection / Action Points

1. When you were younger, did you have traditions that positively affected your family life? Have you brought those traditions into your own family?

2. What traditions do you have for Christmas, Easter, birthdays, etc.? Do you have specific ones that particularly help you celebrate Christ's life, death, and Resurrection—bringing your family into the daily life of the Church? If not, are there traditions that you are attracted to and can start this year?

3. Are there traditions that you and your spouse can compromise on? Are both of your families represented in your current family?

CHAPTER 7

Spiritual Life

Each Member of the Family Growing in Holiness for Life

MYLÈNE

"Will my kids still have faith?" This is the question every Catholic parent asks themselves, and it is why we have written this book. After all, the most important thing that we can ever hope to pass on to our children is a living faith in God. Not only will this bring peace and meaning to their lives, but it promises them the eternal hope of heaven. As parents, we get to participate in the work of God's creation and so much more! God entrusts us with the task of nurturing, guiding and forming his little creation to become the person he intended. What an honour! We must not take this entrustment lightly. How can we dare match with our human efforts the weight of this privilege and responsibility? How does one even start?

St. John Paul II has a sweet, simple perspective for us as we brave the frontier of parenting life-long disciples : "What really matters in life is that we are loved by Christ and that we love him in return. In comparison to the love of Jesus, everything else is secondary. And, without the love of Jesus, everything is useless."[36] This was the starting point for my parents in introducing the spiritual life to us. Their priority was that we would know and understand that Jesus loves us, and that true life would be found when we love him in return. Everything they taught and showed us about the Catholic faith was to serve the ultimate goal of us being loved by Jesus and loving Jesus in return. They knew this deep rootedness in Christ's love would naturally move us to want others to be loved by him too.

---
36. Pope John Paul II, *Address of His Holiness John Paul II During His Visit to the Tomb of St John Neumann, St Peter's Church*, Philadelphia, 4 October 1979.

ANGÈLE – Our Approach to Prayer and Piety in the Home

When it comes to raising children who are missionary disciples, you are correct in assuming that our family's spiritual life—our way of living out piety, prayer, and devotional practices—plays a major role in that development. What is our life of faith like in the home? I would describe it as rich, real, and sincere. We live an authentic spirituality where we, as the parents, are striving to grow in holiness and mission. André and I take our own spiritual growth very seriously, the hallmark of which is our daily one hour of personal prayer and Scripture reading. We do spiritual reading, listen to worship music, and we are often in spiritual conversations with visitors in our home. Our faith is woven into everything we do, it seems.

But on the other hand, we are pretty normal. We are a crazy, loud, messy family. We play keep-up together[37], watch movies, eat chips, and bicker about who is supposed to empty the dishwasher. Our spiritual life isn't really removed from the everyday. Everything just sort of blends together, so it's a bit challenging to distinguish what our spiritual life is like in our home because it's pretty integrated and natural. As you hear us try to explain it, you might be surprised that it isn't heavily reliant on practices of piety. Many good Catholic families are much more prayerful than we are, so be sure to find more models of family life than ours as you find your own way.

What is the point of it all? Typically the measure of being a successful Catholic parent these days is if our kids will keep going to Mass once they've grown up. For us, we wanted more; the point of living our vocation as Catholic parents is to raise children who will be lifelong disciples of Jesus Christ. We want to raise our children to know they are loved by God. We want to prepare our children to be ready to give God their 'yes' when they are at an age of reason to make an adult decision. All the spiritual practices of our family have this as the aim for each of our children's lives.

When André and I were deciding how we would live our spirituality in the home, we came to some particular approaches and, I have to admit, they are largely reactionary to my own issues growing up. The deal with me is that I have many bad attitudes and reactions. I was such a drama queen growing up. Now take that kind of a kid and give her a mother who is really into spiritual stuff, a mom who loves to pray for long periods of time, watch Christian TV programs, read spiritual books, and go to prayer meetings and church events. Although my mom loved something very good (*ahem* God), as a child I didn't perceive it as a good. I perceived it as a threat. My drama queen interpretation of it all was that

---

37. You know, that game where you stand in a circle and try to keep the soccer ball up in the air.

she enjoyed God stuff more than she enjoyed me. Well, based on how bitter I was about it all, she probably did enjoy those things more than hanging out with a pouting pre-teen. I'm not sure that my mom did anything wrong in how she lived her spirituality with me, but I can tell you that it left an impression on me of how I wanted to live out my spirituality with my own kids.

One of the impressions my 'inner child' had about my mom was that she was always praying, that she was not accessible to me when she was praying, and that she would prefer to pray than be with me. (I know—my thinking was so messed up.) To make sure we don't inadvertently perpetuate the same message to our kids, we make it a point to be present and available to our kids even when praying—never to give off a vibe that we are too busy for them. Before the kids were in school, my preference was actually to pray before the kids were awake or while they were watching a cartoon. Since I didn't like interruptions, this was how I approached it. André on the other hand, as a multi-tasking extrovert, has no problems with interruptions. He is comfortable praying with the kids around, and being open to conversation with them or getting up to help them. Either way, the message we want to send our kids is that we love God and we pray—*and* I am your parent and you are my priority.

In other words, we are intentional that our children perceive we are putting their needs ahead of our own spiritual preferences. Of course we would prefer to sit for an hour or more at a convenient time of the day with a coffee and croissant and enjoy a prolonged time of fulfilling prayer, but the duty of the moment is to take care and be accessible to our children at that 'convenient time of the day.'

Another way we put the needs of the child ahead of our own spiritual preferences related to our involvements, especially in the church community. What I mean is, I might very well prefer to be in several ministries and out at events and retreats on many evenings and weekends, but that wouldn't necessarily be the best for the children and their stability and routine. Many times I sacrificed and put the needs of the kids first. I don't regret it one bit. I believe that the investment in the children—giving them my full attention and establishing proper routines for them along with their sense of trust and security—paid dividends. As the kids have gotten older, I have had more freedom for evening and weekend involvements.

A few times, we packed up the kids and brought them along to church events (which were catered towards adults, not families). The kids spent their time running around and having fun while the event was going on. But, honestly, we weren't watching the kids and it went past their naptime or bedtimes. Don't get me wrong—the kids loved it. But we paid for it afterwards with trying to settle down our hyped-up kids for a late bedtime. Plus, I suspect people were annoyed with their running around (and all the things they did when I wasn't looking). In the end, we opted to always consider the kids' needs first, so André and I would decide which of us (if at all) would go to an event and which of us would stay home to keep the kids in their routine. Now if you know us, you would probably laugh because we aren't as regimented as this might come across. We are a pretty flexible family and we do go out with our kids on crazy adventures (like mission trips) but even then we are careful about keeping the kids in stable routines—especially for their sleeping patterns (because sleep makes everything much easier to deal with all around. Am I right?).

There is an element of sacrifice here. In complete freedom and self-gift, we put the needs of the children before our preferences. They never sensed that we preferred to be doing something else, because ultimately we were preferring them. We chose to orient our lives to the good of the family over a personal spiritual good.

Alongside church events, we also discern our very good and holy ministry opportunities outside of the home. How much is too much? Is it going to take a toll on our kids' well-being? How can we make it a win-win? We also have to ask ourselves if we are hiding behind our family as an excuse not to give to the community. Are we being generous enough to the wider community? Whether we are too involved to the detriment of our children or avoiding involvement to the detriment of the call to mission, it is important we are honest with ourselves and the Lord and keep our call to be missionary and parents in the forefront of every discernment.

Another way we put the needs of the child ahead of our own is how we approached spiritual practices with the children as a family. Our approach is *meeting them where they are at*. Again, the principle is not doing what I prefer, but what is best for the child. So it looks something like this. I might really desire to do all 20 decades of the rosary every night as a family at home, because I enjoy the rosary and see it as a good, pious thing to do as a family, but can the kids have that capacity to stay engaged in it? Probably not, right?

So what we did (when the kids were little), was to take into account the number of children, their ages, personalities, the time of day, whether they were sick or not—there were so many factors to consider. Weighing all these things and being willing to surrender our preferences, we would often just pick a better time, or keep it to simply one decade. Oftentimes, in order to meet the kids where they were at, we chose to do something that was more suitable for our situation, such as reading a Bible story and having them act it out, or André and I praying a rosary aloud as they were falling asleep listening to our voices. Honestly, night prayer as a family rarely happened.

Surely this approach comes across as 'not very pious'—especially for a dedicated missionary family. I get it. But that's not what we were aiming for; we were merely trying to be age-appropriate in the expression of piety. We wanted our children to feel comfortable and respected in our family spiritual practices so that they could learn to pray and love God in engaging ways. Remember that the win is to prepare our children to have a personal relationship with Jesus and become life-long missionary disciples. When our children were younger, our role was to find what would meet their spiritual needs and actively till the soil in their little souls to be open and docile to the Holy Spirit. As they grew older, I knew that all the adult devotions and practices I really enjoy would also be waiting for them to enjoy and discover.

When we consider the model of discipleship we use in CCO and apply it to parenting, we remember that we are companions, leading and guiding the kids on their own path to Jesus. As parents, we could say that we are expert mountaineering guides—leading these children on easy and sure paths that their little feet can handle and in ways that do not discourage them from the journey. The experiences on the mountain with their mom and dad should inspire them to want to hike on the mountain themselves and, someday, be a great mountaineer guide too.

As a result, you will see in this chapter that our spiritual practices as a family are very simple and manageable. They are engaging, not intimidating. They are age-appropriate and they are interesting. In doing them, the child is coming to know that God is personal, real, powerful, and loving. What you are about to read in this chapter is an attempt to describe a mood, a disposition, an approach. It is not so much about concrete actions but about modelling and fostering a positive, personal faith life so kids can see it, aspire to it and take their own steps into it. These little mountaineers aren't expected to carry the same size of backpack on the journey that their dad is. He's wearing a heavy-duty framed MEC backpack. Kids should just be wearing some kind of Disney kiddie backpack, big enough for a small water bottle, granola bars, and room to collect treasures along the way.

So what kind of spiritual practices did we fill their kiddie backpacks with? Here are some practical points about how we approached Catholic practices:

Rosary/Chaplet:

So based on what I already said, it's not like we *don't* do rosaries. I write all of this a bit sheepishly; I'm sure it's shocking to hear that full-time missionaries don't pray *daily* rosaries with their kids. We're exposed. We're so busted right now. But to answer truthfully the question asked of us, "How did you guys raise faithful kids?" we have to admit that it wasn't through evening family rosaries. The family rosary did happen certain years for us during Lent. We would light some candles to make it pretty and sometimes do only a decade—because longer than that would have caused behavioural meltdowns (from me, frustrated with kids messing around and not focusing). And the rosary is always prayed on road trips, but even here little children were encouraged and not forced or expected to join André and me as we prayed aloud. I often casually ask, "Who would like to lead this decade?" and see what happens.

Mass:

You first need to know that I'm not above bribing to get kids to Mass. In fact, I recommend it. This can apply to Sunday Mass or daily Mass. Now, there are certain children and ages when Sunday Mass is a fight. They will create quite a fuss about it all, but it is extremely important that you never ever give in and not go to Mass! This is non-negotiable. Never ever flinch as they will sense that there is a chance that they won't have to go. We always spoke very matter-of-factly about it. "We're going to the 9:45am Mass tomorrow." It was never said as a question. When complaining happened we would say, "Oh, we are all going to Mass. That is happening. And then after Mass we are going to McDonald's (or Denny's ...or wherever) for brunch. But if you're not well behaved at Mass or don't get ready on time, we aren't going out to eat. But we **are** going to Mass in 30 minutes. You decide how this plays out." This sort of approach was common when the kids were in Grades 1, 2, 3, 4 etc. By the time we got to the higher grades, going to Mass was so normal that fights didn't really happen. We have always had, even if we ate at home, a really fun brunch to motivate them (can you say "hashbrown patties with mountains of ketchup"?).

There was also the added benefit of our parish community, where the kids had friends awaiting them, children's liturgy, cookies and juice in the hall, and possibly social plans made spontaneously with other parents standing around after Mass to go for a hike or something. By sticking as much as possible to one Mass time, we more easily formed our community of faith. Mass wasn't so bad when you were a kid in our world. The kids enjoyed seeing our priests over the years and that was an advantage too. Growing up in the habit of keeping Sunday morning to honour the Lord has been a great life-lesson of faith for our kids.

When it came to daily Mass attendance with the kids, I really didn't push it. After all, this is not an issue of serious obligation to the observance of the Lord's day. (Again, for me, I didn't push it out of my perspective of not burdening my children with the many desired spiritual practices or events I would personally love to be doing.) Maybe I was overly sensitive to this, but I approached it with a concern for where the kids were at. Going to Mass with babies is generally a breeze compared to bringing toddlers or multiple little folks. If we did go to Mass, I wanted to make it an extra positive experience, so I would use fun bribes. There was one year when I only had Caleb at home, before Natalie was born. I was able to convince him to come with me to daily Mass once a week by bribing him with a trip to Tim Horton's (an iconic Canadian coffee shop) for a 'small decaf double-double' which he would order for himself. Basically, it's an eight-ounce coffee with no caffeine, two spoons of sugar and two portions of cream. What's not to love?! Of course, no Canadian coffee at Tim's is complete without a doughnut with sprinkles on top, eh? Let's just say Caleb didn't complain about going to Mass on a Wednesday. It was a "date" and it was just the right balance for his developing spiritual muscle (although perhaps a detriment to his physical muscle, ha!).

Regnier Family Practices:

Did we do any strong Catholic spiritual family practices then? It seems like I am explaining away practices more than shedding light on them.

Well, I guess what we did accomplish in forming our family's spirituality was:

- We strove to observe the Lord's day well. It was a non-negotiable priority and important part of our family life. We worshipped God in our community, we had a family day, and we did our best to refrain from shopping and work.

- We lived a strong parish community life. Our kids felt at home in our parish and with our parishioners.

- Our children were familiar and comfortable with the rosary and chaplet, even though we didn't do them daily.

- We went, as a family, to the Sacrament of Reconciliation at least twice a year, usually followed by a trip to, yes, Tim Horton's for doughnuts.

- The stories of the Saints and angels came up in timely moments as they applied to family conversations and experiences or on their particular feast day. Often they were spoken of in a true and familial way—as real and present friends in heaven.

- Our children appreciated the liturgical seasons of the Church as we celebrated our family traditions.

Through it all, we focused on leading our kids into personal encounters with God (Father, Son, and Holy Spirit) *in age-appropriate ways*. They were encouraged to pray in very comfortable and conversational ways, and to live and make choices in a way that honoured God who should be at the centre of their lives.

A Note to Parents on Your Prayer Lives

ANDRÉ – To the Dads

I would like to take just a few moments to speak directly to all the men and fathers who are reading this book. You may feel that your faith is not strong enough, or that your wife is better at talking about this 'spiritual stuff'. Your sentiment is that you will support what she is doing 100 percent, but at the end of the day, passing on the faith is her domain. But I want to encourage you, no—*challenge* you to embrace your role as the spiritual head of your family. Don't pass off your responsibility and just hope for the best. It is not about perfection; it is a process of growth, understanding, and effectiveness.

One of the most powerful images I had of my own father growing up was seeing him in his room on his knees in prayer. I once heard a man describe how, as a child, he knew God must be all powerful because his dad, who was all powerful in his mind, was willing to bow before God.

It's no mystery that the faith, or lack thereof, of fathers is a key indicator in whether children stay in the faith or not. Your role is not only to make sure they get to Mass on time or remind them to pray. You need to live out your faith in a personal and intentional way if you want to raise kids to become missionary disciples.

You cannot give what you do not have. So that means you need to take time daily for prayer. You need to be living your life for Christ, constantly seeking to go deeper in your relationship with him. You need to be living a sacramental life. You need to take your faith seriously. Then you can teach your kids to pray well. Only then can you speak to them of the truth of God and his Church. Then you can teach them how to deal with the world that is hostile towards faith. As a father, your faith has to be visible in your daily family life. I encourage you to initiate a conversation with your wife, and when appropriate, with your kids about the spiritual life in the home and the direction the family should take to grow as missionary disciples.

ANGÈLE – How do Moms Find Time for Prayer?

André addressed the dads, and I would like to speak a bit to those young moms out there who are struggling to know how to pray.

I first want to prepare you and encourage you to be free to adapt to your changing schedule and seasons depending on your littles. This may mean that prayer is a ten-minute conversation with the Lord while nursing a child. It might also mean praying half an hour before they wake up. It could mean making prayer your first priority when the kids are down for their nap. It might mean doing a fifteen-minute prayerful reflection on your day and your actions and God's presence when you crawl into bed. (This is the Ignatian *Consciousness Examen*. See more about it in section 5 of the bonus features.) It might mean listening to a meditation on a podcast while driving or making a meal. You can think of this prayer time as healthy "me time" in a certain way. It is personal, inspiring, and self-reflective. The kind of prayer you desire is to hear a truth from the Lord, especially in the Scriptures. You can seek the Lord's presence in what has transpired in the day, and to reflect on your own life. What were the graces that led you to success and repentance? After reflecting, resolve to rely on the Holy Spirit to help you improve in areas of weakness and sin. Journaling, if possible, is a great catharsis and outlet for moms (and everyone).

Prayer

Looking back, I am very appreciative of the way my parents approached prayer with us. Prayer is a common part of the Catholic family experience, everything from grace before meals, to night prayer, to a family rosary on roadtrips. It enters into the regular flow of life both naturally and with intention. My parents were careful to introduce prayer in a way that met us where we were at, and this looked different throughout the many seasons of family life. What was important throughout it all was that faith was witnessed to us in an authentic manner and prayer was suggested in a loving, rather than overly strict, way. Elizabeth will share how this also benefited her faith life.

ELIZABETH

I would not be who I am without my family and I definitely would not have the faith that I have without my parents. I would argue that the most effective way my parents inspired us to take our faith seriously, was showing us their own faith. Mom and Dad's faith was attractive. They *loved* Jesus and, even though they weren't perfect, their faith was authentic and I knew that. They were living their faith normally, not hiding us from it, but also not forcing it on us. Their faith, and in particular the example of my mother, is actually what led me to accept my own faith personally.

As a child, I loved my faith and I loved Jesus. Because of this, I was full of joy and freedom. I really believed I was a princess; I loved to get all dressed up and twirl around. I was confident in who I was because of the love of my family and God.

However, when I got to Grade 7 and started to grow up, things began to change. I became very aware of what other people thought about me. I cared so much about being liked that I would do anything to win their approval. One day my friends made it very clear that they were atheists—that they no longer believed in God. I was shocked, but was afraid to be made fun of—and I honestly wondered if they were right, so I went along with them and chose to reject God. I came home and announced it to my parents, saying that I would still go to Mass but I didn't really care anymore. I started to change, trying desperately to be like my friends at school and ultimately hoping that this would make me happy. The joy, freedom, and love I grew up with quickly began to vanish.

I remember coming home from school one day and finding a letter from my mom on my bed. In it, she told me how much she loved me and how much God loved me. She spoke about her personal relationship with Jesus and about how much he desired to be my friend. This letter deeply impacted me. I realized that I wasn't happy and felt a deep emptiness inside me. I knew something was missing from my life but I longed to be fulfilled! It was like there was a God-shaped hole in my heart. I knew that Jesus was calling out to me and inviting me to allow him to fill the emptiness that I was experiencing. I wanted that joy, freedom, and love I once had, and I knew that I could have that, again, with Jesus. So I chose to place Jesus at the centre of my life, to live for him.

That decision completely reorientated my life. I started to pray regularly and seek God in everything. He gave me more joy than I thought possible, and I wanted all my decisions to reflect the new relationship I had.

So I am grateful for the faith of my parents. Along with their personal witness and teachings, they definitely employed other resources to help us grow in our faith, such as the rosary. We would go through phases of being very committed to it and phases when we weren't. As we got older, I went through times of enjoying the rosary and times when I couldn't wait to get through it to do something else.

One memory that my siblings and I regularly laugh about is an example of what not to do during the family rosary. We had a babysitter who really wanted us to pray the rosary with her. My two youngest siblings started giggling about something and, as children often do, they couldn't stop laughing. Our babysitter was frustrated and so she made the two kids kneel in front of the statue of Our Lady and finish their rosary looking into the eyes of Mary so that they would feel remorse for their distraction. It was a little ridiculous, but like I said: an example of what not to do!

We also laugh when we remember how we would often grab at opportunities to skip the rosary. On rare occasions, Dad would doze off to sleep during the rosary. The funny thing was that, if Mom wasn't there, the next action was for all of us kids to tip-toe out of the room to go play.

Although my parents really desired to make the family rosary a habit, sometimes they would only do a decade with us, or a shorter prayer time that didn't include the rosary. When we prayed through praise and worship music, there were no complaints; that was always a winner with our musical hearts! Overall, I see the benefit of age-appropriate introductions to prayer that my parents used. They were such a huge part of my openness to Jesus as a girl.

Prayer with children won't look perfect. There *will* be distractions, giggles, and rolled eyes. Its guaranteed. It's comforting to know that our God welcomes his little ones to him, fully knowing their nature and embracing it.

It was a delicate balance to both meet us where we were at and to challenge us to something greater. This approach will look different for every family. It is something worth discerning carefully. My mom already explained their unique approach and how rote prayers were existent in our family life, but they were not the sole focus. We were taught that prayer was more than *just* intercession. It also involved a personal exchange with God. My dad, especially, saw that personal prayer times were a component of the spiritual life to foster.

ANDRÉ – Teaching Children How to Pray

Over the last 30 years, we have been involved with building up young leaders in the Church who are committed to bringing about the renewal of the world. A lot of work has gone into equipping people with the skills, knowledge, and attitudes that are required for this great task. These young leaders, moved by the Holy Spirit, are like sponges taking in any information they can to help them prepare to become effective missionary disciples. But in order to see fruit, it is essential that we first teach and encourage them to have a personal prayer life, that is, time set aside daily where they speak to and hear from God.

As practising Catholics, there is typically a familiarity with communal prayer such as Mass, Eucharistic Adoration, the rosary etc. The real struggle hits when it comes to finding consistent time for personal daily prayer. From my observations over the years, what seems to distinguish the "practising Catholics" from the missionary disciples is that the latter has an established and consistent daily prayer life. This is one of the great struggles of the Christian life—the ability to spend time with God on our own each day, but with it comes a fruitful and joyful relationship with the Lord. It provides the intimacy of knowing Jesus in a real way, as someone living and present in your life.

Being acutely aware of this struggle, Angèle and I looked for opportunities to develop this discipleship in our children's lives. We desired for them to have their own personal prayer lives. We were confident that the devotions and practices of the faith would take root best in the fertile soil of an intimate prayer life.

At a very young age, our kids saw us praying each morning. My prayer time as a father was not my private time where no one could bother me. It was the opposite. I can remember Jo when he was around four years old, sitting on the stairs, wearing his pyjamas, and eating his toast while watching me praise God aloud. I was aware how powerful a visual that was for him. Prayer was not a mystery for him. Rather it was ordinary and it was daily. One time, I called him down to come and sit on my knee and he sat there quietly as I began to read the Gospel and meditate on what God was saying to me. He was learning the place of Scripture in prayer. He absorbed silence and reflection. It was all there for him to take in.

As they grew up, we encouraged our children to have their own prayer times and we recommended that they do it in the morning. Whenever they were facing a decision, we suggested that they go upstairs in their room to read Scripture and listen to what the Lord was saying in Scripture.

I would love to say that my three oldest children took up the challenge and that all through high school they got up early and prayed. Alas, this was not the case. Yet, we continued to encourage them and model to them the importance of personal prayer. We would let them know how God had spoken to us and answered us in prayer. Although they faltered establishing a habit of prayer, we were still confident that, as they matured and had deeper encounters with God, they would find their way to consistency.

Through God's grace and the encouragement and modelling of many people, our three oldest kids became, and continue to be, committed to having at least one hour of prayer time in the morning each day. This was fostered by their peers when they were members of NET Canada or on campus with CCO. We are now able to have open conversations about our prayer lives with our kids; what a blessing!

With that said, as we look back, we realized that we encouraged and modelled prayer to our older children, but we did not actually teach them *how* to pray. Though they now have prayer lives, it would have been a benefit to them to know *how* to pray even while in high school. Realizing this, Angèle and I decided that, with our two youngest, we would teach them how to pray so they would have the tools and the knowledge.

Lent is such a great time for starting good spiritual resolutions. It provides 40 days to do what we can to prepare our hearts to celebrate the passion and victory of Christ at Easter. One year, along with all the other sacrifices, I decided to use each week of Lent as an opportunity to teach our young girls how to pray. Natalie and Janna were 13 and 10 years old at the time.

The first week, I focused on how to worship. Starting on the day after Ash Wednesday, I gathered them for ten minutes in the morning before school. Personal prayer is ideally done in the mornings, so I wanted to form this habit early. I asked them to bring their Bibles downstairs where a fun breakfast was ready for them. (I had learned a few things since the days of the smoothie-incentive-Lenten-prayer-time fails with the older kids.) We sat down and I began explaining in simple terms why we start prayer with worship. Worshipping God helps put our hearts and our thoughts in the right place. To help them understand, I asked them where their thoughts went when I said, "God is good and all-powerful." Janna responded first, "I feel safe knowing he is good." After a little bit more of self-reflection, Natalie followed up by describing God as "strong and almighty." Then I asked another question, "What does it mean to feel safe around God?" They were quick to share what it means—that he cares about them and all of their problems. I invited them to continue to reflect on that in silence. For a couple of minutes, they closed their eyes and reflected on this profound truth.

The next day we continued the exercise with new descriptions of God. While I wanted them to understand worship, I also wanted to expand their vocabulary when it came to describing God's attributes. I had them reflect a little longer on the words of worship they were bringing up. I could see that it was not having a profound impact on them but I knew they were learning. My perspective was for the long game. I wanted to teach them how to pray, so that in the future they would be able to hear and encounter God in prayer.

The day after, to help inspire and guide their time of worship, I brought out the Psalms, using the psalm of the day. I asked them to read the first few lines and identify what they learned from the psalm about God and his relationship with us. For example, the first line of Psalm 18 says, "I love you Lord, my strength." Janna chimed in, "God makes us strong!" We then spent a few minutes reflecting on that truth.

In the second week, I introduced repentance, which I see as the natural overflow of worship. The more we see the greatness of God, the more we realize our weaknesses and failures. I wanted them to understand repentance as more than just a time of confessing all of their sins (although that is part of it). I taught them to look also at attitudes or struggles they may have in their relationship with God. I described how, when meditating on God's love for us, we might realize that we do not love him the way we should. This is an opportunity to repent and communicate to God our need for mercy and help. I shared with them how I often speak to God of how I am so easily distracted in my prayer and that I need his help. After all, repentance is simply us expressing our need for God's help and mercy because of our weaknesses and failures. I asked them to try and make this the most honest part of their prayer.

In the third week, I taught them to meditate on the Gospel of the day with a simple form of Lectio Divina. Prayer started with a short time of worship and acknowledgment of our weaknesses which then led to reading the Gospel of the day. They would take some time of reflection after the reading to identify what stood out to them. What was the Holy Spirit trying to teach them? I wanted them to know that the Bible is more than just a book. Rather, in the Scriptures, God is actually speaking to us and our job is to learn how to hear what he is saying. We can approach the Scriptures confident that God will always speak to us through them. I followed this up by encouraging them to start a prayer journal—to write down what they hear God saying and then reflect on integrating that into their lives.

The last week, they learned how to intercede for others and for the needs in their own lives. This week was quite easy to understand. I wanted them not only to ask but to have confidence that God hears and answers their prayer. This confidence is based on what they have come to realize in their worship and in the Gospels.

NATALIE – Personal Prayer

I always knew I wanted to have a prayer life because, every morning when I woke up, I would see Mom and Dad praying. I loved this. I especially liked coming down the stairs and seeing Dad praying in the living room when I was getting ready for school. God is first in my dad's life and I thought it was pretty cool that he prayed for a long time. I also liked that if ever I needed my dad while praying, he helped me right away. He never told me to stop interrupting his prayer, but would pause prayer time to help me with whatever I needed. He would even stop and ask me if I needed anything if he noticed me walk by.

I didn't have an actual daily prayer life until I was in Grade 9. The summer before, I went to Steubenville Youth Conference and fell in love with Jesus. I wanted to maintain a friendship with him and knew I needed to pray. It was hard since my school starts early and I had to wake up at 5:45am, but I did it because I saw that it was important. I experimented with what Dad taught me and tried different methods but also learned that I don't really need to follow a strict order or way. It's like talking with a friend, and if you're friends with someone you don't really need to care about how you're talking with them—just talk normally. So I developed my prayer life over time. There were definitely rough times where I felt bored, but then there were times where I felt more in love, like any normal relationship.

Tilling the Soil

Christ's parable of the sower is a particularly powerful and relevant one:

> *"Now the parable is this: the seed is the word of God. The ones on the path are those who have heard; then the devil comes and takes away the word from their hearts, so that they may not believe and be saved. The ones on the rock are those who, when they hear the word, receive it with joy. But these have no root; they believe only for a while, and in time of testing fall away. As for what fell among the thorns, these are the ones who hear; but as they go on their way, they are choked by the cares and riches and pleasures of life, and their fruit does not mature. But as for that in the good soil, these are the ones who, when they hear the word hold it fast in an honest and good heart, and bear fruit with patient endurance."*
> Luke 8:11-15

One look at the people around us and we can see that the word of God that has radically transformed our own lives can have little to no effect on people who hear the same word. This is disheartening, to say the least, and it is our ultimate hope, as parents, that our children will have good soil, so that the seed of God's word will flourish in their hearts.

As parents, we have the opportunity to till our children's soil; to remove any rocks, weeds, and thorns so that their soil is primed and ready to receive the word of God without hindrance. This was a priority for my parents in the methods they chose to transmit the faith to us. They wanted to create a fertile planting ground, tilling the soil for our eventual mature commitment to him. Our parents prepared us through practical teaching as well as encouraging encounters with God.

Teaching and Formation

My parents made it a priority to teach us the matters of the faith. This was done through little conversations that came up when we asked complicated questions such as, "What is heaven like?" (To which my mom always responded that there were rainbows to slide down and clouds made out of cotton candy that we could bounce on like trampolines. I am not so sure she can source this formation to any official Church teachings....)

Even though there were a few whimsical improvisations, our parents heavily leaned on books, programs, and media to pass the Church's teachings on to us. Jo, who successfully absorbed every little piece of information about the faith they fed us (unlike the rest of us, who mostly remember Mom's catechesis of a candyland heaven), will share how these external resources nurtured his growth in the faith.

JO – Love for Scripture

If I ever wonder why I was always called the "Catholic kid" in elementary school, I just remember how whenever our teacher asked the class, "What do your parents do?" my arm would shoot up—I couldn't wait to share with the class that my parents were missionaries. In fact, in Grade 6, when it came time for the public speaking competition, I chose to give my speech on my dad and his work with CCO. My faith was something I was proud of and I was vocal about it. Mom and Dad's missionary hearts made me want to go deeper on my spiritual journey.

Another important aspect of my spiritual journey while growing up were the many Christian clubs and groups that Mom and Dad made available to us. These were fun, engaging, and memorable things we did as children that made faith tangible and relevant in our little lives. This helped us enter into our relationship with God in an age-appropriate way. Mom and Dad had us take part in Vacation Bible School camps, Christian soccer camps, Catholic kids clubs, and other similar things. As a kid, going to Church wasn't something separate from fun; it was a major part of it. This is important because now, as a CCO missionary, I see that many young people view the Heavenly Father in the same way they view the Church. If Church is perceived as boring, unrelatable, and not something you can connect with or feel joyful around, then that's *exactly* how you will feel about God. These groups gave me a positive, engaging, and life-giving view of God and his Church. This set the stage for me to be open to having God in my life when I grew up.

Another thing our parents did to nurture and till the soil of our hearts was to provide us with Catholic/Christian resources growing up. We listened to Christian music, watched VeggieTales[38], listen to Christian cassette tapes and read Christian books. I want to highlight one of my favourites: my comic book Bible.

Mom and Dad wanted us to know the Scriptures in order for us to come to know Christ in a personal way. So to reach us where we were at, they bought us a comic book Bible, which is, literally, a comic book of the WHOLE Bible from Genesis to Revelation. As soon as we got it, I ran up to my room and spent the next few weeks reading the whole thing. I was learning details about the story of Elijah or Solomon I had never heard before and was discovering Bible stories I had never known. The Bible became more than a book; it became an adventure I wanted to be part of. You might be thinking, "sure it may have been fun to read, but how accurate or detailed could a comic book really be?" Well, a week after I finished, we happened to have CCO staff over to the house and they pulled out a "Bible Trivia" game. They probably were expecting to win—after all they were full-time Catholic missionaries who lead Bible studies for a living. But lo and behold, these adults were utterly demolished by a child's knowledge of the intricate details of the Scriptures. Immediately the staff were grilling me: "How did you get so smart?" and "Where did you hide your cheat cards?" I quickly produced my humble comic book Bible, which I lent to one of the staff members because he wanted to do some Scripture study—comic book style. Suffice it to say, I have since moved on to the genuine article, but that little book set me on a journey with the Scriptures.

As Catholics, we often get a bad rap for not knowing our Bibles. As St. Jerome said, "Ignorance of Scripture is ignorance of Christ."[39] Personally, I love my Bible (I'm not talking about the comic book kind). I read it almost everyday in prayer; it's beat up, highlighted, underlined, and circled. It is a physical manifestation of my walk with Jesus. The Lord speaks clearly and powerfully to me through the Scriptures.

---

38. VeggieTales (TV series). Created by Phil Vischer & Mike Nawrocki. Big Idea Entertainment. 1993 – .

39. St Jerome. Cited in the Catechism of the Catholic Church, 133.

Along with these little encounters, there were a multitude of resources, discussions, and activities that my parents used to instruct us in the faith and help us to understand things such as the Mass, the Saints, Mary, and the virtues. These were important in giving us an intellectual foundation for grasping the Catholic faith.

As children get older, forming, teaching and equipping becomes more complex. While there are an abundance of valuable resources to equip parents on the how-to's of forming our children in the faith, Alana will discuss a simple strategic principle that CCO uses to help us know where to start in forming people in the faith.

ALANA

Just reading Angèle's description of heaven for the kids makes me laugh and feel relief to see the simplicity and child-like approach that can be taken with raising missionary disciples. Being the youngest of six kids, and not having any younger siblings to teach, I never really experienced first hand what it would be like to raise a child to love Jesus and live for him. The idea of raising children who are practising their faith is daunting enough, let alone the view to train them up as missionary disciples! If you're feeling, what I'm feeling, it's kind of overwhelming. However in spending more every-day time with the Regniers, especially since being engaged to Caleb, I have been able to have real-time experience of seeing the spiritual life of missionary disciples in the making, and it is actually quite simple—though very intentional.

From my experience in CCO on campus and with training missionaries, I am reminded of a strategic tool that we use to work with our students to become complete in holiness and mission. I wanted to give you this practical tool, as I've seen it woven clearly throughout André and Angèle's parenting technique. It makes sense of course—they founded CCO—how could they not live out those principles in their family life?

Introducing: the A.S.K. model. What is this you may ASK? Okay bad joke. A.S.K. stands for Attitudes, Skills, and Knowledge. An important distinction is that: Attitudes are *caught*, Skills are *trained*, and Knowledge is *taught*. As I am working with someone in areas of their personal holiness or missionary identity, I am asking myself—what are the necessary attitudes, skills or knowledge that I need to impart in order for them to grow in this area?

Hopefully this model can help you in terms of identifying where to begin in working with your child to grow. As an example, let's look at prayer. Many families may have trained the necessary *skills* for prayer; rote prayers, family prayer, reading Scripture or listening to worship songs, etc., or even taught the importance of prayer and how it helps us to grow in our relationship with God (knowledge). But all of the skills and knowledge of prayer without the attitude can leave our efforts falling flat. Let's face it, attitudes can be harder because we have less control over them.

Attitudes are caught, and therefore need to be modelled and fostered. Let's say you've worked with your child to develop a personal prayer life and they've been equipped in the necessary skills and knowledge, but they still aren't praying—it could likely be an attitude problem. So how can I model or foster this? I feel like this is what I have witnessed the most in the Regnier family. All the kids have testified that they *loved* seeing their parents praying in the morning as they grew up. They've caught a positive attitude towards prayer. As André showed us earlier, an attitude towards prayer can be modelled by the parent through their example and attitude while teaching the skills and knowledge. Attitudes can also be fostered through positive reinforcement such as smoothies (even if they go mouldy), fun breakfasts or other special things to encourage a positive attitude. I've noticed on regular occasions that André and Angèle share vulnerably about their personal prayer. They model the attitude we should have towards prayer.

I continually learn from André and Angèle in this way (A.S.K.) as they seize teachable moments to form us in our spiritual life—in holiness and mission. A recent example would be how they helped Caleb and I navigate where we would get married; Saskatchewan or Ottawa. It may seem minor in the grand scheme of things, but this wasn't just another 'hmm, what should our wedding colours be?' kind of decision. It meant family and friends on either end, travelling over 3,000 km to spend our day with us. That is 1864.114 miles for all you friends South of the border. It was heart-wrenching! We had to take into consideration our families and friends and the consequences for them, and ultimately the desire and vision that we had for the day that we would become united in the sacrament. We experienced André and Angèle fostering in us an attitude of abandonment, and modelling a love for Jesus that desires to give him the greatest glory. They practically equipped us with practical skills to discern and the necessary knowledge to know what good discernment looks like, all while asking us questions to help us gather more data to work through our decision. When the necessary attitudes, skills, and knowledge are imparted, a person is set up for success for growth in their spiritual life.

So I believe the A.S.K. model can be a helpful diagnostic tool for you in helping your children grow in their spiritual life. When a child doesn't want to go to Mass on Sundays, they get easily distracted during Mass, they don't want to partake in family prayer, they don't want to go to youth group, they don't want to watch spiritual movies—whatever it might be—I encourage you to ask yourself; is this an attitude that needs to be caught (modelled/ fostered), a skill to be trained, or knowledge to be taught?

Encountering God

A large emphasis my parents made was intentionally encouraging personal encounters with God. This was done by providing opportunities to encounter God, as well as by celebrating the spiritual moments that occurred organically. Janna and Caleb will describe some examples of how they did this.

JANNA

I recently received the sacrament of Confirmation. Mom and Dad spent time with me, talking about how important it is to open my heart to the Holy Spirit. I knew it was a very important sacrament where I would receive the Holy Spirit and I couldn't wait. I was also very excited to receive spiritual gifts at my Confirmation, especially *the* gift. You see, my dad has a tradition where he prays over us kids after our Confirmation to hear God say what spiritual gift he'd like to give us. Knowing this was happening soon, I asked my dad over and over what gift I would get and he just kept telling me to prepare my heart and wait.

My Confirmation day came and I was excited. I waited for something to happen. The time came where the Bishop blessed me and I received the Holy Spirit. I didn't feel anything but I knew it happened. Mylène (my godmother) made me a picture frame with four of my special saints. Then my dad invited everyone to pray over me. If anyone heard something from the Lord, they said it out loud for me to hear. It was really special and made me feel good. But Dad never told me my gift! I told him, "Dad I am waiting!!"

He started with telling me that Confirmation is about maturity, and that I am invited to go deeper in my relationship with the Lord. Dad said that he felt the Lord has given me *"the fear of the Lord"* in a special way. Huh? Am I supposed to be scared of Jesus? Knowing I was confused, he explained that it means that I have wonder and awe for God. I felt so happy! I knew it was the right gift for me. So I smiled and hugged him.

CALEB

Mom and Dad have been instrumental in showing me the reality that God is close and personal. They had the opportunity to help me form my understanding of who God is, how he sees me, and how deeply he loves me and desires to be with me. This was and always will be my view of who God is.

So how did Mom and Dad instill this in me? I believe a big part of it was seeing and seizing spiritual moments in order to reveal God's desire to show himself to me. Even when I was little, Mom and Dad would celebrate small encounters I would have with God. This helped reveal *spiritual realities*. Rather than force these ideas upon me, they would look for opportunities to point out how God had been working in my life. For example, when I was in elementary school, I decided I wanted to pray for my aunt and uncle/Godparents who smoked cigarettes. I knew they were trying to quit, and I really hoped that they would be able. I remember praying for them before going to bed. Some time later, they had successfully quit smoking and my aunt called me to thank me for praying for her, and that she knew my prayers helped them. Mom and Dad celebrated with me and explained to me how the Lord hears my prayers. They explained to me that I was using the gift of intercession, and that it is so powerful. I was in awe. I felt so seen by God; I felt like God had blessed me with power from on high. I could have died and went to heaven right then and there. But in all seriousness, I truly felt and understood the power of God! This whole experience impacted me deeply. Why would I ever want to refuse a God who is *so* close, who desires to hear my prayers? Mom and Dad could have smiled and simply said, "Aww, that's so cute that you prayed!" but instead, they took an opportunity to reveal something greater to me.

Opportunities like this happened so often. I can even remember feeling amazed at how much God loved me because of my electric toothbrush, of all things. In grade two, I had a super cool electric toothbrush that was shaped like a dolphin. I loved it and it made me so excited to brush my teeth (maybe I should get one for myself now). When the battery died, I was heartbroken (it used those small batteries that look like little dimes—they're called LR44 batteries; yes, I googled it). I didn't know where to buy them and I felt defeated. One day after Mass, I went outside of the church and was thinking about how sad I was about my toothbrush when, right beside me on a ledge, I noticed a little crucifix, the size of my thumb. Interested in this treasure, I picked it up to check it out. As I flipped it over, I saw a LR44 battery attached to the back. Seriously, I found some sort of a light-up cross with the exact battery I needed for my electric toothbrush attached to the back. It was just what I needed! I grabbed it and sprinted to go tell my parents. My adrenaline was pumping; how could this be possible!? I told

Dad and he got excited with me; he even told a couple of people at Church about what happened. This may be a strange and funny story and my dad could have simply thought it was adorable or laughable, but he chose to delight in it. He encouraged me and reaffirmed my excitement that indeed, God had heard my little cry for an LR44 battery. God performed a miracle! I then knew that he was concerned with the littlest details of my life. By seizing this opportunity to encourage me, for the rest of my childhood, I always knew that God was good and that he cared to provide for me.

Even when I was in high school and I would share about an experience I had at a retreat or in my prayer time, my parents would always delight in those encounters, and help me to understand the significance of that moment with God.

I see now how important it was for me to grow up knowing God is personal. In *Forming Intentional Disciples*, Sherry Weddell describes the correlation between knowing that God is personal and attending Mass on Sunday. She also presents sobering research on the amount of people sitting in our pews on Sundays who do not believe a personal relationship with God is possible. Sherry explains:

> *"Certainly, one of the most fundamental challenges facing our Church is this: The majority of adult Catholics are not even certain that a personal relationship with God is possible. In short, statistical reality bears out this prophetic passage from Pope John Paul II Catechesi Tradendae (On Catechesis in Our Time): It is possible for baptized Catholics to be "still without any explicit personal attachment to Jesus Christ; they only have the capacity to believe placed within them by Baptism and the presence of the Holy Spirit." (25) ... The majority of Catholics in the United States are sacramentalized but not evangelized. They do not know that an explicit, personal attachment to Christ—personal discipleship—is normative Catholicism as taught by the apostles and reiterated time and time again by the popes, councils, and saints of the Church."*[40]

Let us change this. Let this stop here. I am certain that being only sacramentalized without a personal attachment to God would not have been enough to keep me practising my faith. If we desire for our children to have an authentic conversion, to have a personal attachment to Christ, it is essential to till the soil by instilling an understanding that God desires a personal relationship with them.

---

40. Sherry A. Weddell, *Forming Intentional Disciples: The Path to Knowing and Following Jesus*, (Huntington, IN: Our Sunday Visitor, 2012), p 46.

My parents' decision to see and delight in these small spiritual encounters that we had with God made a significant impression on our young hearts. We felt treasured by God and saw that he was doing something in our lives. Furthermore, talking about these encounters made them feel more real, and more worthy of awe. These encounters didn't get shoved under the bushel basket; they were brought into the light. Our parents guided us through these little moments, helping us to see their value, getting excited for us, and showing us how to respond to the Lord with grateful hearts. They were involved in our faith journeys, just as much as they were involved in our school or extracurricular activities. Marc and I try to do the same with our children. Though they are young, we trust that God wants to encounter them *now* so we try to encourage an understanding of God's personal love for them.

MARC – Fostering Toddler Faith Encounters

I see fatherhood as an opportunity to role-model through my words and actions the love of God the Father to my children. In this way, I am fostering their spirituality from the ground up. I am not just showing them the faith and teaching them about Catholicism; I am revealing God the Father's love to them.

As parents we may often think that we have all the time in the world, and we delay opportunities to teach them to grow in their faith until they are older and can understand more. This is something Mylène and I regularly fall into. However, I have no doubt in my mind that God is already speaking to Max and Audrey and, therefore, it is my great privilege as a parent to help my children hear God's voice and be attuned to his promptings. Jesus said, "Let the little children come to me, and do not stop them; for it is to such as these that the kingdom of heaven belongs." (Matthew 19:14) He desires children to know him personally. God is a God for children just as much as he is a God for teens and adults, and so this encouragement of faith in young children should be just as crucial.

As you know, every year as a family, we make a trip to St. Joseph's Oratory in Montréal. The day always seems to be a spiritually rich day. One year, I wanted to dedicate the trip to Max. I spent a large amount of time with him to make sure he had a great experience. At the end of the day we were lighting candles for intercession in front of a statue of St. Joseph with the multitude of candles gleaming below it. I was giddy with excitement to see the reaction on my son's face. I knelt down at Max's level and told him how much I loved him and enjoyed being with him. I then invited him to light a candle and repeat after me this prayer, "Jesus, come into my heart."

Max lit the candle, prayed, and afterwards, while holding him in my arms, I asked him if he felt Jesus in his heart. Max responded, "Jesus isn't in my heart yet, Dad. He is coming in five minutes." Over the course of the day I asked Max multiple times if Jesus came into his heart yet, and I always received the same response, "No, not yet, Dad." Later that evening, we were at a fast-food joint for supper and I asked him after the meal, "Max, is Jesus in your heart yet?" Max, feeling fulfilled after a full hamburger, fries, and a drink said, "Yeah Dad, Jesus is in my heart." I told him, "Max, I don't think Jesus is just in your heart; I think he is in your belly!" Max loved my 'dad joke' by the way.

This might seem like such a small moment with Max choosing to light a candle and pray, but I am convince that it will bear fruit in his spiritual life that I guided him, delighted in him, and affirmed him on opening his heart. These little moments matter. I am a firm believer that, if Max can choose over and over again to open his heart to Jesus at a young age, I will have laid a strong foundation for him in future matters of faith. This doesn't mean that he won't make his fair share of mistakes or stray away from his faith, but it does mean that he will have an awareness that God is real, God loves him, and longs to delight in him.

Conclusion

In being a parent myself now, I am able to witness first-hand these tiny moments where God encounters my children as they understand more and more his love for them. God is using us as parents to reflect and image himself to our children. Using the analogy of tilling the soil, we must ensure that the soil is prepared to receive a seed. Reflecting on my own childhood, I see that I really did know that God was everything. My parents succeeded in passing this belief onto me. Here are some reminders of how they did that:

- ■ Live your faith authentically in front of your children. Spirituality shouldn't be removed from the day to day, but should be naturally incorporated.

- ■ Aim higher than making your children good Catholics; aim for them to be disciples of Christ. This starts with your own discipleship. As you take time for daily prayer and Scripture reading, and live a dynamic relationship with the Lord, you lay the foundation to help your children become disciples when they're ready.

- ■ Remember to place your child's needs ahead of your own spiritual preferences. Do pious things as a family, always taking into account the ages, personalities, and time of day for your children.

- Teach your children the necessary attitudes, skills, and knowledge of being a disciple. When you are struggling to pass on the faith, ask yourself which area they are lacking in, and then you will know if you need to train, teach, or model something.

- Use resources that make the faith fun and interactive for children so that they see from an early age that faith can be fun.

- When spiritual opportunities present themselves, delight in them and explain the spiritual reality to your children. Don't assume your child isn't old enough to understand—seize the moment to show them God is real and good!

As my parents followed these principles while passing on the faith, I learned that God was not cruel, impersonal, distant, or irrelevant. I saw that God was personal, he provided for us, and he was deeply involved in the little moments as well as the big ones. I saw the relationship with God that my parents had and it excited me to imagine what God could do in my life! A relationship with God attracted me in every way as I saw it manifested in my parents and the village around me.

Reflection / Action Points

1. How do you make time for the Lord in your own personal prayer life, while showing your children that they are also your priority?

2. How do you incorporate faith into your regular life as a family? Do your children see you pray or overhear you have spiritual conversations?

3. André spoke to fathers, reminding them that they are the spiritual leaders of the home. Fathers, how are you leading your family? Are you making time for prayer every day? André encouraged you to initiate a conversation with your wife (and if appropriate, with the children) about the spiritual life in the home. Find time to do that this week.

4. Are there attitudes, skills, and knowledge that your children need to grow in the faith? Remember that attitudes are modelled by parents and caught by children. In particular, are there certain attitudes that you need to work on modelling for the sake of your children?

Concluding Thoughts

Letting Dad Have the Last Word

ANDRÉ

So there you have it. This is our secret sauce for how Angèle and I raised our children, and how our children responded to their Catholic upbringing. We hope you have gained from the principles as outlined by the chapter headings. We have tried to keep your gaze on the vision and the purpose and not to be prescriptive. (We did however give lots of practical examples and approaches just to appease all of you who were begging us for the nitty gritty; the "how did you do that?!") I might add that the secret sauce isn't just those particular principles; it's that Angèle and I wrestled to agree on what *our parenting philosophy* would be. Yes, to be united in our methods, but mainly to have a unified approach at a macro level. We knew what we were going for—*to raise children who would be life-long disciples, missionaries and lovers of Jesus Christ.*

Before you close the book, I would like to leave you with some thoughts to consider as you go forward in your journey as a Catholic parent in today's world. Yes, I do like to have the last word.

As you have seen in this book, we are not a perfect family by any means. We fight, we have made mistakes (big and small), and we have failed time and time again. I hope that brings you consolation! We do not want you to feel that you must be perfect to raise your family. Raising families seems to be more of an art: always learning and adjusting as we go. In the early years, we made some wrong decisions and allowed our own weaknesses to affect how we interacted with the family. When we saw a weakness or a blindspot in our parenting or family life, we readjusted. We worked at how we responded to the kids. We sought the Lord for the grace to grow in maturity, love, kindness and mercy.

In your efforts and zeal to form your children as missionary disciples, I advise you to simply slow down a bit to be cognizant of the tone, the way, the attitude in which you execute your missionary discipleship parenting. The attitudes and motivations behind your efforts can have a profound effect on the way your children appropriate your formation. To illustrate this, I will share with you an area where Jo and Caleb resisted my influence in the realm of sports.

You have to understand that my whole life was characterized by being competitive in sports—in my mind, every game or scrimmage merited the same intensity as the Olympics. I loved athletics and throughout my life I received satisfaction from working hard to win. When my boys were in elementary school, I imposed those competitive expectations on my kids. It did not turn out well. In fact, it caused a lot of conflict and bitterness in my relationship with my boys. I forced them to go to intensive sport camps, got upset when they didn't spend their free time practising, and showed disappointment when they did not try hard enough. From an early age, I think they sensed this intensity and began to reject playing sports at all. My approach led them to have a negative perception of athletics. Their attitude led me to become more and more frustrated with them—I could not understand why they were not wanting to become better athletes, or why they did not enjoy going to games and practices like myself and so many of their peers enjoyed doing. Resentments rose on my end and on theirs and sports became a highly sensitive topic in our family. Something that should have brought life to my kids and been an exciting part of their upbringing instead became the source of a wound in their hearts. After time and discussion with Angèle, I came to see how I was forcing my expectations on the boys, rather than supporting them in their desires. We made the needed changes in behaviour and attitude and it had positive effects on our relationships. To this day though, the boys aren't big fans of sports. This is in a large part due to the way I introduced it to them.

While we often joke about this stage in our family life today, it was a raw struggle at the time. I present this example because I feel that this could have easily been the same way that I approached the faith with my kids. In fact, I think many parents have a similar type of interaction with their kids when it comes to their Christian faith. Parents may tend to pass on the faith in a way that is intense with high expectations, that looks a lot like "sports-obsessed dad mode". This is especially acute in the teenage years. The child senses their parents' desperation and sees the faith as a burdening expectation that is placed on them instead of something to be accepted out of their free will.

As parents, our pride also must be kept in check. I was seeing my kids' peers excelling and working hard in sports and I wanted my sons to be out there with them. My sons saw sports as a source of pain, disappointing their father, and not being good enough. A similar pattern can happen when it comes to our kids and their involvement in the faith. We might be seeing other Catholic families whose kids seem to be living more virtuous, pious lives but we must be sure not to project this envy onto our children. As parents, I urge you to be careful not to allow your children to see the faith as a source of negative experiences. With sports, all of my efforts resulted in bitter rebellion. A bitter rebellion of the faith is the last thing we want our children to experience.

> *"Children, obey your parents in the Lord, for this is right. 'Honour your father and mother'—this is the first commandment with a promise: 'so that it may be well with you and you may live long on the earth.'*
>
> *"And, fathers, do not provoke your children to anger, but bring them up in the discipline and instruction of the Lord." Ephesians 6: 1-4*

Yes, we all want our children to be perfect and be the best, even when it comes to faith. But let's watch our own vainglory in this. Let's be careful to assess our motivations, to renounce any ounce of pride that influences our interactions towards our children. Let's not be obstacles that prevent our kids from growing up in "the freedom of the glory of the children of God" (Romans 8:21).

As we guard our hearts and our motivations, let us too grow up in the freedom of the glory of the children of God. Let's earnestly seek the Lord's heart, the Lord's mission and lean in to hear him assure us that we are his beloved children too. Let us be multiplying missionary disciples, bringing God into the lives of our children, brick by brick.

And as I close this book, I want the final words of this book to be a blessing from our family to yours: We pray that the Lord will abundantly shower you with his love, peace and mercy. May he bless you, and your children, and your children's children for his greater glory and the salvation of the world. Amen

*   *   *   *   *

"Now this is the commandment—the statutes and the ordinances—that the Lord your God charged me to teach you to observe in the land that you are about to cross into and occupy, so that you and your children and your children's children may fear the Lord your God all the days of your life, and keep all his decrees and his commandments that I am commanding you, so that your days may be long. Hear therefore, O Israel, and observe them diligently, so that it may go well with you, and so that you may multiply greatly in a land flowing with milk and honey, as the Lord, the God of your ancestors, has promised you."

"Hear, O Israel: The Lord is our God, the Lord alone. You shall love the Lord your God with all your heart, and with all your soul, and with all your might. Keep these words that I am commanding you today in your heart. Recite them to your children and talk about them when you are at home and when you are away, when you lie down and when you rise. Bind them as a sign on your hand, fix them as an emblem on your forehead, and write them on the doorposts of your house and on your gates."
Deuteronomy 6: 1-9

Bonus Features

Extra Content from André and Angèle

1) André Explains the Heart of Becoming a Disciple of Jesus Christ.

As a Catholic, the idea of being a disciple of Christ is much more extraordinary than simply obediently following the example and teachings of Jesus and the Church. It is a matter of love.

There are two elements that speak to this love. The first is that it involves love in the context of a personal relationship with Jesus Christ. The second is knowing that we have the power to choose to be open to this relationship of love. As parents, we want to lead our kids to understand that God is personal and help them choose to embrace that relationship. *In order to help our kids do this, we have to know how to choose that relationship for ourselves.*

The most appropriate place to begin is where the Catechism begins—with God's desire that we "share in his own blessed life" that we would "know" and "love him" and "become...his adopted children"[41]. These phrases speak of relationship which is the fundamental nature of the Blessed Trinity—the Father, the Son and the Holy Spirit. Theirs is an active relationship of unitive love.

The idea that God desires for us to share in his life and be in a personal relationship with him should capture our attention. It should also resonate with our own humanity, since we are social beings in our very nature. Relationships are integral to how we function and what we desire in our

---

41. Catechism of the Catholic Church. 1, (Prologue)

lives. We all know the basic principles of how to build new relationships or restore broken ones.

This leads to the fundamental Christian truth that our relationship with God is broken due to sin. Sin is more than a judgment or criticism of our behaviours—the things we do or do not do. Properly understood, sin can even shed light on the nature of love and relationship. Sin is always a failure to love. We all see how quickly we fall into this state: we fail to sacrifice for others, we think uncharitable thoughts, we take the selfish route. Looking honestly at our lives, we know that we've done wrong things. We've hurt other people. It makes sense to us as social beings that such behaviour (sin) has negative consequences on our relationships. We humans understand that relationships require care, engagement and sacrifice; and we experience the richness of love when we give of ourselves.

When we look at sin from the lens of relationship, we can understand how our choices and behaviours are at the heart of our spiritual problem. The axis of sin is not about failure to meet God's expectations and requirements—it's that we've done something to break the relationship.

Out of love for us, the Father sent his only Son, Jesus to reconcile us back into relationship with the Blessed Trinity. He accomplishes this restoration on the cross by taking our sins and failures upon himself. We are forgiven. This is *the* good news.

In a relationship it is not good enough for us simply to know that someone loves us. For love to reach its fulfillment, we need to receive the love and reciprocate that love. As is true in human relationships, it is within our freedom to allow Jesus to restore the relationship he offers to us. Will we trust him and allow him into our lives? Will we really open our hearts up to relationship with him? Prayerfully reflect on the words of Pope Benedict XVI where he explains that giving our lives to Jesus Christ is only a matter of opening our heart to him.

> *"If we let Christ into our lives, we lose nothing, nothing, absolutely nothing of what makes life free, beautiful and great. No! Only in this friendship are the doors of life opened wide.*
>
> *Only in this friendship is the great potential of human existence truly revealed.*
>
> *Do not be afraid of Christ! He takes nothing away and he gives you everything. When we give ourselves to him, we receive a hundredfold in return. Yes, open, open wide the doors to Christ—and you will find true life."* [42]
>
> *Pope Benedict XVI*

---

42. Pope Benedict XVI, *Homily of His Holiness Benedict XVI for the Inauguration of his Pontificate*, St. Peter's Square, 24 April 2005.

Take a moment and invite the Holy Spirit to reveal this truth to you right now. In your imagination picture Jesus giving up his life for you. Think about his resurrection from the dead, promising to you a new life—a relationship with the Father and the Son and the Holy Spirit for eternity. Think about the friendship he offers you. Linger in that.

How do we accept God's love in Jesus Christ and love him in return? The following illustration helps us to identify how we are living our relationship with Jesus. It also helps us to understand the kind of relationship he desires to have with us: a relationship of friendship, intimacy, commitment, fidelity, mercy and love.

The Relationships Diagram

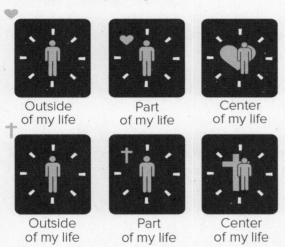

Outside of my life Part of my life Center of my life

Outside of my life Part of my life Center of my life

The top three images represent levels of commitment in three kinds of human relationships. The first image represents someone who is single; there is no romantic relationship in their life. The second image represents someone who is dating. This relationship is a part of their life, but commitment is limited. The third image represents someone who is married; there is an intimate relationship and a permanent mutual commitment.

Let's compare this to our *relationship with God*

The bottom three images represent levels of commitment in a relationship with God. The first image represents someone who does not have a relationship with Jesus. As far as this person is concerned. Jesus is outside of their life. The second image represents someone who acknowledges Jesus as a part of their life, but has not completely committed to him. Jesus is just one aspect of their life among many others. The third image represents a Christ-centered relationship. This relationship is primary and contral, influencing all decisions and every aspect of their life.

Which image best represents your relationship with God?

Which image would you like to have represent your relationship with God?

If you want to open your life, your heart to this relationship with Jesus Christ, I invite you to pray this prayer right now:

> *"Jesus, I know that you are the Son of God, who have given your life for me. I want to follow you faithfully and to be led by your word. You know me and you love me. I place my trust in you and I put my whole life into your hands. I want you to be the power that strengthens me and the joy which never leaves me."*[43]

Amen! God acts when we make a conscious decision to accept the love that he offers. His response is love and mercy. The Scriptures speak of this, "whoever opens the door, I will come." (Revelation 3:20) Like the return of the prodigal son, there is cause for rejoicing. If this is the first time you have made such a decision, this is holy ground my friend. Take a moment and thank the Lord for loving you. Take 10 to 15 minutes to pray and read the Scriptures (daily). Tell someone the decision you made today. Confirm the mercy and receive sanctifying grace by going to the sacrament of Reconciliation.

Opening ourselves to a relationship with Jesus Christ is a very important and exciting moment in our spiritual lives. It is a decision that we must cling to and reaffirm daily, opening our lives more fully to his love for us. I assure you, by daily building on this new relationship, and with the help of the Holy Spirit, you will be stepping into an exciting and fulfilling period in your life. You will see and relate to God in a whole new way, as you will with his Church. You will never be the same.

This is the alive, dynamic relationship that you desire for your children. Make it joyfully yours and they will be drawn to it too. This relationship makes faith and Church relevant and life-giving. Instead of *forcing* faith and the Church on your children, you can *draw them* to it through the context of your authentic relationship of love and devotion to God and his Kingdom. You can raise your children to know what it is, and how to have a personal relationship with God. With this foundation, these little disciples of Christ can easily be grown to have a "missionary" mindset like your own.

---

43. Pope Benedict XVI, Words of the Holy Father at the Beginning of the Eucharistic Celebration, World Youth Day Cuatro Vientos Air Base, Madrid, Sunday, 21 August 2011.

2) Angèle's Tips for Going to Mass with Children

Let's talk about how to get through Mass with kids—commonly experienced in our section of the pew as 'mass confusion'. Since we have 1,430 Masses under our belt (yes, I did the math), we feel qualified to pass on a few insights from our extensive field research.

Here's our **'Must-Have Diaper Bag Mass Essentials'**

- Dry, quiet, (not sticky) snacks.
  YES: cheerios, raisins, cheese cubes.
  NO: carrots, bananas, yogurt.
- Dripless sippy cup or bottle.
- Soft Toys—that do NOT squeak, rattle, roll, or bang easily. It's amazing how many toys have the potential for noise. Yes, soft cloth books and stuffed animals. No hot wheels cars, balls, rattles, electronic toys, or lego.
- Books! Especially Christian children's books.
- Crayons and colouring sheets. (Not too many crayons—too many leads to chaos with rolling crayons). Bonus points if you print off some Christian colouring sheets.

Pro tip: do not give kids snacks *until the homily*. Snacks are your greatest defensive distraction tactic and you don't want to pull it out of your bag of tricks prematurely.

You get the idea on what to pack, so let's talk about behaviours and noise. Our approach to managing the monkey-business was rooted in three beliefs:

1. That kids need boundaries
2. That kids need to learn respect
3. That kids cannot be expected to behave like adults

With these principles in mind, we brought our kids to Mass ready for success. We would stake out our 'pew pen'. The 'pew pen' was a section of a church pew that would become our little home away from home for that hour. We would make sure to be fairly close to the front so the kids could get a good view, and it had to have access to a side aisle for stealthy escapes if needed.

It seems kids just need to test those boundaries. Their little heads are scheming, "I wonder how far I could get towards that nice old lady?" I would usually "draw the boundary" with jackets or the diaper bag. "You shall not pass!"—that's a Lord of the Rings reference there for ya.

Now, the aisle gatekeeper has an important role. We were adamant that children were not allowed to wander out of the 'pew pen'. We know first-hand that letting a child wander backfires. At first, it's really cute when a toddler starts wobbling around, exploring and checking out the parish landscape and entertaining parishioners. Once your darling angel has had a taste of the freedom to wander, you will have a dickens of a time getting them to comply to the 'pew pen' boundary at the next Mass. Learning that the hard way, we made a point to keep our 'pew pen' intact. André and I rarely sat side-by-side at Mass with the kids because we had jobs to do—being physical barriers to their escape at either end of the 'pew pen'. (P.S. Wandering cuties are also a distraction for grown adults who have a hard enough time focusing on Mass.) When kids are school-aged, your physical presence in the pew is not so much about guarding the "exits", it's about managing sibling fights. The quickest and quietest way to stop the bickering is just to move yourself between the warring parties. No need to say anything. This is a classic teacher move. (Yes, I have a Bachelor of Education—you're welcome.) Your physical presence should neutralize the situation, not to mention the distraction they are creating for others.

Speaking of distracting others, we made it a point to keep our kids looking forward, not backwards for the sake of the people behind us. Here you can cue: stupid faces, trying to make others laugh, staring awkwardly, and worse—activating other kids to get silly; all without you knowing it is happening, even though they are right beside you. Nope, our little monkeys' faces were gently rotated to face forward with Mom or Dad's loving hand and a stroke of their hair.

When it came to kid noise (talking, crying, whining, fighting, silliness, struggling, banging or just restlessness), if we could not get the kids to be quietly distracted with our arsenal of tricks in the diaper bag, then we would swiftly and stealthily go with the child to the back of the church before he/she became a distraction. Out of respect for fellow parishioners, we moved.

Now, I'm not saying that 'children should be seen and not heard', because the non-distracting hum of children in a parish is actually a very healthy sign and a reason to rejoice in these days where there is a crisis of faith and an attack on the family. I also hope you don't hear my comments sounding like a grumpy old grandma who can't stand any squawks coming out of kids. No. Kids, being kids, can't be expected to stay perfectly quiet and motionless in a pew pen when they are sick, teething, learning to walk, and so on. Out of understanding for the child *and* respect for those around us, we would scoop up the child and move to a better location that gave freedom to pace with the little one while allowing us to see or hear the liturgy. Something we were concerned about was to not leave the pew too often, because this could inadvertently train a toddler to equate 'acting up' with 'getting out'. Classic conditioned behaviour scenario right?

In order to communicate that we had every intention of being at Mass and sitting in the pew, we held the child in our arms the whole time we were in the back, and would return to the pew as quickly as possible. We did not let the child run. If the child had to move, we held their hand and walked them or let them walk in a very confined area. A child allowed to wander will not want to sit still when returning to the pew. I've seen what happens when we had lazy parenting in the narthex—our kids quickly learned the advantages of getting out of the pew: the freedom to run, or to sneak a "church hall cookie" well before after-Mass cookie time. Basically, kids are quick to figure out how to work the system, and that's why André took over the role of taking the kids out because he was strong enough to hold them the whole time. (Have you ever seen André's muscles?!)

We found that we needed to be watchful and intent to form the child to the desired behavioural outcome—that of being well-behaved and reasonably quiet in the pew during Mass. We were committed to establishing the right behaviours early on, because we are lazy and didn't want to deal with behavioural issues in Mass for the rest of our lives! The investment of being firm, timely, controlled, calm and loving in the toddler years paid off big time. But that formative process doesn't have to be military style with proper posture and austerity. What we were going for was being in a pew without causing a disturbance. Very often our kids were seated on the kneeler using the pew as their colouring desk or dining room table. Even with their quiet little activities during Mass, I was regularly astonished at how they were listening, often commenting on things Father said during the van ride back from Mass.

So you probably have gathered that we would strongly discourage young parents from a permissive parenting style which gives a long leash for noise and wandering. Rather, play the long game. Focus on developing the right habits in your child, for their own piety and out of respect for the community and the liturgy. Even though we've all gotten the glare, the head turns, or snide comments from intolerant parishioners from time to time, let's keep it classy parents, and do our best not to have our families be an unnecessary distraction to others and a pain point for ourselves.

I became aware during those couple of years just before we had Natalie (when we didn't have any toddlers) that I, too, naturally turned my head whenever I heard a noise at church. I wasn't grumpy or anything; it was just a knee-jerk reaction. I heard a noise and I turned my head to see where it came from—that's it. I thought about being at Mass in the 1990s when I perceived every head turn in my children's direction as judgment. Maybe those people turning their heads were just responding to a noise stimulus like I was. I've also come to know some dear elderly folks over the years and I have seen them react to loud, sudden noises. They've told me that their hearing aids intensify those sounds in a sharp and painful way for them. This all gave me perspective that some of the reactions towards my kids in the past may have just been physiological responses, not attitudinal.

So when we had the younger girls, I honestly didn't take offense at the turn of heads. I noticed that when I gave people the benefit of the doubt, I was way more confident and relaxed having our family at Mass and I think that vibe affected the whole experience. Having said that, I assure you that I know there are people in any given parish who are not child-friendly and will say unfortunate things to you. Lord have mercy. But there are also some sweet souls who have said to us, "You have a such well-behaved, pleasant family. It's so nice to see." And then there was dear Monsignor Latour at our parish, who used to always say at the end of Mass, "Thank you for bringing your beautiful children to Mass today." How sweet is that? Savour those sweet moments! You're doing a great job!

3) Angèle's Tips for Disciplining Children

When it comes to discipline in the childhood years, the most reasonable methods for us were '1-2-3 Magic'[44] and time-outs. Giving time-outs is a popular method and we used it sometimes, but honestly, it didn't always suit every child's personality. (By the way, a practical tip for reasonable time-outs is the minute:age ratio. If a child is five years old, they get five minutes in time-out. It also seemed very fair to the kids as well. This also works for me with finishing the food on your plate. "Since you're eight years old, you have to eat eight more good bites.") The problem we had with time-outs, was that certain kids just wouldn't sit in the time-out spot. Period. Unless maybe we had used duct tape to keep them there—and even then I don't know.

We used the '1-2-3 Magic' method a lot. Basically, you state the behaviour you need the child to do, warn them that you will count to three and if they don't do what you asked them to do before "three" is spoken, then they will face the consequences. If they do it again, say "one" out loud. Then "two" if it happens again. But if you are required to say "three" by the wrong behaviour continuing, you have to—and this is the catch—be prepared to immediately do what you said. What happened to us a lot is that we said "one, two, three" too fast. We'd say a quick "one..." and then "two..." and then it would be like, "Oh man, that kid's not stopping and I'm painted into a corner here—I've got to say "three", but I was *really* banking on the

---

44. Thomas W. Phelan, Ph D, *1-2-3 Magic: Effective Discipline for Children 2-12* (Naperville, Il: Sourcebooks, Inc., 2016).

kid to act better before I got to three." So in desperation, we would come up with excessive or unreasonable consequences. For example, saying to our kids, "If you don't stop jumping on Grandma's couches, we are going home." But we just drove two hours to Grandma's house for Thanksgiving supper, so it's really an empty threat. When we weren't reasonable, consistent, and timely (too quick in this instance), we were up the creek. We would end up stalling by turning a blind eye and not saying "three" when we should have or saying "this is your last chance…" (which is de facto extending the count to four or more).

The '1-2-3 Magic' is fantastic when you are committed to being consistent, timely, and reasonable. It's really effective and we had great success with it. But once you start muddying the rules and execution of the '1-2-3 Magic', you're hooped. It's an uphill battle to reestablish compliance to the method. Again, the problem here is not with the kids or with the method. The problem is with the parent. We are our own worst enemy. We botched the system, compromised on reasonableness, consistency, and timeliness and we were left with the consequences. But if you are smart and play this method well, you will have great results. It is extremely satisfying to say a solitary number "ONE!" firmly and immediately hear the lament of a child totally busted in their bad behaviour, some shuffling, and quick readjustment to quiet submission as a child's behaviour is brought appropriately in line.

4) Angèle's Tips for Reasonable Context Appropriate Consequences

Here are some examples of reasonable context-appropriate consequences:

- Apply a direct consequence of their actions. "You can keep throwing around that Lego, but you will not eat supper until it is all cleaned up properly."

- Take away something they are enjoying at the moment—especially if it is the cause of their disobedience. For example, take away that toy, turn off that tv show, remove their treat, or leave the park.

- Have them do something to make up for what they did to a sibling, such as giving them a gift (some of their candy or their time on a video game).

- Remove money from their allowance. This really only works well with the following method: at the beginning of the week, give them their allowance in a clear jar in anticipation of the work they will be doing for chores. Let's say it's $7 for the week ($1/day). It is put in the jar as cash in good faith that they will do what they are supposed to do. However, should they disobey and not change their behaviour with warning, let them see that you are removing a loonie out of their allowance. The key here is actually to see the money going away. It has to be concrete and tangible.

- My favourite consequence for fighting or hurting a sibling is that they have to do that person's chores (in addition to their own of course.)

- Employ some kind of a points system to encourage and reward good behaviours (chores, attitudes, etc.) and deduct points for bad behaviours. A classic motivator is the loss or gain of TV or video game time. Although these systems can be very effective, be prepared for the required diligence and consistency to monitor the points-giving. (Personally, I found that these were too cumbersome and I could never stay on top of allocating points and what-not. The whole system only lasted for maybe five days under my purview.)

5) Angèle Tips for Doing the Examen

The "examen" (or "examen of consciousness") is an Ignatian practice of prayerfully reviewing your day just before going to bed. It is only meant to be 15 minutes long. Since it is a reflection of consciousness (not conscience per se), you reflect on when you were conscious of God's loving presence or conscious of feeling far from him. Here are the steps of an examen of consciousness.

1. Welcome the Holy Spirit

Begin by asking the Holy Spirit for the grace to see and to understand his working in your life.

2. Review the day

Look back on your day. Pay attention to your experiences. What stands out? What affected your inner life? (What made you feel close to him? What made you feel far from him?)

3. Consolations

With gratitude, recall those moments, experiences, and thoughts which inspired you to love or serve God more. Thank him for the ways you encountered his loving presence, guidance and strength today.

4. Desolations

Notice when you felt spiritually discouraged or far from God. What was going on? Where did those feelings come from?

Are there truths about God that you need to cling to?

Are there lies that you need to reject?

Notice your failures and shortcomings today. Ask yourself, "what led to those behaviours"? Ask the Lord to forgive you.

5. Resolutions

Ask God to show you ways to be stronger and improve—by exercising virtues and remembering the truths of his promises and/or by rejecting vices and lies of the enemy.

Ask the Holy Spirit for his guidance and strength moment by moment tomorrow.

6) Angele's Comments on Finances and a Large Family

We wanted to add a brief word about finances and family. Money is a funny thing. Salaries are never enough, and for us, we tend to spend in pace with the salary we are receiving. "Can we afford to have more kids?" is a common question couples ask themselves nervously. But have you ever noticed that people with large families are generally those that 'can't afford it'? They are often single-income families. I think sometimes these couples are perceived as (financially) irresponsible for having so many children. I think these families would say it all boils down to priorities.

As a missionary family, which lives directly by God's providence through the donations of good people, we know what it is like to live by a budget. We know what it is to make decisions on how to spend your money when family is the clear priority. We don't regret any of that. Sure, we don't own a cottage or a boat, but it's not like our kids have never enjoyed either of those things. We chose not to have our kids in every top level extra-curricular activity—we made home life the greater priority. Losing out on things like annual all-inclusive vacations, brand-name clothing, seasons-tickets to NHL games, or the latest home trends paled in comparison to the richness of the self-gift of raising a beautiful family for God's glory. We made careful decisions on how to spend and save our money with the help of a budget and common sense. And when we got to enjoy an NHL game, or stay at a cottage, or get a nice brand-name outfit, it was truly appreciated as a gift from God with great delight.

Every family needs to learn basics in how to budget; it's amazing how so many do not know how to manage money. We lived month-to-month: covering living expenses while paying off student loans or a mortgage and yet we tucked away money every month for emergencies and financial investments too. I'm not going to lie—there were some seasons when we felt the pressure and concern keenly, forcing us to double down and make even simpler choices on groceries or entertainment. Sometimes we were afraid, but the storm never lasted long. Never, in any of that, did we cut back on the principle of tithing. We gave, at a minimum, 10 percent of our paycheque back to the Lord. Honestly, generosity to the Lord and to family life has not left us lacking anything we *really* needed.

I find it heartbreaking when financially stable folks say they can't afford to have a second or third child. I have to wonder what is at the heart of this statement. Is it about safeguarding a certain standard of living? I'm not sure. Maybe at the heart of it, is a fear of not having enough money for the future. When it comes to saving for our old age, we felt like children were a great investment to secure our future. Surely our five children will rally around us when we are elderly and make sure we are taken of. Because there are so many of them, no one child will be overwhelmed with the task. That's not to say we aren't saving for our retirement—we are. But we are also confident that the love and investment we made in our children will reap us invested love in our own vulnerable old-age, should we need it. The providence of God and the love of family speaks to me of safety and reminds me of the Scripture verse that says, "Perfect love casts out all fear." [1 John 4:18]

7) CCO's Apostle's Prayer[45]

Lord, when you called Abraham, he responded, "Ready"

When you called Isaiah, he answered, "Here I am Lord."

When the angel Gabriel called out to Mary, she responded,

"I am the handmaid of the Lord. Let it be done to me according to your word."

Lord, I hear you calling my name.

I hear you entrusting me with the task of building your kingdom.

Like those holy men and women who have gone before me, I give you my 'yes'!

I will go anywhere you want me to go.

I will do anything you want me to do.

I will say anything you want me to say.

Holy Spirit I welcome you and ask you to guide me.

Form in me an apostle's heart filled with love for Christ and zeal for souls.

I will commit myself with courage and generosity to the New Evangelization.

I will build brick-by-brick, the city of God inside the city of man.

Amen

---

45. Catholic Christian Outreach (CCO). CCO's Apostle's Prayer.

References

Arthur (TV series). Directed by Greg Bailey. Cookie Jar Group and WGBH-TV. 1996 – .

Saint Augustine (translated by Henry Chadwick), *The Confessions*, Oxford World Classics, OUP Oxford, 2008.

Benedict XVI. Homily in St Apollinaris Wharf, Port of Brindisi. 2008. Web.

Benedict XVI. Homily in St Peter's Square. 2005. Web.

Benedict XVI. Interview of the Holy Father Benedict XVI in Preparation for the Upcoming Journey to Bavaria. 2006. Web.

Benedict XVI. Words of the Holy Father at the Beginning of the Eucharistic Celebration, World Youth Day, Madrid. 2011. Web.

Ben-Hur. Directed by William Wyler. Metro-Goldwyn-Mayer. 1959.

Berenstain, Stan and Berenstain, Jan. *Berenstain Bears Get the Gimmies*, Random House Books. 1988.

Catechism of the Catholic Church. Libreria Editrice Vaticana. 1993.

Catholic Christian Outreach (CCO). CCO's Apostle's Prayer. Web.

Cinderella. Directed by Kenneth Branagh. Walt Disney Motion Pictures. 2015.

Discovery Faith Study. Catholic Christian Outreach. 2012.

Francis. Homily of Pope Francis during Mass for the Family Day on the Occasion of the Year of Faith in St. Peter's Square (Vatican). 2013. Web.

Jesus of Nazareth. Directed by Franco Zeffirelli. ITC Entertainment & RAI. 1977.

John Paul II. Address of His Holiness John Paul II During His Visit to the Tomb of St John Neumann, Philadelphia. 1979.

John Paul II. *Familiaris Consortio*. Libreria Editrice Vaticana. 1981. Web.

John Paul II. *Gratissimam Sane*. Libreria Editrice Vaticana. Web.

John Paul II. Homily of John Paul II in Perth (Australia). 1986. Web.

John Paul II. Homily of the Holy Father During Mass with Young People, Czech Republic. 1997. Web.

John Paul II. *Redemptoris Missio*. Libreria Editrice Vaticana. 1990. Web.

John Paul II. Wednesday General Audiences: Theme: Theology of the Body. 1979 – 1984.

John Paul II. Address by the Holy Father John Paul II at the Evening Vigil with Young People, 27 July 2002, Toronto. Web.

Lencioni, Patrick. *The Advantage: Why Organizational Health Trumps Everything Else In Business*, San Francisco: Jossey-Bass A Wiley Imprint. 2012.

Les Miserables. Directed by Bille August. Columbia Pictures. 1998.

Loes, Harry Dixon. "This Little Light of Mine." c.1920.

Lord of the Rings (Film series). Directed by Peter Jackson. New Line Cinema. 2001 – 2003.

New Revised Standard Version Bible: Catholic Edition. Copyright © 1989, 1993 National Council of the Churches of Christ in the United States of America.

Paul VI. *Evangelii Nuntiandi*. Liberia Editrice Vaticana. 1971. Web.

Paw Patrol (TV series). Directed by Jamie Whitney, Charles E. Bastien. Guru Studio and Spin Master Entertainment. 2013 – .

Phelan, Thomas W. Ph D, *1-2-3 Magic: Effective Discipline for Children 2-12*. Naperville, Il: Sourcebooks, Inc., 2016.

Pokemon Trading Card Game. Creatures Inc.(Japan), Media Factory (Japan), The Pokemon Company (Japan), Creatures Inc. (United States), Wizards of the Coast (Hasbro) (United States), The Pokemon Company International (United States). 1996 – .

Regnier, Angèle. *Forgiveness is Key*. Algonquin, IL Ministry23, LLC. 2016.

Rowling, J.K. Harry Potter (Book series). Bloomsbury Publishing (UK). 1997 – 2007.

Silence. Directed by Martin Scorsese. Paramount Pictures. 2016.

Terminator 2: Judgement Day. Directed by James Cameron. Tristar Pictures. 2011.

The Count of Monte Cristo. Directed by Kevin Reynolds. Buena Vista Pictures. 2002.

The English Oxford Living Dictionaries. Web.

The Mission. Directed by Roland Joffé. Warner Bros. 1986.

The Passion of the Christ. Directed by Mel Gibson. Newmarket Films. 2004.

The Prince of Egypt. Directed by Brenda Chapman, Steve Hickner & Simon Wells. DreamWorks Pictures. 1998.

The Robe. Directed by Henry Koster. 20th Century Fox. 1953.

The Scarlet and The Black. Directed by David Butler. CBS. 1983

The Simpsons (TV series). Created by Matt Groening. 20th Television. 1989 – .

The Ten Commandments. Directed by Cecil B. DeMille. Paramount Pictures. 1956.

The Ultimate Relationship. Catholic Christian Outreach. 2011.

VeggieTales (TV series). Created by Phil Vischer & Mike Nawrocki. Big Idea Entertainment. 1993 – .

Weddell, Sherry A. *Forming Intentional Disciples: The Path to Knowing and Following Jesus*. Huntington, IN: Our Sunday Visitor. 2012.

Wiersbe, Warren W. *The Wiersbe Bible Commentary: Old Testament*. Colorado Springs, David Cook. 2007

Zoolander. Directed by Ben Stiller. Paramount Pictures. 2001.

There are many great programs for evangelization, yet CCO's Faith Study series is unique: it creates an environment for intentional accompaniment through personal relationships. The Faith Studies enable you to proclaim the Gospel message clearly and simply in a small group setting. By the end of the five book series, participants will be missionary-ready disciples.

Titles are available in English, French and Spanish. Some are currently available in Chinese.

Level 1—DISCOVERY invites you to encounter Jesus through a simple but challenging look at the Gospel message.

Level 2—SOURCE introduces you to the Holy Spirit and the impact that the third person of the Trinity can make in the lives of faithful Catholics.

Level 3—GROWTH examines the fundamental practices which nurture our Christian life such as prayer, sacraments and fellowship.

Level 4—TRUST helps you grow in trusting the Lord in all aspects of life so as to live in greater freedom.

Level 5—COMMISSION focuses on revealing your missionary identity.

THE ULTIMATE RELATIONSHIP

The Ultimate Relationship booklet provides an easy way for anyone to share the Gospel message in a clear, simple and personal way. The Ultimate Relationship is currently available in fourteen languages, including English, French and Spanish.

CLEAR & SIMPLE

Clear & Simple goes beyond any particular evangelistic program to communicate the heart of relational ministry and focuses on how to have intentional spiritual conversations.

FORGIVENESS IS KEY

Through the pages of Forgiveness Is Key, God will draw you into his mercy and greater freedom.

5 TENETS TO RENEW THE WORLD

Five principles for evangelization that guide Catholic Christian Outreach and will give you building blocks for success in your apostolate.

CATHOLIC MISSIONARY IDENTITY

Rediscovering our foundational missionary identity is essential for the Catholic Church to experience renewal.

BRICK BY BRICK

With real life stories, tons of humour, and practical advice, this three-generation family illustrates seven key principles of discipleship parenting that bore great fruit raising their children to be missionary disciples.

ORDER TODAY AT: www.cco.ca/store

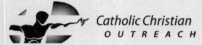

Catholic Christian
OUTREACH

Catholic Christian Outreach (CCO) is a university student movement dedicated to evangelization. We challenge young adults to live in the fullness of the Catholic faith with a strong emphasis on becoming leaders in the renewal of the world.

CCO was founded by André and Angèle Regnier in 1988 at the University of Saskatchewan. From the humble beginnings of a handful of students, the movement now serves thousands of students across Canada and in Uganda.

CCO's goal is to make the message of the gospel accessible for the next generation and to raise them up as leaders who will bring that message to all people. In imitation of Jesus himself, they employ a multiplication model of ministry by investing spiritually in the lives of a few, who can in turn invest in the lives of others. CCO proclaims Jesus to students, equips them to be mature disciples of Christ, and then commissions them to evangelize and equip others to do the same.

CCO Beyond the Campus

CCO is a global leader in the new evangelization, and it's materials and methods are used extensively throughout the world in parishes, dioceses and campuses.

Through CCO's **Connect: Parish** program, parishes can benefit from 30 years of experience on the leading edge of the New Evangelization. CCO offers workshops, coaching, and a game-changing plan to help parishes form missionary disciples of Jesus and establish a multiplying movement. CCO's resources and approach have proven to be effective in creating parish cultural transformation. Whether parishes are looking to simply test-out some of the resources or are ready to commit to full-scale evangelization and discipleship efforts, CCO is ready to help.

The **Missionary Disciple Podcast** is where leaders can be equipped to become effective missionary disciples of Jesus. CCO Co-founders André and Angèle Regnier, along with their host Gerhard share practical wisdom on how to be active in the mission of sharing Jesus and his mission with the world.

www.cco.ca

Are you a CCO alum?

Join the CCO Alumni community for support, encouragement, fellowship and ongoing formation as you live out the mission in the 'real world'. Get connected at http://bit.ly/ccoalumni